Learning Dart
Second Edition

Learn to develop high-performance applications
with Dart 1.12

Ivo Balbaert

Dzenan Ridjanovic

[PACKT] open source *
PUBLISHING   community experience distilled

BIRMINGHAM - MUMBAI

Learning Dart
Second Edition

First published: January 2014

Second edition: September 2015

Production reference: 1220915

Published by Packt Publishing Ltd.
Livery Place
35 Livery Street
Birmingham B3 2PB, UK.

ISBN 978-1-78528-762-6

www.packtpub.com

Credits

Authors
Ivo Balbaert
Dzenan Ridjanovic

Reviewers
Rokesh Jankie
Hans Van den Keybus
Marko Vuksanovic

Commissioning Editor
Nadeem N. Bagban

Acquisition Editor
Sonali Vernekar

Content Development Editor
Divij Kotian

Technical Editor
Chinmay S. Puranik

Copy Editor
Akshata Lobo

Project Coordinator
Nikhil Nair

Proofreader
Safis Editing

Indexer
Mariammal Chettiyar

Graphics
Jason Monteiro

Production Coordinator
Arvindkumar Gupta

Cover Work
Arvindkumar Gupta

About the Authors

Ivo Balbaert is currently a web programming and databases lecturer at CVO Antwerpen (www.cvoantwerpen.be), a community college in Belgium. He received a PhD in applied physics in 1986 from the University of Antwerp. He worked for 20 years in the software industry as a developer and consultant in several companies, and, for 10 years, as a project manager at the University Hospital of Antwerp. In 2000, he switched over to partly teach and partly develop software (KHM Mechelen, CVO Antwerp).

He also wrote *Programmeren met Ruby en Rails*, an introductory book in Dutch about developing in Ruby and Rails, by Van Duuren Media.

In 2012, he authored *The Way To Go*, a book on the Go programming language by IUniverse.

In 2014, he wrote *Learning Dart* (in collaboration with *Dzenan Ridzanovic*) and *Dart Cookbook*, both by Packt Publishing.

Finally, in 2015, he wrote *Getting started with Julia* and *Rust Essentials*, both by Packt Publishing.

I would like to thank Dzenan Ridzanovic for his efforts in updating the book's projects.

Dzenan Ridjanovic is a university professor who is planning his early retirement to focus on the development of web applications with Dart, HTML5, web components, and NoSQL databases. For more than 10 years, he was a director of research and development in the Silverrun team (http://www.silverrun.com/), which created several commercial tools to analyze, design, and develop data-driven applications. He was the principal developer of Modelibra (http://www.modelibra.org/) tools and frameworks for model-driven development in Java. Currently, he is developing the dartling framework for the design and code generation of Dart models. His projects are on GitHub (https://github.com/dzenanr), where he is considered a Dart expert (http://osrc.dfm.io/dzenanr). He writes about his projects on the *On Dart* blog (http://dzenanr.github.io/). His courses are available on *On Dart Education* (http://ondart.me/). He markets his Dart efforts on the *On Dart* G+ page (https://plus.google.com/+OndartMe). Dzenan Ridjanovic wrote a book in 2009, under the Creative Commons License, entitled *Spiral Development of Dynamic Web Applications: Using Modelibra and Wicket* (http://www.modelibra.org/).

About the Reviewers

Rokesh Jankie graduated in 1998 with a master's degree in computer science at Leiden University, The Netherlands. He specialized in algorithms and NP-complete problems. Scheduling problems that can be NP-complete was his area of focus. He started working for the University of Leiden, ORTEC consultants, and Ponte Vecchio, and later worked for Qualogy. At Qualogy, he used what he had experienced till that point to set up a product. Qualogy works in the field of Oracle and Java technology. With the current set of technologies, interesting products can be delivered and that is QAFE (see www.qafe.com for more information).

QAFE Inc. has a very dynamic team, which works in an agile way (going to production weekly, quickly adjusting to market needs, and so on). There is no distinction between senior developers and junior developers and very good software engineers are recruited. This gives a new dynamic to the team and makes it a great experience on a daily basis.

He has also reviewed *Dart in Action* by Manning, *HTML5 and CSS3 Responsive Web Design Cookbook*, and *HTML5 Canvas Cookbook* by Packt Publishing.

> I'm very grateful to my parents and wife for supporting my enthusiasm for computer science. My two-year-old son inspires me to be the best dad and he makes sure that I work hard to create a better future for him through the applications of computer science in daily life and the sharing of knowledge on this subject. Reviewing this book is a part of that journey.

Hans Van den Keybus started off hacking MySpace layouts when he was still in high school.

Having a degree in arts, his initial projects were in games and animation development for several major designing companies. Soon he developed an interest in structuring the code behind these projects.

He built an expertise in OOP, design patterns, and microarchitectures. Currently, he's working on an enterprise portal—developed in Google Dart—for his customers MSC and Maersk, while he's also running his own company, 'dotdotcommadot.'

Whenever Hans is not programming, he's probably doing a gig in some underground venue with his equally underground grindcore band, or cruising on his motorcycle.

He also reviewed *Dart Essentials, Packt Publishing* authored by *Martin Sikora*.

Marko Vuksanovic is a consultant specializing in software development and delivery. He received his master's degree in electrical engineering and computing from the University of Zagreb, Croatia, in 2009. At the moment, Marko is employed by ThoughtWorks Australia, where he helps deliver outstanding products to the clients. He spent the last 10 years working with web applications, and, during this period, he was involved in numerous open source as well as closed source projects. He is very active within the Dart community; he used to contribute to the Angular.dart project. His other interests lie in protocols, information security and machine learning space.

When not providing services to his clients, Marko spends time acquiring new skills, breaking things, reverse engineering, writing articles, or enjoying some time off at one of Australia's beaches or a nearby tennis court.

www.PacktPub.com

Support files, eBooks, discount offers, and more

For support files and downloads related to your book, please visit www.PacktPub.com.

Did you know that Packt offers eBook versions of every book published, with PDF and ePub files available? You can upgrade to the eBook version at www.PacktPub.com and as a print book customer, you are entitled to a discount on the eBook copy. Get in touch with us at service@packtpub.com for more details.

At www.PacktPub.com, you can also read a collection of free technical articles, sign up for a range of free newsletters and receive exclusive discounts and offers on Packt books and eBooks.

PACKTLIB®

https://www2.packtpub.com/books/subscription/packtlib

Do you need instant solutions to your IT questions? PacktLib is Packt's online digital book library. Here, you can search, access, and read Packt's entire library of books.

Why subscribe?

- Fully searchable across every book published by Packt
- Copy and paste, print, and bookmark content
- On demand and accessible via a web browser

Free access for Packt account holders

If you have an account with Packt at www.PacktPub.com, you can use this to access PacktLib today and view 9 entirely free books. Simply use your login credentials for immediate access.

Table of Contents

Preface

Developing a web application (or software in general) is still a challenging task. There is a client- or browser-side and a server-side with databases. There are many different technologies to master in order to feel comfortable with a full client-server stack. There are different frameworks with different objectives. There are different programming languages as well that a developer must learn, each one more suitable either for the server-side or for the client-side.

Learning Dart will make a developer become more productive by using Dart both for clients and servers. Using the same language, a developer will lose neither performance nor flexibility. Dart can be used within its virtual machine or its code may be compiled to JavaScript. In both the cases, the performance benchmarks show promising scores (https://www.dartlang.org/performance/). Dart is both an object-oriented and a functional language. A mix of both the approaches is possible with Dart, providing great professional freedom and programming background flexibility. In addition, Dart provides many libraries and tools (http://pub.dartlang.org/) to allow a developer focus on the tasks at hand and not be concerned with all the aspects of software development.

With Polymer.dart (https://www.dartlang.org/polymer-dart/), a new approach of developing web applications with web components will allow a developer to divide a web page in sections and reuse an already developed and tested web component for each section. In the near future, different catalogs of web components will appear, enabling, after waiting for many years, an engineering approach to software development. A web component may be derived from other web components. It may pass data to its components. A web component may inherit its behavior from another web component. It may access an already instantiated web component.

The spiral approach

The spiral approach to software learning and development, which preserves a project history as a series of code snapshots or spirals, is used in this book.

The following three points are important in the spiral approach:

- The history of development is preserved.
- Simple solutions are provided first. Later on, these solutions may be replaced by more advanced solutions.
- Only the concepts used in a spiral are explained.

All three points are important to teach and learn these technologies.

Learning new software concepts and technologies is a challenging task. Learning in spirals, from simple to more advanced concepts but with concrete software applications, helps readers get a reasonable confidence level early on, and motivates them to learn by providing more useful applications. With each new spiral, the project grows and new concepts are introduced. A new spiral is explained with respect to the previous one. The difference between the two consecutive spirals is that the next spiral introduces the new code and modifies or deletes the old. This is called learning by anchoring to what we already understand. With a new spiral, we can go back to what we did previously and improve it. In this way, learning in spirals can touch the same topic several times, but each time, with more details in a better version.

What this book covers

Learning Dart, Second Edition, has 11 chapters. It begins with the basic elements of Dart and ends with a client/server application that uses MongoDB (http://www.mongodb.org/) for data persistence on the server-side.

Chapter 1, Dart – A Modern Web Programming Language, will help you understand what Dart is all about. Dart is presented as a major step forward in the web programming arena.

Chapter 2, Getting to Work with Dart, will help you get a firm grasp on how to program in Dart. The code and data structures in Dart and its functional principles are explained by exploring practical examples.

Chapter 3, Structuring Code with Classes and Libraries, will make you understand how to use Dart classes to organize code. Dart libraries will be introduced to show how complex software may be packaged.

Chapter 4, Modeling Web Applications with Model Concepts and Dartlero, will let you design graphically a small model in the Model Concepts tool, which is developed in Dart. A model is then represented in Dart as several classes that inherit some data and operations from the classes of the Dartlero model framework; this is also done in Dart.

Chapter 5, Handling DOM in a New Way, covers how to access HTML elements in Dart. Some elements will be even created in Dart and placed properly in the Document Object Model (DOM) of a web page. Dart will also handle user events, such as a click on a button. Finally, you will be able to create a simple game in Dart.

Chapter 6, Combining HTML5 Forms with Dart, will let you enter some data in a form. The data will be validated by HTML5 and Dart. Then, the valid data will be saved in the local storage of a browser.

Chapter 7, Building Games with HTML5 and Dart, will let you create a well-known memory game step by step, based on what you have learned already. Each step will be a new spiral represented as a complete project in Dart Editor. The first spiral will draw only a rectangle, while the last spiral will be a game that you may show to your friends.

Chapter 8, Developing Business Applications with Polymer Web Components, will help you create several web components using Polymer.dart. These web components will be used in the different sections of a single-page application. Three different projects with web components will be presented in this chapter.

Chapter 9, Modeling More Complex Applications with dartling, will let you discover how a graphical model can be transformed into a JSON document and then used to generate a complete model in Dart by using the dartling domain model framework together with its tools. The dartling follows the Model View Controller (MVC) pattern to separate a model from its views.

Chapter 10, Local Data and Client-Server Communication, will let you store application data in a local database called IndexedDB. The data will then be sent as a JSON document to a Dart server. Asynchronous programming with futures will be covered in this chapter.

Chapter 11, Data-Driven Web Applications with MySQL and MongoDB, will help you learn how to use database drivers to save (and load) data to (and from) a relational database and a NoSQL database. Data sent from a browser as a JSON document will be easily saved in MongoDB in the same JSON form. Two clients will exchange data with the server so that both of them will be up-to-date.

For this second edition, all the code and projects were updated to Dart version 1.11. Moreover, sections on the following topics were added:

- enums

- Async and await

- The Observatory tool

- Running a Dart server on an App Engine Managed VM

What you need for this book

In order to profit from this book, you need to have some basic experience in programming. It is also useful to have some understanding of HTML and CSS. What you really need to bring is your enthusiasm to learn how to become a web developer of the future. All the software used in the book is freely available on the Web:

- `https://www.dartlang.org/`

- `https://github.com/Ivo-Balbaert/learning_dart`

- `https://github.com/dzenanr`

- `http://www.mysql.com/`

- `http://www.mongodb.org/`

One of the authors has already taught three times an introductory course to programming with some material from this book. Other educational resources for Dart can be found at `http://ondart.me/`.

Who this book is for

The book is intended for (web) application programmers, game developers, and other software engineers. Because of its dual focus (Dart and HTML5), the book can appeal to web developers who want to learn a modern way of developing web applications and to developers who seek how to use HTML5. The audience includes mainstream programmers with an object-oriented background (Java, .NET, C++) as well as web programmers who use JavaScript to seek a more structured and tooled way of developing. Both groups will leverage their existing knowledge and expertise: the book will offer the first way of developing modern web applications using techniques they already know; it will give the second a more productive and engineered way of developing (business) web applications. The following article describes well what Dart has to offer for web developers of the future:

`http://news.cnet.com/8301-1023_3-57613760-93/mixbook-sees-perfect-storm-for-googles-dart-language-q-a/`

Conventions

In this book, you will find a number of styles of text that distinguishe between different kinds of information. Here are some examples of these styles, and an explanation of their meaning.

Code words in text, database table names, folder names, filenames, file extensions, pathnames, dummy URLs, user input, and Twitter handles are shown as follows: "The last clause in the `try` statement should be `on Exception catch(e)` or, even better, a simple `catch(e)` to stop any type of error or exception."

A block of code is set as follows:

```
import 'dart:math';                                          (1)

void main() {
  var n = 0; // number of rabbits                            (2)

  print("The number of rabbits increases as:\n");            (3)
  for (int years = 0; years <= 10; years++) {                (4)
    n = (2 * pow(E, log(15) * years)).round().toInt();       (5)
    print("After $years years:\t $n animals");               (6)
  }
}
```

When we wish to draw your attention to a particular part of a code block, the relevant lines or items are set in bold:

```
try {
  int inp = int.parse(input);
} on FormatException {
  print ('ERROR: You must input an integer!');
}
```

Any command-line input or output is written as follows:

```
Observatory listening on http://127.0.0.1:49621
```

New terms and **important words** are shown in bold. Words that you see on the screen, in menus or dialog boxes for example, appear in the text like this: "Navigate to **Tools | Preferences | Run and Debug**, and change **Break on Exceptions** to **None**".

> Warnings or important notes appear in a box like this.

> Tips and tricks appear like this.

Reader feedback

Feedback from our readers is always welcome. Let us know what you think about this book—what you liked or may have disliked. Reader feedback is important for us to develop titles that you really get the most out of.

To send us general feedback, simply send an e-mail to feedback@packtpub.com, and mention the book title via the subject of your message.If there is a topic that you have expertise in and you are interested in either writing or contributing to a book, see our author guide on www.packtpub.com/authors.

Customer support

Now that you are the proud owner of a Packt book, we have a number of things to help you to get the most from your purchase.

Downloading the example code

You can download the example code files for all Packt books you have purchased from your account at http://www.packtpub.com. If you purchased this book elsewhere, you can visit http://www.packtpub.com/support and register to have the files e-mailed directly to you.

Errata

Although we have taken every care to ensure the accuracy of our content, mistakes do happen. If you find a mistake in one of our books—maybe a mistake in the text or the code—we would be grateful if you would report this to us. By doing so, you can save other readers from frustration and help us improve subsequent versions of this book. If you find any errata, please report them by visiting http://www.packtpub.com/submit-errata, selecting your book, clicking on the **errata submission form** link, and entering the details of your errata. Once your errata are verified, your submission will be accepted and the errata will be uploaded on our website, or added to any list of existing errata, under the Errata section of that title. Any existing errata can be viewed by selecting your title from http://www.packtpub.com/support.

Piracy

Piracy of copyright material on the Internet is an ongoing problem across all media. At Packt, we take the protection of our copyright and licenses very seriously. If you come across any illegal copies of our works, in any form, on the Internet, please provide us with the location address or website name immediately so that we can pursue a remedy.

Please contact us at copyright@packtpub.com with a link to the suspected pirated material.

We appreciate your help in protecting our authors, and our ability to bring you valuable content.

Questions

You can contact us at questions@packtpub.com if you are having a problem with any aspect of the book, and we will do our best to address it.

1
Dart – A Modern Web Programming Language

In this chapter, we will investigate:

- What Dart is all about
- Why it is a major step forward in the web programming language arena
- Getting started with Dart programming

We will get started with the Dart platform and have a look at its tools. Before this, we will be programming and taking a dive into a simple functional to-do list program so that you realize how familiar it all is.

What is Dart?

Dart is a new general and open source programming language with a vibrant community developed by Google Inc. and its official website is http://www.dartlang.org. It was first announced as a public preview on October 10, 2011; it has now reached version 1.10. World class language designers and developers are involved in this project, namely, Lars Bak and Kasper Lund (known for their V8 JavaScript engine embedded in the Chrome browser, which revolutionized performance in the JavaScript world), and *Gilad Bracha* (a language theorist known for the development of the **Strongtalk** and **Newspeak** languages and for the Java specification). Judging by the huge amount of resources and the number of teams working on it, it is clear that Google is very serious about making Dart a success.

> Take your time to familiarize yourself with the https://www.dartlang.org/ site. It contains a wealth of information, code examples, presentations, and so on to supplement this book, and we will often reference it.

Dart looks instantly familiar to the majority of today's programmers coming from a Java, C#, or **JavaScript (JS)** (ActionScript) background; you will feel at ease with Dart. However, this does not mean that it is only a copy of what already exists; it takes the best features of the statically typed "Java-C#" world and combines these with features more commonly found in dynamic languages such as JS, Python, and Ruby. On the nimble, dynamic side Dart allows rapid prototyping, evolving into a more structured development familiar to business app developers when application requirements become more complex.

Its main emphasis lies on building complex (if necessary), high performance, and scalable-rich client apps for the modern web. By modern web, we mean that it can execute in any browser on any kind of (client) device, including tablets and smartphones, taking advantage of all the features of HTML5, and it is ported to the ARM-architecture and the Android platform. Dart is designed with performance in mind by the people who developed V8. Because the Dart team at Google believes web components will be the foundation for the next evolution of web development, there is strong Dart support for the Polymer framework (web components are pieces of the web code containing HTML and Dart or JavaScript that you can reuse in different pages and projects. In other words, it is a reliable infrastructure of widgets). However, Dart can also run independently on servers. Because Dart clients and servers can communicate through web sockets (a persistent connection that allows both parties to start sending data at any time), it is, in fact, an end-to-end solution. It is perfect on the frontend to develop web components with all the necessary application logic, nicely integrated with HTML5 and the browser document model (DOM). On the backend server side, it can be used to develop web services, for example, to access databases, or cloud solutions in Google App Engine or other cloud infrastructures.

Moreover, it is ready to be used in the multicore world (remember, even your cell phone is multicore nowadays), because a Dart program can divide its work among any number of separate processes called **isolates**, an actor-based concurrency model as in Erlang.

Dart is a perfect fit for HTML5

To appreciate this fully, we have to take a look at the history of client-side web development.

A very short history of web programming

A web application is always a dialog between a client-browser requesting a page and the server responding with processing and delivering the page and its resources (such as pictures and other media). In the technology of the early dynamic web (the 90s of the previous century, extending even until today), the server performed most of the work: compiling a page, executing the code, fetching data from a data store, inserting the data in the page templates, and in the end, producing a stream of HTML and JavaScript, which was delivered to the browser. The client digested this stream, rendering the HTML into a browser screen while executing some JavaScript, so processing on the client side was minimal. The whole range of applications using Perl, Python, Ruby, PHP, JSP (Java Server Pages), and ASP.NET follows this principle. It is obvious that the heavy server loads impact negatively the number of clients that could be served as well as the response time in these applications. This mismatch is even clearer when we realize that the power of the client platforms (with their multicore processors and large memories) is heavily underutilized in this model.

The plugin model, within which the browser started specialized software (such as the Adobe Flash Player) to handle all kinds of media and other resources, partly tipped the balance to the client side. Following this trend, a whole range of technologies for developing **Rich Internet applications** (**RIA**) were developed that executed application code in the browser at the client side instead, ranging from Java applets around 1995 to Microsoft Active X Objects, culminating in the Adobe Flex and Microsoft Silverlight frameworks. While they have their merits, it is clear that they are more like a parasite in the browser; a virtual machine that executes, for example, ActionScript or C# code that is alien to the browser environment.

Dart empowers the web client

Empowering the client is the way to go, but this should better be done with software technology intimately linked to the browser itself: HTML and JavaScript. In order to eliminate the need for alien plugins, the power of HTML needs to be enlarged. This is precisely what is achieved with **HTML5**, for example, with its `<audio>` and `<video>` tags. **JavaScript** is the ubiquitous language of the web and it can, like Dart, request/send data from/to the server without blocking the user experience through technologies such as Ajax. However, flexible and dynamic as JavaScript may be, today it is also often called the assembly language for the web.

JavaScript is not the way to go

Why is this? JavaScript was, from the beginning, not designed to be a robust programming language, despite its name that suggests an affiliation with Java. It was designed to be a simple interpreted language, which could be used by nonprofessional programmers and that would be complemented by Java for more serious work. However, Java went away to prosper on the server and JavaScript invaded the browser space. Today, JS is being used to develop big and complex web applications, with server components such as Node.js, far beyond the original purpose of this language. Most people who have worked on a large client-side web application written entirely in JS will sooner or later come to the conclusion that its use in these applications is overstretched and the language was not meant to build this kind of software.

Understanding program structure is crucial in large, complex applications: this makes code maintenance, navigating in code, debugging, and refactoring easier. Unfortunately, JS code is hard to reason about, because there is almost no declarative syntax and it is very hard to detect dependencies between different scripts that can appear in one web page. JavaScript is also very permissive: almost anything (spelling mistakes, wrong types, and so on) is tolerated, making it hard to find errors and unpredictable results. Furthermore, JS allows you to change the way built-in core objects function, a practice often called monkey patching (for a reason!). Would you trust a language in which the following statement is true in its entirety and all of its comparisons?

```
10.0 == '10' == new Boolean(true) == '1'
```

Because of this sometimes undefined nature of JS, its performance is often very unpredictable, so building high performance web apps in it is tricky.

Google, GWT, and Dart

Google is the web firm par excellence: its revenue model is entirely based on its massive web applications, such as Gmail (some half a million lines of JS), Google Docs, Google Maps, and Google Search. So, it is no wonder that these teams encountered the difficulties of building a large JS application and strived for a better platform. Due to the fundamental flaws of JS and its slow evolution, something better was needed. A first attempt was **Google Web Toolkit** (**GWT**), where the development was done in Java, which was then compiled to JS. Although it was reasonably successful because it enabled a structured and tooled approach to application building, it was clear that the use of Java is somewhat awkward in a web environment. Thus, arose the idea for Dart: a kind of hybrid platform between the dynamic nature of JS and the structured and toolable languages such as Java and C#. In order for Dart to run in all modern web browsers like GWT, it must be compiled to JS. Google has provided a special build of Chromium, called Dartium, which provides a **Dart VM** to execute Dart code on the fly without any compilation step. This is useful for testing in Dart Editor (Chrome or any other browser can be used to test the JS version of your Dart app).

Advantages of Dart

This way, Dart can get a better performance profile than JS (remember that the same experts who developed the V8 JS VM are forging Dart, see `http://www.dartlang.org/performance/`) and, at the same time, maintain the simple and rapid development process of JS in the browser: the edit code, save, and refresh browser cycle to view the latest version, rather than having to stop, recompile, and run for every little change. Dart delivers high performance on all the modern web browsers and environments ranging from small handheld devices to server-side execution. When it runs on its own VM, Dart is faster than JS (currently, around 1.5 times the performance of JS). Moreover, through **snapshotting** (a mechanism inherited from Smalltalk), a Dart app has a fast application startup time in contrast to JS, where all the source code has to be interpreted or compiled from the source.

Dart executes in the browser after having been compiled to JS, so Dart runs everywhere JS does. The Dart VM can also run standalone on a client or server.

Another big advantage compared with GWT is that Dart is much better integrated with the web page and like JS can directly manipulate the page elements and the document structure, that is, the **Document Object Model (DOM)**. Like JS, it has intimate access to the new HTML5 APIs, for example, drawing with the canvas, playing audio and video clips, or using the new local storage possibilities. Following the RIA model explained earlier, Dart executes the full application code in the browser, requesting data from the server and rebuilding the page user interface when needed. Because Dart wants to be a part of the web, not just sit on the top, the team has also built a Dart to JavaScript interop layer to call JavaScript from Dart and the other way around. Together with its out-of-browser and server capabilities, Dart is also conceived to build complex, large-scale web applications. This can be clearly seen from its object-oriented nature, and Dart code is built with code clarity and structure (using libraries and packages) in mind. To summarize it:

- Dart compiles to JavaScript
- Dart is faster than JavaScript while running in its VM (as a server standalone application, or in Dartium, which is a special build of the Chromium browser)
- Dart is better suited for large scale applications

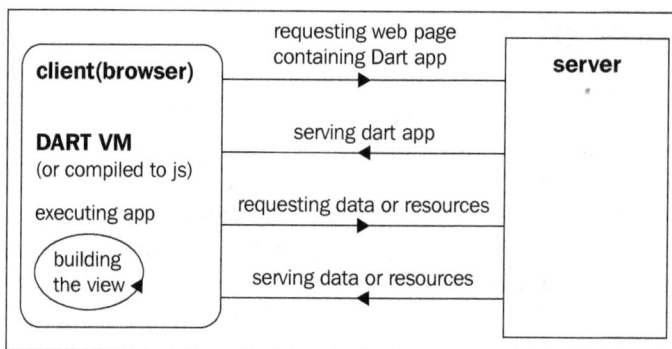

The Dart web model

Getting started with Dart

The Dart project team wants us to get an optimal development experience, so they provide a full but lightweight IDE: the **Dart Editor**, a light version of the well-known Eclipse environment. Installing this is the easiest way to get started, because it comprises the full Dart environment. Another awesome editor is **WebStorm** from JetBrains (see `https://www.dartlang.org/tools/webstorm/`).

Installing the Dart Editor

Because Eclipse is written in Java, we need a **Java Runtime Environment (JRE)**, version 6 or higher, on our system (this is not needed for Dart itself, only for the Dart Editor). To check whether this is already the case, go to `http://www.java.com/en/download/installed.jsp`.

If it is not the case, head to `http://www.oracle.com/technetwork/java/javase/downloads/index.html`, click on the **JRE DOWNLOAD** button, choose the JRE for your platform, and then click on **Run** to start the installation.

Then, go to `http://www.dartlang.org/` and click on the **GET STARTED** and **Download Dart** menu item. Under **Download the SDK**, choose the appropriate button (according to whether your installed OS is 32-bit or 64-bit) to download the editor.

> This is also the page where you can download the SDK separately, or the Dartium browser (a version of Chromium to test your Dart apps) or download the Dart source code.

You are prompted to save a file named `darteditor-os-nn.zip`, where OS can be Windows, Linux, or MacOS, and nn is 32 or 64. Extracting the content of this file will create a folder named `dart` containing everything you need: `dart-sdk`, `dartium`, and `DartEditor`. This procedure should go smoothly, but if you encounter a problem, please review `http://www.dartlang.org/docs/editor/getting-started/`.

> In case you get the following error message: **Failed to load the JNI shared library C:\Program Files(x86)\Java\jre6\bin\client\jvm.dll**, do not worry. This happens when JRE and Dart Editor do not have the same bit width. More precisely, this happens when you go to `http://www.java.com/` to download JRE. In order to be sure what JRE to select, it is safer to go to `http://www.oracle.com/technetwork/java/javase/downloads/index.html`, click on the **JRE DOWNLOAD** button, and choose the appropriate version. If possible, use a 64-bit versions of JRE and Dart Editor. There could be another problem related to JRE. After unzipping a Dart Editor file, it is recommended to copy the `jre` folder from the Java folder to the `dart` folder (where the `DartEditor.exe` file is located). Again, it is important to copy the correct bit width version. If the 64-bit version of Dart Editor is used, the 64-bit version of JRE must be copied. This version is in the `Program Files/Java` folder under the `jre7` name (don't copy the `jre7` folder from Program Files (x86) / Java, this is the 32-bit version). Finally, after the `jre7` folder is copied, it must be renamed from `jre7` to `jre`.

Other options for working with Dart code

If you are more familiar working in the Eclipse environment, you can simply use the Dart Eclipse plugin (`https://www.dartlang.org/tools/eclipse-plugin/`), which provides the same functionality as Dart Editor. Another rich working environment alternative is built in the WebStorm environment from IntelliJ: `https://www.dartlang.org/tools/webstorm/`.

If you need a cloud environment, you can use DartPad for simpler projects: `https://dartpad.dartlang.org/`.

Your first Dart program

Double-click on `DartEditor.exe` to open the editor. Navigate to **File | New Project** or click on the first button below the menu (**Create a new Dart Project...**). Fill in an application name (for example, `dart1`) and choose the folder you want the code file to be created (make a folder such as `dart_apps` to provide some structure; you can do this while using the **Browse** button). We will leave the **Console application – A simple command-line application** selection.

With these names, a `dart1` folder is made as a subfolder of `dart_apps` and a `main.dart` source file is created in `dart1\bin` with the following code (we'll explain `pubspec.yaml` and the packages folder in one of the following examples). For now, replace its contents with the following code:

```
void main() {
  print("Hello, World!");
}
```

> **Downloading the example code**
>
> You can download the example code files for all the Packt books you have purchased from your account at `http://www.packtpub.com`. If you purchased this book elsewhere, you can visit `http://www.packtpub.com/support` and register to have the files e-mailed directly to you.

Here, we see immediately that Dart is a C-syntax style language, using { } to surround code and ; to terminate statements. Every app also has a unique `main()` function, which is the starting point of the application.

This is probably the shortest app possible, but it can be even shorter! The void keyword indicates (as in Java or C#) that the method does not explicitly return an object (indeed print only produces output to the console), but the return types can be left out. Furthermore, when a function has only one single expression, we can shorten this further to the following elegant shorthand syntax:

```
main() => print("Hello, World!");
```

Now, change the printed string to "Becoming a Dart Ninja!" and click on the green arrow button (or press *Ctrl + R*) to run the application. You should see something like the following screenshot (where the **Files**, **Apps**, and **Outline** items from the **Tools** menu were selected):

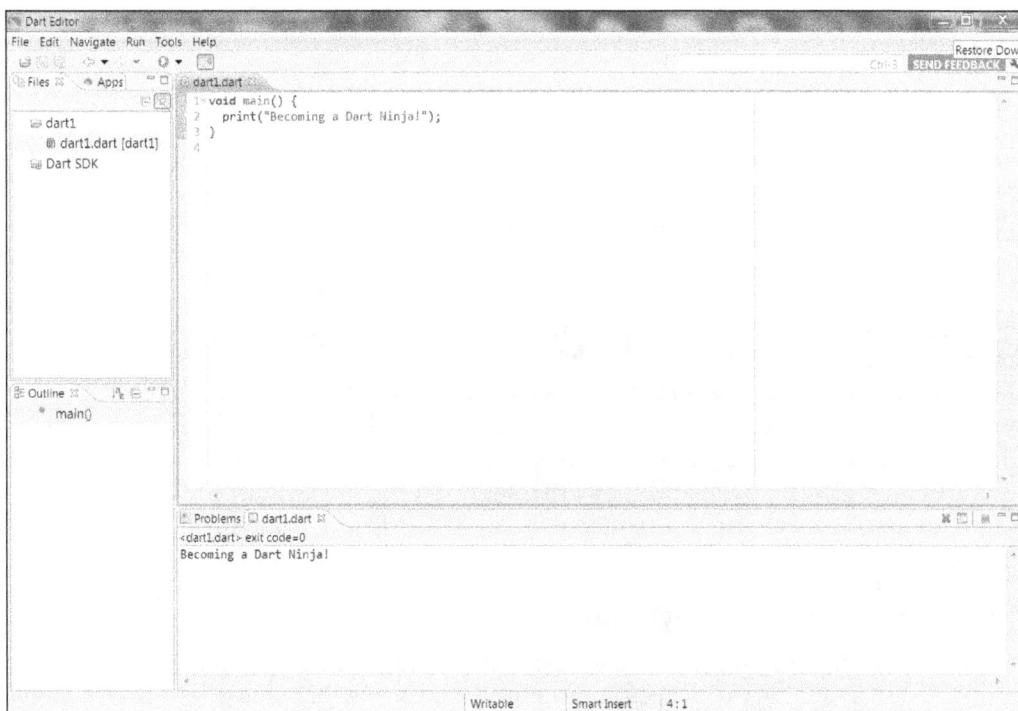

The Dart Editor

You have successfully executed your first Dart program!

Near the bottom of the screen, we see our string printed out together with the exit code=0 message meaning that all went well.

The **Files** and **Apps** tabs are useful for browsing through your applications and for creating, copying, moving, renaming, and deleting files. The **Outline** tab now only shows main(), but this tool will quickly become very useful because it provides an overview of the code in the active file.

Because this was a command-line application, we could just as easily have opened a console in our dart1 folder and executed the dart main.dart command to produce the same output as shown in the following screenshot:

```
Administrator: C:\Windows\system32\cmd.exe
E:\dart\Book  - Learning Dart by Projects\BOOK\code\chapter_1\dart1>dart dart1.dart
Becoming a Dart Ninja!
```

A Dart console application

> To let this work, you must first let the OS know where to find the Dart V. For example, in Windows, you change the path environment variable to include C:\dart\dart-sdk\bin if your Dart installation lives in C:\dart.

Getting a view on the Dart tool chain

Dart comes with *batteries included*, which means that a complete stack of tools is provided by Google to write Dart apps, compile, test, document, and publish them. Moreover, these tools are platform-independent (being made for 32- and 64-bit Linux, OSX, and Windows) and they are integrated in the Dart Editor IDE. The Dart Editor contains everything a seasoned developer needs to work with confidence on his app:

- Syntax coloring for keywords
- Auto completion for class members (by typing . after a class name you get a list of available properties and methods of the current class)
- Folding/unfolding code blocks
- Tools to navigate the code (a handy overview of the code with the outline, find callers of a method, and so on)
- Full debugging capabilities of both browser and server applications
- Choose your preferred editor style by navigating to **Tools** | **Preferences** | **Visual Theme**
- Quick fixes for common errors

- Refactoring capabilities
- Direct access to the online API documentation by navigating to **Help |
  API Reference**

The code you make is analyzed while you type, indicating warning (yellow triangles) or errors (red underscores or stop signs). To get more acquainted and experiment with these possibilities, go and read the documentation at http://www.dartlang. org/docs/editor/ and play with one of the samples such as Sunflower or Solar (you can find the samples by navigating to **Tools | Welcome Page**). From now on, use the editor in conjunction with the code examples of the book so that you can try them out and test the changes.

The Dart execution model

How a Dart app executes is sketched in the following diagram:

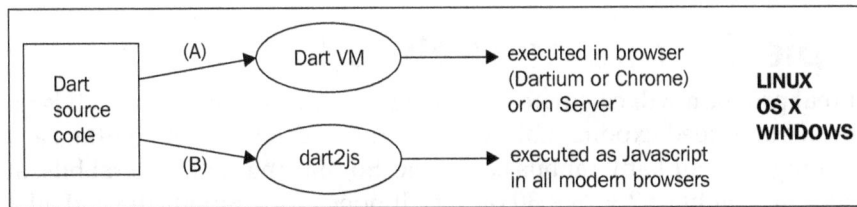

The Dart execution model

The Dart code produced in the Dart Editor (or in a plugin for Eclipse or IntelliJ) can:

- Execute in the Dart VM, hosted in Dartium (Dartium is an experimental version of Chrome to test out Dart) or directly in the operating system (the browser VM knows about HTML, the server VM does not, but can use, for example, IO and sockets, so they are not completely equivalent)
- Be compiled to JS with the dart2js compiler so that it can run in all the recent browsers

Code libraries in Dart are called packages and the **Dart SDK** core contains the basic types and functionalities to work with collection, math, html, uri, json, and so on. They can be recognized by the dart:prefix syntax, for example, dart:html. If you want to use a functionality from a library in a code file, you must import it by using the following as the first statement(s) in your code (dart:core is imported by default):

```
import 'dart:html';
```

The Dart code can be tested with the **unit test** package and, for documentation, you can use the **dartdoc** tool, which generates a local website structured like the official API documentation on the Web. The **pub** tool is the Dart package manager: if your app needs other packages besides the SDK, pub can install them for you (from the **Tools** menu item in Dart Editor, select **Pub Get** or **Pub Update**). You can also publish your apps with it in the `http://pub.dartlang.org/` web repository.

We will see all of these tools in action in *Chapter 2, Getting to Work with Dart*.

A bird's eye view on Dart

It's time to get our feet wet by working on a couple of examples. All the code will be thoroughly explained step by step. Along the way, we will give you a lot of tips and, in the next chapter, we will go into more detail on the different possibilities, thus gaining deeper insight into Dart's design principles.

Example 1 – raising rabbits

Our first real program will calculate the procreation rate of rabbits, which is not only phenomenal but indeed exponential. A female rabbit can have seven litters a year with an average of four baby rabbits each time. So, starting with two rabbits, at the end of the year, you have $2 + 28 = 30$ rabbits. If none of the rabbits die and all are fertile, the growth rate will follow the next formula, where n is the number of rabbits after the years specified:

$$n(years) = 2 \; x \; ek \; x \; years$$

Here, the growth factor $k = ln(30/2) = ln15$. Let's calculate the number after each year for the first 10 years.

Go to **File | New Project** as before, select **Console application**, and type the following code, or simply open the script from `chapter_1` in the provided code listings (don't worry about the `pubspec.yaml` file, we'll discuss it in the web version).

The calculation is done in the following `prorabbits_v1.dart` Dart script:

```dart
import 'dart:math';                                         (1)

void main() {
  var n = 0; // number of rabbits                           (2)

  print("The number of rabbits increases as:\n");           (3)
  for (int years = 0; years <= 10; years++) {               (4)
    n = (2 * pow(E, log(15) * years)).round().toInt();      (5)
```

```
    print("After $years years:\t $n animals");              (6)
  }
}
```

Our program produces the following output:

```
The number of rabbits increases as:

After 0 years:      2 animals
After 1 years:      30 animals
After 2 years:      450 animals
After 3 years:      6750 animals
After 4 years:      101250 animals
After 5 years:      1518750 animals
After 6 years:      22781250 animals
After 7 years:      341718750 animals
After 8 years:      5125781250 animals
After 9 years:      76886718750 animals
After 10 years:   1153300781250 animals
```

So, if developing programs doesn't make you rich, breeding rabbits will. Because we need some mathematical formulas such as natural logarithms log and power pow, we imported dart:math in line (1). Our number of livestock n is declared in line (2); you can see that we precede its name with var. Here, we don't have to indicate the type of n as int or num (so called *type annotations*), as Dart uses *optional typing*.

> Local variables are commonly declared untyped as var.

We could have declared it to be of type num (number) or int, because we know that n is a whole number. However, it is not necessary, as Dart will derive this from the context in which n is used. The other number type is called double, used for decimal numbers. Also, the initialization part (= 0) could have been left out. With no initialization var n; or even int n;, it gives n the value null, because every variable in Dart is an object. The null keyword simply indicates that the object has no value yet (meaning that it is not yet allocated in heap memory). It will come as no surprise that // indicates the beginning of a comment, and /* and */ can be used to make a multiline comment.

> Comment on a section of the code by selecting it and then right-click on **Toggle comment** in the **Edit** menu.

In the lines (3) and (6), we see that within a quoted string, we can use escape characters such as \n and \t to format our output. Line (4) uses the well-known for loop that is also present in Dart. In order to have the count of animals as a whole number, we needed to apply the round() function. The pow function produces double and because 6750.0 animals doesn't look so good, we have to convert double into int with the toInt() function. In the line (6), the elegant string substitution mechanism (also called string interpolation) is used: print takes a string as argument (a string variable: any expression enclosed within " " or ' ') and, in any such quoted string expression, you can substitute the value of variable n by writing $n. If you want the value of an expression within a string, such as a + b, you have to enclose the expression with braces, for example, ${a + b}.

> You don't have to write ${n} while displaying a variable n, just use $n; you can also simply use print(n).

It is important to realize that we did not have to make any class in our program. Dart is no class junkie like Java or C#. A lot can be done only with functions; but if you want to represent real objects in your programs, classes is the way to go (see the *Example 2 – banking* section).

Extracting a function

This version of our program is not yet very modular, we would like to extract the calculation in a separate calculateRabbits(years) method that takes the number of years as a parameter. This is shown in the following code (version 2 line (4) of prorabbits_v2.dart) with exactly the same output as version 1:

```
import 'dart:math';

int rabbitCount = 0;                                    (1)
const int NO_YEARS = 10;                                (2)
const int GROWTH_FACTOR = 15;                           (3)

void main() {
  print("The number of rabbits increases as:\n");
  for (int years = 0; years <= NO_YEARS; years++) {
    rabbitCount = calculateRabbits(years);              (4)
    print("After $years years:\t $rabbitCount animals");
  }
}

int calculateRabbits(int years) {                       (5)
  return (2 * pow(E, log(GROWTH_FACTOR) *
    years)).round().toInt();
}
```

We could have written this new function ourselves, but Dart has a built-in refactoring called **Extract Method**. Highlight the line:

```
n = (2 * pow(E, log(15) * years)).round().toInt();
```

Right-click and select **Extract Method**. Dart will do the bulk of the work for you, but we can still simplify the proposed code by omitting the n parameter.

The `calculateRabbits` function calculates and returns an integer value; this is indicated by the `int` word preceding the function name. We give the function a return type here (int), but the program would have run without the function-type indication because of Dart's type inference.

This new function is called by `main()`. This is the way a Dart program works: all the lines in `main()` are executed in sequence calling functions, as needed, and the execution (and with it, the Dart VM) stops when the } ending of `main()` is reached. Things get a bit more complicated when Futures or Streams are used: these are put in a microtask queue to be executed. Only when there are no more tasks to execute in this queue will the Dart VM stop executing.

We rename the n variable to `rabbitCount`, so we need no more comments.

Renaming a variable is also a built-in refactoring. Select the variable (all the occurrences are then indicated), right-click, and then select **Rename**.

A good programmer doesn't like hardcoded values such as `10` and `15` in a program. What if they have to be changed? We replace them with constant variables indicated by the `const` keyword in Dart, whose name is, by convention, typed in capital letters and parts separated by _, see lines `(2)` and `(3)`.

Take care of your top-level variables, constants, and functions, because they will probably be visible outside of your program (sometimes, called the interface or API of your program). Type them and name them well.

Now, for some practice:

1. Examine this second version by going to **Tools | Outline**.

2. Set a breakpoint on the `rabbitCount = calculateRabbits(years);` line by double-clicking on the margin in the front.

3. Run the program and learn how to use the features of the **Debugger** tool (press *F5* to step line by line, *F6* or *F7* to step over or out of a function, and *F8* to resume execution until the next breakpoint is hit).

4. Watch the values of the `years` and `rabbitCount` variables.

The output should resemble the following screenshot:

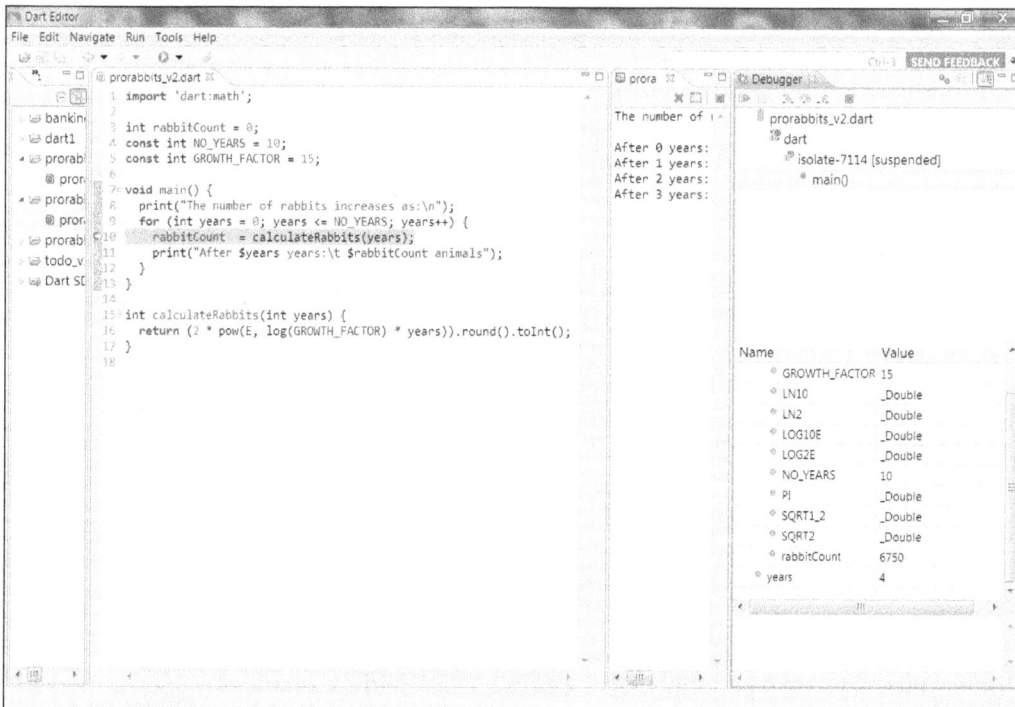

Debugging prorabbits_v2.dart

A web version

As a final version, for now, let us build an app that uses an HTML screen, where we can input the number of years of rabbit elevation and output the resulting number of animals. Go to **File | New Project**, but this time select **Web application**. Now, a lot more code is generated, which needs explaining. The app now contains a `web` subfolder; this will be the home for all of the app's resources. However, for now, it contains a stylesheet (`.css` file), a hosting web page (`.html`), and a startup code file (normally `main.dart`, in our case, `prorabbits_v3.dart`). The first line in this file makes the HTML functionality available to our code:

```
import 'dart:html';
```

We remove the rest of the example code, so only an empty `main()` function remains. Look at the source of the HTML page right before the `</body>` tag, it contains the following code:

```
<script type="application/dart" src="prorabbits_v3.dart"></script>
<script src="packages/browser/dart.js"></script>
```

The first line starts our Dart script.

The Dart VM exists only in Dartium for testing and debugging purposes. For other browsers, we must supply the Dart-to-JS compiled scripts; this compilation can be done in the Editor by navigating to **Tools | Pub Build - Minified Javascript**. The output size is minimal: the "dead" JS code that is not used is eliminated in a process called **tree shaking**. However, where does this mysterious script `dart.js` come from? The `src="packages/browser/dart.js"` value means that it is a package available in the Dart repository at `http://pub.dartlang.org/`.

External packages that your app depends on need to be specified in the `dependencies` section in the `pubspec.yaml` file. In our app, it contains (I have changed the name and description) the following:

```
name: prorabbits_v3
description: Raising rabbits the web way
dependencies:
  browser: any
```

We see that our app depends on the browser package; any version of it is ok. The package is added to your app when you right-click on the selected `pubspec.yaml` file and select **Pub Get**: a `packages` folder is added to your app and, per package, a subfolder is added containing the downloaded code, in our case, `dart.js` (In *Chapter 2, Getting to Work with Dart*, we will explore pub in greater depth and see that it can also be performed from the command-line).

For this program, we replace the HTML `<p id="sample_text_id"></p>` code as shown in the following code:

```
<input type="number" id="years" value="5" min="1" max="30">
<input type="button" id="submit" value="Calculate"/>
<br/>Number of rabbits: <label id="output"></label>
```

The input field with type number (new in HTML5) gives us a `NumericUpDown` control with a default value 5 limited to the range of 1 to 30. In our Dart code, we now have to handle the click-event at the button with `id` as `submit`. We do this in our `main()` function with the following line of code:

```
querySelector("#submit").onClick.listen( (e) => calcRabbits() );
```

The query Selector ("#submit") gives us a reference in the code to the button with ID equal to submit and listen redirects to an anonymous function (see *Chapter 2*, *Getting to Work with Dart*) to handle the e event, which calls the calcRabbits() function shown in the following code:

```
calcRabbits() {
    // binding variables to html elements:
    InputElement yearsInput  = querySelector("#years");     (1)
    LabelElement output = querySelector("#output");         (2)
    // getting input
    String yearsString = yearsInput.value;
    int years = int.parse(yearsString);
    // calculating and setting output:
    output.innerHtml = "${calculateRabbits(years)}";
}
```

Here, in the lines (1) and (2), the input field and the output label are bound to the yearsInput and output variables. This is always done in the same way: the querySelector() function takes as its argument a CSS selector; in this case, the ID of the input field (an ID is preceded by a # sign). We typed yearsInput as InputElement (because it is bound to an input field). This way, we can access its value, which is always string. We then convert this string into an int type with the int.parse() function, because calculateRabbits needs an int parameter. The result is shown as HTML in the output label via string substitution, see the following screenshot:

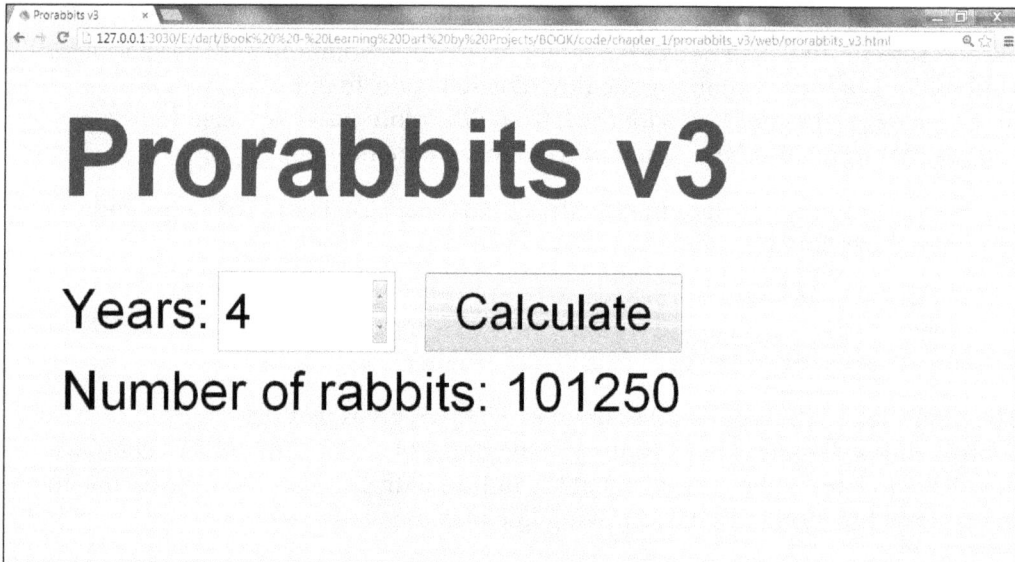

The screen of prorabbits_v3

All the objects in the Dart code that are bound to the HTML elements are instances of the `Element` class. Notice how you can change the Dart and HTML code, and save and hit refresh in Dartium (Chrome) to get the latest version of your app.

Example 2: banking

All the variables (strings, numbers, and also functions) in Dart are objects, so they are also instances of a class. The class concept is very important in modeling entities in real-world applications, making our code modular and reusable. We will now demonstrate how to make and use a simple class in Dart by modeling a bank account. The most obvious properties of such an object are the owner of the account, the bank account number, and the balance (the amount of money it contains). We want to be able to deposit or withdraw an amount of money so as to increase or decrease the balance, respectively. This can be coded in a familiar and compact way in Dart, as shown in the following code:

```
class BankAccount {
    String owner, number;
    double balance;
    // constructor:
    BankAccount(this.owner, this.number, this.balance);     (1)
    // methods:
    deposit(double amount) => balance += amount;            (2)
    withdraw(double amount) => balance -= amount;
}
```

Notice the elegant constructor syntax in line (1), where the incoming parameter values are automatically assigned to the object fields via `this`. The methods (line (2)) can also use the shorthand `=>` function syntax, because the body contains only one expression. If you prefer the {} syntax, they will be written as follows:

```
deposit(double amount) {
    balance += amount;
    return balance;
}
```

The code in `main()` makes a `BankAccount` object `ba` and exercises its methods (see the `banking_v1.dart` program):

```
main() {
    var ba = new BankAccount("John Gates",
        "075-0623456-72", 1000.0);
    print("Initial balance:\t\t ${ba.balance} \$");
    ba.deposit(250.0);
```

```
      print("Balance after deposit:\t\t ${ba.balance} \$");
      ba.withdraw(100.0);
      print("Balance after withdrawal:\t ${ba.balance} \$");
   }
```

The preceding code produces the following output:

```
   Initial balance:                 1000.0 $
   Balance after deposit:           1250.0 $
   Balance after withdrawal:        1150.0 $
```

Notice how when you type ba. in the editor, the list of the BankAccount class members appears to autocomplete your code. By convention, variables (objects) and functions (or methods) start with a lower case letter and follow the CamelCase notation (http://en.wikipedia.org/wiki/CamelCase), while class names start with a capital letter as well as the word parts in the name. Remember Dart is case sensitive!

Making a to-do list with Dart

Since this has become the "Hello World" for web programmers, let's make a simple to-do list and start a new todo_v1 web application. To record our tasks, we need an input field corresponding with InputElement in Dart:

```
   <input id="task" type="text" placeholder=
     "What do you want to do?"/>
```

The HTML5 placeholder attribute lets you specify a default text that appears in the field.

We specify a list tag (UListElement), which we will fill up in our code:

```
   <ul id="list"/>
```

The following is the code from todo_v1.dart:

```
   import 'dart:html';

   InputElement task;
   UListElement list;

   main() {
     task = querySelector('#task');            (1)
     list = querySelector('#list');            (2)
     task.onChange.listen( (e) => addItem() ); (3)
   }

   void addItem() {
```

```
var newTask = new LIElement();        (4)
newTask.text = task.value;            (5)
task.value = '';                      (6)
list.children.add(newTask);           (7)
}
```

We bind our HTML elements to the Dart objects task and list in the lines (1) and
(2). In line (3), we attach an addItem event handler to the onChange event of the
textfield task: this fires, when the user enters something in the field and leaves it
(either by pressing *Tab* or *Enter*). UListElement is, in fact, a collection of LIElements
(these are its children). So, for each new task, we will make LIElement in (4),
assign the task's value to it in (5), clear the input field in (6), and add the new
LIElement to the list in (7). In the following screenshot, you can see some tasks to
be performed:

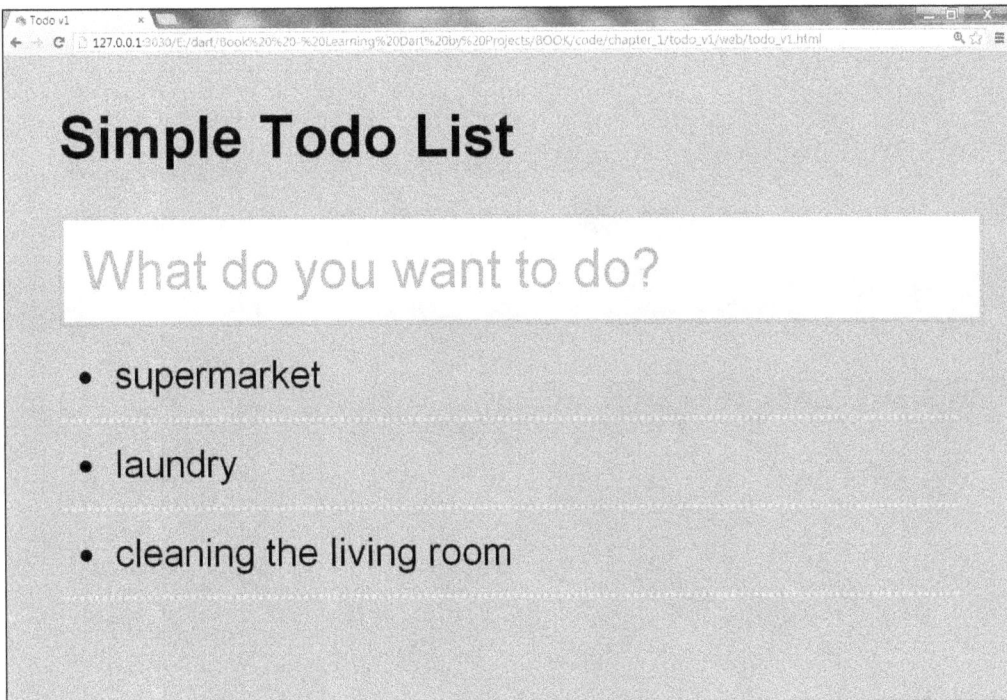

A simple to-do list

Of course, this version isn't very useful (unless you want to make a print of your
screen); our tasks aren't recorded and we can't indicate the tasks are finished. Don't
worry, we will enhance this app in the future versions.

Summary

We covered a lot of ground in this introductory chapter but, by now, you know the reasons for using Dart in the context of web applications. We also saw where Dart apps can live, how they are executed, and the various tools to work with Dart, in particular, the Dart Editor.

You also got acquainted with some simple command-line and web Dart apps and got a feeling for the Dart syntax. In the next chapter, we will explore the various code and data structures of Dart more systematically. Any obscurities that are still there in your mind will surely disappear. More coming soon to a Dart center near you...

2
Getting to Work with Dart

In this chapter, you will get a firm grasp on how to program in Dart. The code and data structures in Dart and its functional principles are explained by exploring practical examples. We will look at the following topics:

- Variables: if, how, and when to type them
- What are the basic types that you can use?
- Documenting your programs
- How to influence the order of execution of a program
- Using functions in Dart
- How to recognize and catch errors and exceptions

You will see plenty of examples, we will also be revisiting the code from *Chapter 1, Dart – A Modern Web Programming Language*. Because most of this will be familiar to you, we will discuss these topics succinctly and emphasize only on the ones which are new or different. You can refer to `http://www.dartlang.org/docs/dart-up-and-running/contents/ch02.html` if you need more detailed explanations. We encourage you to play with the code examples, it is the best way to become familiar with Dart. The full API reference documentation is available at `http://api.dartlang.org`. Experiment in the Dart Editor to find out more if in doubt!

Variables – to type or not to type

In our first example (raising rabbits) in *Chapter 1, Dart – A Modern Web Programming Language*, we started by declaring a `rabbitCount` variable dynamically with `var`. Then, in the second version, we gave it a static `int` type (refer to the `prorabbits_v1.dart` and `prorabbits_v2.dart` files in *Chapter 1, Dart – A Modern Web Programming Language*) and concluded that *typing is optional* in Dart. This seems confusing and it has provoked a lot of discussion: "is Dart a dynamic language like Ruby or JavaScript, or a static language like Java or C#?" After all, some of us were raised in the (static) belief that typed variables are absolutely necessary to check whether a program is correct, a task mainly performed by the compiler (however, the Dart VM has no separate compiler step, and dart2js, the Dart to JS compiler, doesn't check types because JS is fully dynamic).

It turns out that no mainstream language actually has a perfect type system (static types don't guarantee program correctness) and that not letting a program run, because of an obscure type error, blocks the programmer's creativity. However, it is true that static type checks can prevent bugs. On the other hand, the dynamic belief states that typing variables hinders the programmer's fantasy (and wears out the fingers). In their world, grave errors due to wrong types occur only when the program is running; to avoid such calamities, they have to rely on a rigorous unit testing discipline.

Dart takes a pragmatic middle stand: web programming is already accustomed to dynamically typed languages that are more flexible. Dart honors this and adheres to a system of optional or loose typing. You can start out by writing your code without types while you're still experimenting and doing quick prototyping. In a more advanced stage, you can annotate (some of) the code with types. This will enhance the readability of your code for your fellow developers and, as such, it will be additional documentation. Furthermore, it will allow the Dart analyzer tools to check the code for the types used and report possible errors, so it makes more useful developer tools as possible.

As the app becomes larger and more stable, types can be added to aid debugging and impose structure where desired, making the code more robust, documented, and more maintainable. Dart code can evolve from a simple, untyped experimental prototype to a complex, modular application with types. Moreover, as you will experience while working in the Dart Editor, with types, the IDE (Integrated Development Environment) will be able to suggest better autocompletion for the properties and methods of any code object. The two extremes (no typing or everything typed) are not encouraged.

> In general, give everything in your code that can be seen publicly, a type (in the sense that it is visible in and can be used from outside the code, sometimes called the interface) such as top-level variables and functions, including their arguments. This way, other apps can use your code with increased safety.

Using `var` (or `final` or `const`) for an object leaves it untyped. However, in fact, Dart internally considers this object to be of type `dynamic`, the unknown type. The `dynamic` keyword is rarely seen in the code: it is used to denote a type that can change over the course of the running program or when the developer does not know the type of the variable.

To cope with this dilemma, Dart has two runtime modes (ways of executing programs):

- **Checked mode**: This is typically used when you develop, debug, and test. The IDE will warn you when you misuse variables in a typed context (a tool called the `dartanalyzer` continuously checks your code, while saving and even while you type). The types are checked while executing assignments, passing arguments to a function, and returning a result from a function. By default, your program will also run in this mode, breaking the execution when a (typing) error occurs (you can change this behavior by navigating to **Run | Manage Launches | VM settings** and unchecking the **Run in checked mode** checkbox).

- **Production mode**: This is when your program runs for real, that is, it is used by customers. Then, Dart runs as a fully dynamic language and ignores type information, giving a performance boost because the checks don't need to be performed.

Errors (indicated in the Editor by a white x in a red circle) prevent you from running the program. For example, delete an ; or } ending from some source code and see what happens.

Warnings (a black ! in a yellow triangle) indicate that the code might not work. For example, in the following code snippet (from `chapter_2\checked_mode.dart`), a warning is indicated in line (1):

```
int age = 'Dart';                    (1)
print ('$age') ;
```

The warning sign is shown in front of the line and the string with the value 'Dart' underlined in yellow. If you hover the cursor over one of these, you will see the message: **A value of type 'String' is not assignable to 'int'**. If you try to run this example in the default checked mode in Dart Editor, you'll get the following output:

```
Unhandled exception:
type 'String' is not a subtype of type 'int' of 'age'.
#0   main
(file:///E:/dart/Book/code/chapter_2/checked_mode/bin/checked_mode.da
rt:2:14)
```

However, if you uncheck and let it run in the production mode, it will run and the normal Dart output will appear in the console. Dart expects the developer to have thoroughly checked and tested the program.

> Warnings do not prevent you from running a program in the production mode in most cases.

A variable is just a nickname of an object; the same object can have multiple variables referring to it and a variable name can also switch from one object to another, like in the following code:

```
var name = 'John';
name = 'Lucy';     // name now refers to another String object
```

However, sometimes, you don't want this to happen, you want a variable to always point at the same object (such as immutable variables in functional languages or, in other words, a read-only variable). This is possible in Dart using the final keyword, like in the following code (refer to final.dart):

```
final name = 'John';
name = 'Lucy';          //   (1)   warning!
```

Now, line (1) generates a warning: **Final variables cannot be assigned a value**, but the execution is stopped even in the production mode! The var and final keywords used as such refer to a dynamic untyped variable, but final can also be used together with a type, as shown in the following code:

```
final String name = 'John';
```

The const keyword (which we used already in prorabbits_v2.dart in
Chapter 1, Dart – A Modern Web Programming Language) like final also refers to
something whose value cannot change, but it is more restricted. It must be a literal
value (such as 100, Dart, or another const) or a calculation with known numbers,
a so-called compile-time constant. For example, see the following code:

```
const NO_SECINMIN = 60;
const NO_SECINDAY = NO_SECINMIN * 60 * 24;
```

The following is an example that shows the difference:

```
int daysInWeek = 7;
final fdaysInYear = daysInWeek * 52;
const DAYSINYEAR =  daysInWeek * 52;  //  (2) error!
```

Now, line (2) gives an error:

```
'const' variables must be constant value.
```

To summarize it, types are not used for performance optimization and they don't
change the program behavior, but they can help you write and maintain your code; a
little typing goes a long way. A combination of tool support, static analysis, checked
mode assertions, and unit tests can make you feel just as safe in Dart as in any
statically typed language while being more productive.

Built-in types and their methods

Like Ruby, Dart is a purely **object-oriented (OO)** language, so every variable in
Dart points to an object and there are no primitive types like in Java or C#. Every
variable is an instance of a class (that inherits from the Object base class) and has a
type and, when uninitialized, has the null value. However, for easy use, Dart has
built-in types for the numbers, Booleans, and Strings defined in dart:core that look
and behave like primitive types; that is, they can be made with literal values and
have the basic operations that you would expect (to make it clear, we will use full
typing in builtin_types.dart, but we could have used var as well).

A **String** (notice the capital) is a sequence of Unicode (UTF-16) characters,
for example:

```
String country = "Egypt";
String chineseForWorld = '世界';
```

They can be indicated by paired ' or " (use "" when the string contains ' and vice
versa). Adjacent string literals are concatenated. If you need multiline strings, use
triple quotes ''' or """ (handy for defining chunks of HTML!).

Escape characters are not interpreted when the string is prefixed by r, a so-called raw string, which is invaluable while defining regular expressions. The empty string ' ' or " " is not the same as null. The following are all legal strings:

```
String q = "What's up?";
String s1 = 'abc'
            "def";
print(s1); // abcdef
String multiLine = '''
  <h1> Beautiful page </h1>
  <div class="start"> This is a story about the landing
      on the moon </div>
  <hr>
''';
print(multiLine);
String rawStr = r"Why don't you \t learn Dart!";
// output: Why don't you \t learn Dart!
print(rawStr);
var emptyStr = ''; // empty string
```

The num (number) types are int (integer) and double, which are both subtypes of num:

```
int n = 42;
double pi = 3.14;
```

Integers can use a hexadecimal notation preceding with 0x, as shown in the following code:

```
int hex = 0xDEADBEEF;
```

They can be of arbitrary precision, as shown in the following code:

```
int hugePrimeNumber = 4776913109852041418248056622882488319;
```

> You cannot use this feature if you rely on the compilation to JS, because here, we are restricted to JS integers!

Doubles are of a 64-bit precision and can use scientific notation:

```
double d1 = 12345e-4;
```

The num type has the usual abs(), ceil(), and floor() methods as well as round() for rounding. Use either int or num, but double only in the specific case when you need a decimal number that cannot be an integer.

Booleans can only have a true or false value:

```
bool selected = false;
```

In contrast to JavaScript, where any variable can be evaluated as true or false, Dart does not permit these strange behaviors in the checked mode; in the production mode, every value different from true is treated as false.

Conversions

To use numbers as strings, use the toString() method and to convert String into int, use int.parse():

```
String lucky = 7.toString();
int seven = int.parse('7');
```

Likewise, converting String into double is done with double.parse():

```
double pi2 = double.parse('3.1415');
```

If you want to retain only a certain amount of decimal numbers from double, use toStringAsFixed():

```
String pi2Str = pi2.toStringAsFixed(3);
    //   3.142 (notice rounding occurs)
```

To convert between the num types, use toDouble() for int to double and toInt() for double to int (truncation occurs!).

Operators

All the operators in Dart follow the normal priority rules, when in doubt or for clarity, use () around the expressions that must be executed first.

We have our familiar number operators (+, -, *, /, and %) in Dart, and assignments with these can be shortened as +=. Use ~/ to get an integer result from a division. Likewise, we have prefixed and postfixed ++ and -- to add or subtract 1 to or from a number, and <, <=, >, and >= to check the order of the numbers or strings.

> Strings a and b can be concatenated with + as a + b, but string interpolation such as '$a $b' executes faster, so we will prefer this.

Numbers have also bitwise- and shift-operators to manipulate individual bits.

To see if the two variables have the same content, use ==. Or, to check for different content, use !=. These expressions result in Boolean values, such as b1 and b2 in this snippet (brackets are only used for clarity):

```
var i = 100;
var j = 1000;
var b1 = (i == j);
var b2 = (i!= j);
print('$b1'); // false
print('$b2'); // true
```

For numbers and strings, == is true when both the variables have the same value.

> The == operator can be redefined for any type; generally, it will check whether both the arguments have the same value. Use the identical(a,b) function to check whether variables a and b refer to the same object.

For strings, both hold true; the same string is only one object in memory, and if the string variable gets a new value, it references another address in memory. Strings are immutable:

```
var s = "strings are immutable";
var t = "strings are immutable";
print(s == t); // true, they contain the same characters
print(identical(s, t)); // true, they are the
    // same object in memory
```

Boolean values or expressions can be combined with an AND operator (&&) or an OR operator (||), or negated with a NOT operator (!).

Because we will be working a lot with objects and types in the Dart code, it is important to be able to test if an object is or is! (not) of a certain type (class):

```
var b3 = (7 is num); // () are not necessary
print('$b3');          // true
var b4 = (7 is! double);
print('$b4');          // true, it's an int
```

A very useful built-in function, which can be used for micro unit testing, is `assert`; its parameter is a Boolean expression. When this is true, nothing happens at runtime; but when it is false, the program stops with `AssertionError`. You can sprinkle them around in your code to test certain conditions that must hold; in the production mode, the `assert` statements are ignored. So, for the last example, we could have written:

```
assert(b4 == true) or shorter assert(b4)
```

We will use these throughout the example code, but will not print them in the text for brevity.

The `[]` indexing operator is used to obtain an element from a collection (a group of variables) at a certain index; the first element has a `0` index.

To convert or cast a `v` variable to a certain `T` type, use the `as` operator: `v as T`.

If `v` indeed is of this type, all is well and you will be able to access all of `T`'s methods, but if this fails, an error will be generated.

Some useful String methods

Strings are all-pervasive and Dart provides handy methods to work with them. For details, refer to the documentation at `http://api.dartlang.org/docs/releases/latest/dart_core/String.html`.

We will show some examples in `string_methods.dart`:

- You can test that the owner of a bank account (a string) is not filled in with `owner.isEmpty`, which returns a Boolean value:
  ```
  assert("".isEmpty);
  ```

- `length()` returns the number of UTF16 characters:
  ```
  assert('Google'.length == 6);
  ```

- Use `trim()` to remove the leading and trailing whitespace:
  ```
  assert('\thello  '.trim() == 'hello');
  ```

- Use `startswith()`, `endswith()`, and `contains()` to detect the presence of subwords:
  ```
  var fullName = 'Larry Page';
  assert(fullName.startsWith('La'));
  assert(fullName.endsWith('age'));
  assert(fullName.contains('y P'));
  ```

- Use `replaceAll()` to replace a substring, notice that the original string was not changed (strings are immutable!):

```
var composer = 'Johann Sebastian Bach';
var s = composer.replaceAll('a', '-');
print(s); // Joh-nn Seb-sti-n B-ch
assert(s != composer); // composer didn't change
```

- Use the `[]` operator to get the character at index i in the string:

```
var lang = "Dart";
assert(lang[0] == "D");
```

- Find the location of a substring inside a string with `indexOf()`:

```
assert(lang.indexOf("ar") == 1);
```

- Extract a part of a string with `substring()`:

```
assert("20000 rabbits".substring(9, 13) == 'bits');
```

While printing any object, the `toString()` method, which returns a string, is automatically called. If no particular version of this method was provided, the `toString()` method from the `Object` class is called, which prints the type of the object, as shown in the following code:

```
print('$ba');        //      produces Instance of 'BankAccount'
```

> If you need a readable representation of an object, give its class a `toString()` method.

In `banking_v2.dart`, we provide the following method:

```
String toString() => 'Bank account from $owner with
   number $number and balance $balance';
```

Now, `print('$ba');` produces the following output:

```
Bank account from John Gates with number 075-0623456-72
   and balance 1000.0
```

If you need many operations to build your strings, instead of creating new Strings at each operation and thus using more memory, consider using a `StringBuffer` object for better efficiency. A `StringBuffer` object like `sb` in the following code doesn't generate a new `String` object until `toString()` is called. An example is given in the following code:

```
var sb = new StringBuffer();
sb.write("Use a StringBuffer ");
```

```
sb.writeAll(["for ", "efficient ", "string ", "creation "]);
sb.write("if you are ");
sb.write("building lots of strings.");
var fullString = sb.toString();
print('$fullString');
sb.clear();  // sb is empty again
assert(sb.toString() == '');
```

Dates and times

Almost every app needs time information, so how can we do it in Dart? The dart:core package has a DateTime class for this. In our banking app, we could add the dateCreated and dateModified attributes to our BankAccount class. In the constructor, dateCreated would be initialized to the moment at which the account is created; in our deposit and withdraw methods, we could update dateModified. This is shown in the following code (refer to banking_v2.dart):

```
class BankAccount {
  String owner, number;
  double balance;
  DateTime dateCreated, dateModified;

  BankAccount(this.owner, this.number, this.balance)  {
    dateCreated = new DateTime.now();
  }

  deposit(double amount) {
    balance += amount;
    dateModified = new DateTime.now();
  }
  // other code
}
```

We can print this out with the following command:

```
print('Bank account created at: ${ba.dateCreated}');
```

The output produced is as follows:

```
Bank account created at: 2013-02-10  10:42:45.387
```

The `DateTime.parse(dateString)` method produces a `DateTime` object from a string in one of the suitable formats: `20130227 13:27:00` or `2010-01-17`. All the weekdays and month names are defined as `const int`, such as `MON` and `JAN`. You can extract all the date parts as an int with methods such as `second`, `day`, `month`, and `year`, as shown in the following code:

```
ba.dateModified.weekday
```

A time span is represented by a `Duration` object, `difference()` gives the duration between two `DateTime` objects, and you can `add` and `subtract` a duration from `DateTime`.

List

This is the basic collection type to make an ordered group of objects; it can be of a fixed size (called an array in other languages) or it can grow dynamically. Again `length` returns the number of elements in the List; the last element has a `length - 1` index. An empty list with length equal to `0` and an `isEmpty` property equal to `true` can be created in two ways: literal or with a constructor (refer to `lists.dart`):

```
var empty = [];
var empty2 = new List(); // equivalent
assert(empty.isEmpty && empty2.isEmpty && empty.length == 0);
```

We can either define and populate a List with a literal by using `[]` like in the following code:

```
var langs = ["Java","Python","Ruby", "Dart"];
```

Or, we can define a `List` object with a constructor and an `add()` method:

```
var langs2 = new List();
langs2.add("C");
langs2.add("C#");
langs2.add("D");
print(langs2); // [C, C#, D]
```

A read-only List with constant elements resulting in better performance can be defined as shown in the following code:

```
var readOnlyList = const ["Java","Python","Ruby", "Dart"];
```

The `[]` operator can be used to fetch and set list elements:

```
var langBest = langs[3];
assert(langBest=="Dart");
langs2[2] = "JavaScript";
```

But using an index greater than or equal to the length of the List, provokes `RangeError` in runtime (with no compile-time check!):

```
langs[4] = "F#";   // RangeError !
```

To check whether a List contains a certain item, use the method with the name:

```
print('${langs.contains("Dart")}'); // true
```

When you know the type of the List elements, the List itself can be typed, for example, `langs` and `langs2` are both of the `List<String>` type.

A string can be `split` over a certain character or pattern (which could be a space `" "` or even `""`), producing a `List<String>` named `parts` in the following code, which can then be further analyzed:

```
var number = "075-0623456-72";
var parts = number.split('-');
print('$parts'); // produces [075, 0623456, 72]
```

In simple scenarios, data records are written line after line in text files, each line containing the data of one object. In each line, the data fields are separated by a certain character, such as `";"`. We could read in and split each line of the file, and obtain a list of fields for each object to be shown on a screen or processed further. Conversely, a List can be joined by concatenating all its elements in one String (here, with a separator `'-'`):

```
var str = parts.join('-');
assert(number==str);
```

A List with n elements is used mostly to support an efficient search of the whole List or a large number of the List's elements. The time it takes to search a List grows linearly with n; it is of the $o\ (n)$ order.

To summarize it, a List is an ordered collection of the items that can be retrieved or changed by index (0-based, working via index is fast), and that can contain duplicates. You can find more useful functions in the API, but we will be coming back to the List again in *Chapter 3, Structuring Code with Classes and Libraries*, in *The collection hierarchy and its functional nature* section. (For API docs, see the documentation at http://api.dartlang.org/docs/releases/latest/dart_core/List.html).

Maps

Another very useful and built-in type is Map, basically a dictionary of (key:value) pairs, where the value is associated with the key. The number of pairs is the length of the Map constructor. Keys must be unique, they may not be null and the lookup of the value from the key is fast; mind, however, that the order of the pairs is not guaranteed! Similar to List, a Map constructor can be created literally with {} as shown in the following code:

```
Map webLinks = {  'Dart': 'http://www.dartlang.org/',
  'HTML5': 'http://www.html5rocks.com/'};
```

The keys must be of the string type for a literal Map. Or, it can be created with a constructor (refer to maps.dart):

```
Map webLinks2 = new Map();
webLinks2['Dart'] = 'http://www.dartlang.org/';       (1)
webLinks2['HTML5'] = 'http://www.html5rocks.com/';
```

The empty Map created with var map = {} or var map = new Map() has length as 0; the length of Map is not fixed. You can fetch the value corresponding to a certain key with:

```
var link = webLinks2['Dart']; // 'http://www.dartlang.org/'
```

If the key is not in the Map constructor, you will get null (it is not an error):

```
var link2 = webLinks2['C'];   // null
```

To check whether your Map contains a certain key, use the containsKey() method:

```
if (webLinks2.containsKey('C'))
  print("The map webLinks2 contains key 'C");
else
  print("The map webLinks2 does not contain key 'C'");
// prints: The map webLinks2 does not contain key 'C'
```

To obtain a List of the keys or values, use the methods with the same name:

```
var keys = webLinks2.keys.toList();
print('$keys'); // [Dart, HTML5, ASP.NET]
// getting the values:
var values = webLinks2.values.toList();
print('$values');
// printed output:
// [http://www.learningdart.org/, http://www.html5rocks.com/,
// http://www.asp.net/]
```

Setting a value is done with the syntax shown in line (1); this applies both to inserting a new key-value pair in the map or changing the value for an existing key:

```
webLinks2['Dart'] = 'http://www.learningdart.org/';  // change
webLinks2['ASP.NET'] = 'http://www.asp.net/';  // new key
```

A very handy method is putIfAbsent, which makes your code a lot cleaner. It takes two parameters: a key and a function that returns a value. The method tests whether the key already exists; if not, the function is evaluated and the value returned is assigned to the key (for example, we use a very simple function that directly returns a value, but this could be a calculation or a database lookup operation):

```
webLinks2.putIfAbsent('F#', () => 'www.fsharp.net');
assert(webLinks2['F#']=="www.fsharp.net");
```

Again, for performance reasons, use the const maps when the keys and values are literals or constants:

```
var cities =  const {'1':'London','2':'Tokyo','3':'Madrid'};
```

A Map constructor can also be explicitly typed, for example, Map with integer keys and String values:

```
Map<int, String>
```

A Map constructor with *n* elements is used mostly to support an efficient direct access to a single element of the map based on its key. This will always execute in the same time regardless of the size of the input dataset; the algorithm is of the order O(1).

(For the API docs for Map, see the documentation at http://api.dartlang.org/docs/releases/latest/dart_core/Map.html).

Documenting your programs

Documenting an application is of utmost importance in software engineering and Dart makes this very easy. The single-line (//) and multiline comments (/* */) are useful (for example, to comment out code or mark lines with // TODO), and they have counterparts /// and /** */ called documentation comments. In these comments (to be placed on the previous line), you can include references to all kinds of objects in your code (classes, methods, fields, and so on) and the **Dartdoc** tool (in Dart Editor, go to **Tools | Generate Dartdoc**) will generate an HTML documentation, where these references become links. To demonstrate, we will add docs to our banking example (refer to banking_v2doc.dart):

```dart
/**
 * A bank account has an [owner], is identified by a [number]
 * and has an amount of money called [balance].
 * The balance is changed through methods [deposit] and [withdraw].
 */
class BankAccount {
  String owner, number;
  double balance;
  DateTime dateCreated, dateModified;

  BankAccount(this.owner, this.number, this.balance)  {
    dateCreated = new DateTime.now();
  }

  /// An amount of money is added to the balance.
  deposit(double amount) {

  }

  /// An amount of money is subtracted from the balance.
  withdraw(double amount) {

  }
}
```

This results in the following documentation while viewing `banking_v2doc\docs\index.html` in a browser:

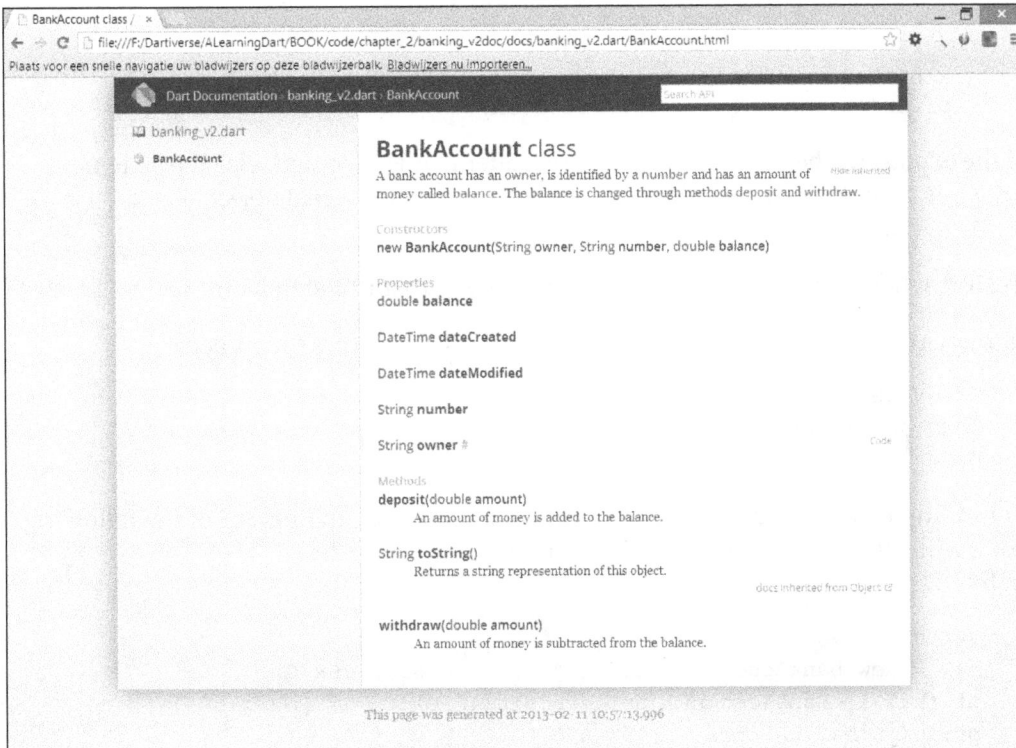

Generated Dart documentation

Changing the execution flow of a program

Dart has the usual control structures with no surprises here (refer to `control.dart`).

The `if...else` statement (with an optional `else`) is as follows:

```dart
var n = 25;
if (n < 10) {
  print('1 digit number: $n');
} else if (n >=  10 && n < 100){
  print('2+ digit number: $n'); // 2+ digit number: 25
} else {
  print('3 or more digit number: $n');
}
```

Single-line statements without { } are allowed, but don't mix the two. A simple and short if...else statement can be replaced by a **ternary operator** (?...:), as shown in the following example code:

```
num rabbitCount = 16758;
(rabbitCount > 20000) ? print('enough for this year!') :
   print('breed on!');    // breed on!
```

If the expression before ? is true, the first statement is executed, else the statement after : is executed. To test whether a variable v refers to a real object, use: if (v != null) { ... }.

Testing whether an object v is of type T is done with an if statement: if (v is T).

In this case, we can safely cast v to type T and access all of T's members:

```
if (v is T) {
   (v as T).methodOfT()
}
```

For example, if ba2 is not of type BankAccount, the code in line (1) of the following code will generate an error. We can avoid this with an if test in line (2):

```
var ba1, ba2;
ba1 = new BankAccount("Jeff", "5768-346-89", 758.0);
if (ba1 is BankAccount) ba1.deposit(42.0);
print('${ba1.balance}'); // 800.0
(ba2 as BankAccount).deposit(100.0); <-- NoSuchMethodError   (1)
if (ba2 is BankAccount) {                                    (2)
   (ba2 as BankAccount).deposit(100.0);
   print('deposited 100 on ba2'); // statement not reached
} else {
   print('ba2 is not a BankAccount'); // ba2 is not a BankAccount
}
```

We can replace multiple if...else if with a switch case statement; switch tests the value of an integer or String variable in () against different constant values in the case clauses:

```
switch(ba1.owner) {
  case 'Jeff':
    print('Jeff is the bank account owner'); // this is printed
    break;
  case 'Mary':
    print('Mary is the bank account owner');
    break;
```

```
default:
    print('The bank account owner is not Jeff, nor Mary');
}
```

Each case must end with break or continue with a label; use default when no other case matches; multiple cases can be combined.

Repetition can be coded with a for loop if the number of repetitions is known or with a while or do...while loop if the looping depends on a condition:

```
var langs = ["Java","Python","Ruby", "Dart"];
for (int i = 0; i < langs.length; i++) {
  print('${langs[i]}');
}
```

Notice that the condition i value should be less than the length of the List.

If you don't need the i index, the for...in loop will provide a simpler alternative:

```
var s = '';
var numbers = [0, 1, 2, 3, 4, 5, 6, 7];
for (var n in numbers) {
  s = '$s$n ';
}
print(s);  // 0 1 2 3 4 5 6 7
```

In each loop, the n variable will take the value of the next collection element.

Conditions can also be tested in a while loop:

```
while (rabbitCount <= 20000) {
  print('keep breeding');
  rabbitCount += 4;
}
```

This is specifically the case when no counter is present.

Don't get involved in an infinite loop by forgetting a statement that changes the condition! You can always break out from a loop with a break statement:

```
while (true) {
  if (rabbitCount > 20000) break;
  rabbitCount += 4;
}
```

Likewise, skip the execution of the body of the loop with a `continue` statement:

```
s = '';
for (var n in numbers) {
  if (n % 2 == 0) continue; // skip even numbers
  s = '$s$n ';
}
print('$s');  // 1 3 5 7
```

Using functions in Dart

Functions are another tool to change the program flow; a certain task is delegated to a function by calling it and providing some arguments. A function does the requested task and returns a value; the control flow returns where the function was called. In Java and C#, classes are indispensable and they are the most important structuring concept.

However, Dart is both functional and object-oriented. Functions are first-class objects themselves (they are of the **function** type) and can exist outside of a class as **top-level functions** (inside a class, they are called **methods**). In `prorabbits_v2.dart` of *Chapter 1, Dart – A Modern Web Programming Language*, `calculateRabbits` is an example of a top-level function; and `deposit`, `withdraw`, and `toString`, from `banking_v2.dart` of this chapter, are methods to be called on as an object of the class. Don't create a static class only as a container for helper functions!

Return types

A function can do either of the following:

- Do something (have a so-called side effect): the return type, if indicated, is `void`, for example, the `display` function in `return_types.dart`. In fact, such a function does return an object, namely `null` (see the print in line (1) of the following code).

- Return an `exp` expression, resulting in an object different from `null`, explicitly indicated by `return exp` like in `displayStr` (line (2)).

The { `return exp;` } syntax can be shortened to `=> exp;`, as shown in `display` and `displayStrShort`; we'll use this function expression syntax wherever possible. The `exp` is an expression that returns a value, but it cannot be a statement like `if`. A function can be an argument to another function, like `display` in `print` line (1), or in line (4), where the `isOdd` function is passed to the `where` function:

```
main() {
  print(display('Hello'));  // Message: Hello.    null    (1)
  print(displayStr('Hello'));  // Message: Hello.       (2)
  print(displayStrShort('Hello'));  // Message: Hello.
  print(display(display("What's up?")));            (3)
  [1,2,3,4,5].where(isOdd).toList();      // [1, 3, 5] (4)
}

display(message) => print('Message: $message.');

displayStr(message) {
  return 'Message: $message.';
}

displayStrShort(message) => 'Message: $message.';
isOdd(n) => n % 2 == 1;


}
```

By omitting the parameter type, the `display` function becomes more general; its argument can be a String, number, Boolean, List, and so on.

Parameters

As all the parameter variables are objects, all the parameters are passed by reference; this means that the underlying object can be changed from within the function. Two types of parameters exist: the `required` (they come first in the parameter list) and the `optional` parameters. Optional parameters that depend on their position in the list are indicated between [] in the definition of the function. All the parameters we have seen so far in the examples were required, but the usage of only optional parameter(s) is also possible, as shown in the following code (refer to `parameters.dart`):

```
webLanguage([name]) =>  'The best web language is: $name';
```

When called, as shown in the following code, it produces the output shown as comments:

```
print(webLanguage());  // The best web language is: null
print(webLanguage('JavaScript')); // The best web language is:
  // JavaScript
```

An optional parameter can have a default value as shown in the following code:

```
webLanguage2([name='Dart']) =>  'The best web language is: $name';
```

If this function is called without an argument, the optional value will be substituted instead, but when called with an argument, this will take precedence:

```
print(webLanguage2());  // The best web language is: Dart
print(webLanguage2('JavaScript')); // The best web language is:
  // JavaScript
```

An example with required and optional parameters, with or without default values, (name=value) is as follows:

```
String hi(String msg, [String from, String to])
                  => '$msg from $from to $to';
String hi2(String msg, [String from='me', String to='you'])
                  => '$msg from $from to $to';
```

Here, msg always gets the first parameter value, from and to get a value when there are more parameters in that order (for this reason, they are called positional):

```
print(hi('hi'));                    // hi from null to null
print(hi('hi', 'me'));              // hi from me to null
print(hi('hi', 'me', 'you'));       // hi from me to you
print(hi2('hi'));                   // hi from me to you
print(hi2('hi', 'him'));            // hi from him to you
print(hi2('hi', 'him', 'her'));     // hi from him to her
```

While calling a function with optional parameters, it is often not clear what the code is doing. This can be improved by using named optional parameters. These are indicated by { } in the parameter list, such as in hi3:

```
String hi3(String msg, {String from, String to}) =>
    '$msg from $from to $to';
```

They are called with name:value and, because of the name, the position does not matter:

```
print(hi3('hi', to:'you', from:'me')); // hi from me to you
```

Named parameters can also have default values (name:value):

```
String hi4(String msg, {String from:'me', String to:'you'}) =>
  '$msg from $from to $to';
```

It is called as follows:

```
print(hi4('hi', from:'you')); // hi from you to you
```

To summarized it:

- Optional positional parameters: [param]
- Optional positional parameters with default values: [param=value]
- Optional named parameters: {param}
- Optional named parameters with default values: {param:value}

First class functions

A function can contain other functions, such as calcRabbits contains calc(years) in prorabbits_v4.dart:

```
String calculateRabbits(int years) {
  calc(years) => (2 * pow(E, log(GROWTH_FACTOR) *
    years)).round().toInt();
  var out = "After $years years:\t ${calc(years)} animals";
  return out;
}
```

This can be useful if the inner function needs to be called several times within the outer function, but it cannot be called from outside of this outer function. A slight variation would be to store the function in a calc variable that has the Function type, like in prorabbits_v5.dart:

```
String calculateRabbits(int years) {
  var calc = (years) => (2 * pow(E, log(GROWTH_FACTOR) *
    years)).round().toInt();                              (1)
  assert(calc is Function);
  var out = "After $years years:\t ${calc(years)} animals";
  return out;
}
```

The right-hand side of line (1) is an anonymous function or lambda that takes the years parameter and returns the expression after => (the lambda operator). It could also have been written as follows:

```
var calc2 = (years) {
  return (2 * pow(E, log(GROWTH_FACTOR) *
    years)).round().toInt();
};
```

In prorabbits_v6.dart, the calc function is made top-level and is passed in the lineOut function as a parameter named fun:

```
void main() {
  print("The number of rabbits increases as:\n");
  for (int years = 0; years <= NO_YEARS; years++) {
    lineOut(years, calc(years));
  }
}

calc(years) => // code omitted, same as line(1)
  //in the preceding code

lineOut(yrs, fun) {
  print("After $yrs years:\t ${fun} animals");
}
```

In the variation to the previous code, prorabbits_v7.dart has the calc inner function that has no parameter, yet it can use the years variable that exists in the surrounding scope. For this reason, calc is called a **closure**; it closes over the surrounding variables, retaining their values:

```
String calculateRabbits(int years) {
  calc() => (2 * pow(E, log(GROWTH_FACTOR) *
    years)).round().toInt();

  var out = "After $years years:\t ${calc()} animals";
  return out;
}
```

Closures can also be defined as top-level functions, as shown by closure.dart. The multiply function returns a function (that itself takes an i parameter). So, mult2 in the following code is a function that needs to be called with a parameter, for example, mult2(3):

```
// short version:  multiply(num n) => (num i) => n * i;
// long version:
```

```
Function multiply(num n) {
  return (num i) => n * i;
}

main() {
  var two = 2;
  var mult2 = multiply(two); // this is called partial application
  assert(mult2 is Function);
  print('${mult2(3)}'); // 6
}
```

This closure behavior (true lexical scoping) is most clearly seen in `closure2.dart`, where three anonymous functions (each of which retains the value of `i`) are added to a `1stFun` list. While calling them (the call is made with the `()` operator after the `1stFun[i]` list element), they know their value of `i`; this is a great improvement over JavaScript:

```
main() {
  var 1stFun = [];
  for(var i in [10, 20, 30]) {
    1stFun.add( () => print(i) );
  }

  print(1stFun[0]()); //   10   null
  print(1stFun[1]()); //   20   null
  print(1stFun[2]()); //   30   null
}
```

While all these code variations might now perhaps seem as just esthetical, they can make your code clearer in more complex examples and we'll make good use of them in the forthcoming apps. The definition of a function comprises of its name, parameters, and return type, which is also called its **signature**. If you find this signature occurring often in your code, you can define it as a function type with `typedef`, as shown in the following code:

```
typedef int addInts(int a, b);
```

Then, you can use `addInts` as the type of a function that takes two values of `int` and returns an `int` value.

Both, in functional and OO programming, it is essential to break a large problem into smaller ones. In functional programming, the decomposition in functions is used to support a divide-and-conquer approach to problem solving. As a last remark, Dart does not have **overloading of functions** (or methods or constructors), because typing the arguments is not a requirement, Dart can't make the distinction. Every function must have a unique name and there can be only one constructor named after the class, but a class can have other constructors as well.

Using enums

Often, you encounter a situation where a variable can only take on a limited number of "named values," like the days in a week or the four compass directions. This concept is known as an **enum** and it was introduced in Dart in version 1.8. Here, is an example (see enums.dart):

```dart
enum Direction {North, South, East, West}

main() {
  Direction dir = Direction.South;
  if (dir == Direction.South) {
    print("Let's go on a trip");
  }
  switch (dir) {
    case Direction.North:
      print("Too cold up there!");
      break;
    case Direction.South:
        print("Let's go on a trip!");
        break;
    case Direction.West:
        print("Better stay home!");
        break;
    case Direction.East:
        print("Which eastern country do you want to visit?");
        break;
  }
}
```

This prints out:

```
Let's go on a trip
Let's go on a trip!
```

The nice thing about enums is that they not only clarify but shorten your code. When used in a switch statement, the Dart tools can warn you when one or more of the cases are missing, so they ensure that all the possible values are handled.

Recognizing and catching errors and exceptions

As a good programmer, you test your app in all possible conditions. Dart defines a number of errors for those things that you should remedy in your code, such as CastError when a cast fails, or NoSuchMethodError when the class of the object on which the method is called does not have this method, and neither does any of its parent classes. All these are subclasses of the Error class, and you should code so that they do not occur. However, when something unexpected occurs while running the app and the code cannot cope with it, Unhandled Exception occurs. Especially, the input values that are read in from the keyboard, a file, or a network connection are dangerous. Suppose the input is such a value that is supposed to be an integer (refer to exceptions.dart); we try to convert it into an int type in line (1):

```
var input = "47B9"; // value read from input,
//   should be an integer
int inp = int.parse(input);                    (1)
```

While running the program on the console with the dart exceptions.dart command, our program will terminate with an exception:

```
Unhandled exception:
FormatException: 47B9
#0      int.parse (dart:core-patch:1586:41)
#1      main (file:///E:/dart/code/chapter_2/
  exceptions/bin/exceptions.dart:4:22)
```

While running in Dart Editor, the default behavior is that the debugger kicks in so you can examine the exception and the values of all the variables (you can change this behavior by navigating to **Tools | Preferences | Run and Debug,** and change **Break on Exceptions** to **None**). The generated FormatException is clear: the input was in the wrong format. A lot of the other exceptions exist such as IntegerDivisionByZeroException, IOException (failure to read or write a file), and HttpException (while requesting a page from a web server); they are all subclasses from the Exception class. When they are generated, they are objects that contain information about the exception. How can we handle this exception so that our program does not crash? For this, Dart follows the familiar try...on/catch... finally pattern:

- try: To try the dangerous statement(s)

- on/catch: To catch the exception (a specific one that you know can occur or a general exception) and stop it from propagating

- finally: It contains code (perhaps to clean up, or close files or connections) that will be executed whether or not an exception occurs, but it is optional.

A minimal exception handler could be as shown in the following code:

```
try {
  int inp = int.parse(input);
} on FormatException {
  print ('ERROR: You must input an integer!');
}
```

This prints out the text in the on part. Use catch if you want to examine the exception object. The last clause in the try statement should be on Exception catch(e) or, even better, a simple catch(e) to stop any type of error or exception. So, the most general exception handler is:

```
try {
  int inp = int.parse(input);
} on FormatException { // or any other specific exception
  print ('ERROR: You must input an integer!');
} on Exception catch(e) { // Any other exception
  print('Unknown exception: $e');
} catch(e) {   // No specified type, handles all
  print('Something really unknown: $e');
} finally {
  print('OK, I have cleaned up the mess');
}
```

If you comment out the on FormatException part, you'll see that $e contains FormatException: 47B9.

Should an abnormal condition occur, you can generate or throw an exception in your code with `throw`. An example is given in the following code:

```
var radius = 8;
var area = PI * pow(radius, 2);
if (area > 200) {          // area is 201.06192982974676
  throw 'This area is too big for me.';
}
```

You can also throw a real `Exception` object with `throw new Exception("…")`. The `throw` keyword produces an expression, so it can be used after a `=>` operator, like this:

```
clearBalance() => throw const UnimplementedError();
```

It is handy to remind yourself while testing that this method hasn't yet been implemented! The bottom line is to test your code exhaustively and provide exception handling for unforeseeable events that your app cannot process in a normal way.

A debugging exercise

The following little program (`debuggingex.dart`) results in `RangeError`. Use the debugger from the beginning to see where it goes wrong and correct it. In Dart Editor, double-click on a narrow column to the left of `for (var i=0; i<=lst.length; i++) {` in order to create a breakpoint (a blue circle). Run the program and use step over to get a new value of the `i` variable. Correct the program to avoid the range error. However, don't use `try...catch` to handle the error, because it is the programmer's mistake:

```
// calculate and print the squares of the list items:
var lst = [1, 2, 3, 4, 5];

void main() {
  for (var i=0; i<=lst.length; i++) {
    print(lst[i] * lst[i]);
  }
}
```

The following screenshot shows `RangeError` in the debugger:

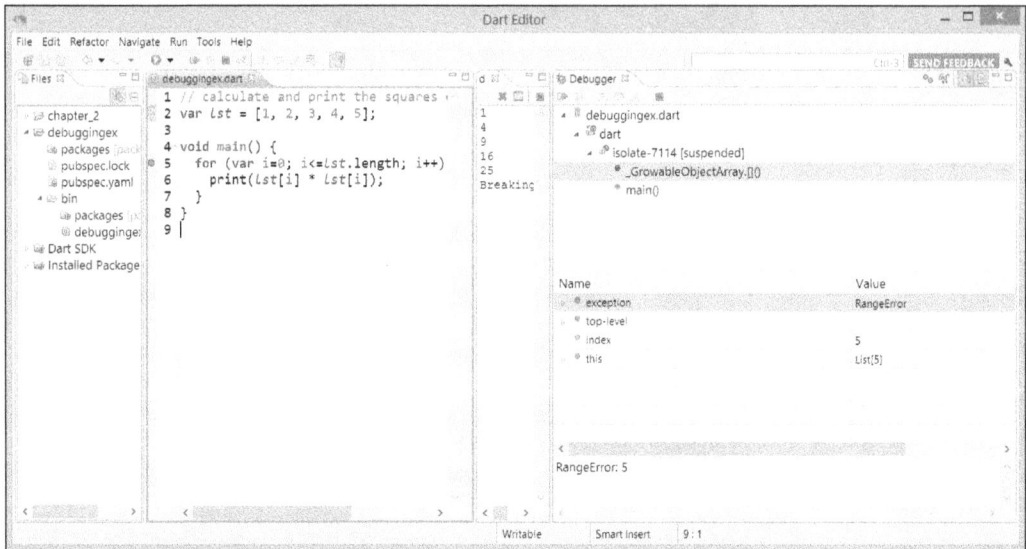

Summary

By now, you have acquired a lot of technical skills and gained insights to how Dart works. We have discussed which typing variables in Dart are relevant and where to apply them: type the public API of your app in order to enhance the tooling and documentation produced with the built-in Dartdoc tool. We also saw that Dart's constructs are very familiar, but their approach is quite refreshing, leading to elegant code. In particular, Dart incorporates quite a few functional ways of coding: the functions are quite powerful and working with collections uses this intensively.

In the next chapter, we will see that Dart is a familiar object-oriented language using classes. Generic types are also available, and we will show how to use libraries to structure your growing code. Using external libraries is easy with the pub tool, and tests can be integrated with the unit testing library.

3

Structuring Code with Classes and Libraries

In this chapter, we will look at the object-oriented nature of Dart. If you have prior knowledge of an OO language, most of this chapter will feel familiar. Although, coding classes is more succinct while introducing some nice new features such as factory constructors, and generalizing the use of interfaces. If you come from the JavaScript world, you will start to realize that classes can really structure your application.

Data mostly comes in collections. Dart has some neat classes to work with collections and they can be used for any type of collections. This is why they are called generic. As soon as you get a few code files in your project, structuring them by making libraries would become essential for code maintainability. Also, your code would probably use existing libraries written by other developers; to make it easy, Dart has its own package manager called pub. Automating the testing of code on a functional level will be done with a built-in unit test library.

We will look at the following topics:

- Using classes and objects
- Collection types and generic classes
- Structuring your code using libraries
- Managing library dependencies with pub
- Unit testing in Dart

We will wrap it all up in a small but useful project to calculate word frequencies in an extract of text.

A touch of class – how to use classes and objects

We saw in *Chapter 1, Dart – A Modern Web Programming Language*, how a class contains members such as properties, a constructor, and methods (refer to `banking_v2.dart`). For those familiar with the classes in Java or C#, it's nothing special and we can already see certain simplifications:

- The short constructor notation lets the parameter values flow directly into the properties:

```
BankAccount(this.owner, this.number, this.balance) { … }
```

- The `this` keyword is necessary here and refers to the actual object (being constructed), but it is rarely used elsewhere (only when there is a name conflict). Initialization of instance variables can also be done in the so-called **initializer list**, like in this shorter version of the constructor:

```
BankAccount(this.owner, this.number, this.balance) :
  dateCreated = new DateTime.now();
```

- The variables are initialized after the colon (`:`) and are separated by a comma. You cannot use the `this` keyword in the initializer expression. If nothing else needs to be done, the constructor body can be left out.

- The properties have automatic getters to read the value (as in `ba.balance`) and, when they are not final or constant, they also have a setter method to change the value (as in `balance += amount`).

> You can start out by using dynamic typing (`var`) for properties, especially when you haven't decided what type a property will become. As development progresses, though, you should aim to change the dynamic types into strong types that give more meaning to your code and can be validated by the tools.

Properties that are Boolean values are commonly named with `is` at the beginning, for example, `isOdd`.

A class has a default constructor when there are no other constructors defined. Objects (instances of the class) are made with the `new` keyword and an is object of the type of the class. We can test this with the `is` operator; for example, if `ba` has the `BankAccount` type, then the following will be true: `ba is BankAccount`. Single inheritance between the classes is defined by the `extends` keyword; the base class of all the classes being `Object`.

Member access uses the dot (.) notation, as in `ba.balance` or `ba.withdraw(100.0)`. A class can contain objects that are instances of the other classes: a feature known as **composition** (aggregation). For example, we could decide at a later stage that the String owner in the `BankAccount` class should really be an object of a `Person` class with many other properties and methods.

A neat feature to simplify the code is the **cascade operator** (`..`). With it, you can set a number of properties and execute methods on the same object, for example, on the `ba` object in the following code (it's not chaining operations!):

```
ba
    ..balance = 5000.0
    ..withdraw(100.0)
    ..deposit(250.0);
```

We'll focus on what makes Dart different and more powerful than common OO languages.

Visibility – getters and setters

What about the visibility or access of class members? They are public by default, but if you name them beginning with an underscore (_), they will become private. However, private in Dart does not mean that it will only be visible in its class; a private field (property), for example, _owner is visible in the entire library in which it is defined, but not in the client code that uses the library.

For the moment, this means that it is accessible in the code file where it is declared, because a code file defines an implicit library. The entire picture will become clear in the coming section on the libraries. A good feature that enhances productivity is that you can begin with public properties, as in `project_v1.dart`. A `Project` object has a name and a description and we will use the default constructor:

```
main() {
  var p1 = new Project();
  p1.name = 'Breeding';
  p1.description = 'Managing the breeding of animals';
  print('$p1');
  // prints: Project name: Breeding - Managing
     the breeding of animals
}

class Project {
  String name, description;
  toString() => 'Project name: $name - $description';
}
```

Suppose now that new requirements arrive; the length of a project name must be less than 20 characters and, when printed, the name must be in capital letters. We want the `Project` class to be responsible for these changes, so we will create a private property, `_name`, and the `get` and `set` methods to implement the requirements (refer to `project_v2.dart`):

```
class Project {
  String _name; // private variable
  String description;

  String get name => _name == null ? "" : _name.toUpperCase();
  set name(String prName) {
    if (prName.length > 20)
      throw 'Only 20 characters or less in project name';
    _name = prName;
  }

  toString() => 'Project name: $name - $description';
}
```

The `get` method makes sure that, in case `_name` is not yet filled in, an empty string is returned.

The code that already existed in `main` (or, in general, the client code that uses this property) does not need to change; it now prints `Project name: BREEDING - Managing the breeding of animals`. If a project name that is too long is given, the code will generate an exception.

> Start your class code with public properties and, later, change some of them to private if necessary with getters and/or setters without breaking the client code!

A getter (and a setter) can also be used without a corresponding property instead of simplifying the code again, such as the getters for area, perimeter, and diagonal in the `Square` (`square_v1.dart`) class:

```
import 'dart:math';

void main() {
  var s1 = new Square(2);
  print('${s1.perimeter}'); // 8
  print('${s1.area}');      // 4
```

```
    print('${s1.diagonal}');   // 2.8284271247461903
}

class Square {
    num length;
    Square(this.length);

    num get perimeter => 4 * length;
    num get area => length * length;
    num get diagonal => length * SQRT2;
}
```

SQRT2 is defined in dart:math. The new properties cannot be changed, because this is only a getter (they are properties derived from other properties). Dart doesn't do function overloading because of optional typing, but allows **operator overloading**, redefining a number of operators (such as ==, >=, >, <=, and < — all the arithmetic operators — as well as [] and [] =). For example, examine the > operator in square_v1.dart:

```
    bool operator >(Square other) => length > other.length
        ? true : false;
```

If s1 and s2 are Square objects, we can now write the code like this: if (s2 > s1) { ... }.

> Use overloading of operators sparingly and only when it seems a good fit and would be unsurprising to fellow developers.

Types of constructors

All OO languages have class constructors, but Dart has only few kinds of constructors covered in the following sections.

Named constructors

Because there is no function overloading, there can be only one constructor with the class name (the so-called **main constructor**). So, if we want more, we must use named constructors, which take the `ClassName.constructorName` form. If the main constructor does not have any parameters, it is called a **default constructor**. If the default constructor does not have a body of statements such as `BankAccount();`, it can be omitted. If you don't declare a constructor, a default constructor will be provided for you. Suppose we want to to create a new bank account for a person by copying data from another of his / her bank accounts, for example, the owner's name. We could do this with the `BankAccount.sameOwner` named constructor (refer to `banking_v3.dart`):

```
BankAccount.sameOwner(BankAccount acc)   {
  owner = acc.owner;
}
```

We could also do this with the initializer version:

```
BankAccount.sameOwner(BankAccount acc): owner = acc.owner;
```

When we make an object via this constructor and print it out, we get:

```
Bank account from John Gates with number null and balance null
```

A constructor can also redirect to the main constructor by using the `this` keyword, as follows:

```
BankAccount.sameOwner2(BankAccount acc): this(acc.owner, "000-0000000-
00", 0.0);
```

We initialize the number and balance to dummy values, because `this()` has to provide three arguments for the three parameters of the main constructor.

Factory constructors

Sometimes, we don't want a constructor to always make a new object of the class; perhaps we want to return an object from a cache or create an object from a subtype instead. The `factory` constructor provides this flexibility, which is extensively used in the Dart SDK. In `factory_singleton.dart`, we use this ability to implement the singleton design pattern (for a general intro to design patterns, see `https://en.wikipedia.org/wiki/Software_design_pattern`) in which there can be only one instance of the class:

```
class SearchEngine {
  static SearchEngine theOne;                                    (1)
```

```
    String name;

    factory SearchEngine(name) {                            (2)
      if (theOne == null) {
        theOne = new SearchEngine._internal(name);
      }
      return theOne;
    }
// private, named constructor
    SearchEngine._internal(this.name);                      (3)
// static method:
      static nameSearchEngine () => theOne.name;            (4)
}

main() {
  //substitute your favorite search-engine for se1:
  var se1 = new SearchEngine('Google');                    (5)
  var se2 = new SearchEngine('Bing');                      (6)
  print(se1.name);                      // 'Google'
  print(se2.name);                      // 'Google'
  print(SearchEngine.theOne.name);      // 'Google'    (7)
  print(SearchEngine.nameSearchEngine()); // 'Google'  (8)
  assert(identical(se1, se2));                          (9)
}
```

In line (1), the theOne static variable (here, of the SearchEngine type itself, but it could also be of a simple type, such as num or String) is declared: such a variable is the same for all the instances of the class. It is invoked on the class name itself, as in line (7); this is why it is also called a class variable. Likewise, you can have static methods (or class methods) such as nameSearchEngine (line (4)) called in the same way (line (8)).

> Static methods can be useful, but don't create a class containing static methods only to provide common or widely used utilities and functionality; use top-level functions instead.

In lines (5) and (6), two SearchEngine objects se1 and se2 are created through the factory constructor in line (2). This checks whether our theOne static variable already refers to an object or not. If not, a SearchEngine object is created through the SearchEngine._internal named constructor from line (3); if it was already created, nothing is done and the theOne object is returned in both cases. The two SearchEngine objects se1 and se2 are, in fact, the same object, as is proven in line (9). Note that the SearchEngine._internal named constructor is private; a factory invoking a private constructor is also a common pattern.

The const constructors

Two squares created with the same length are different objects in memory. If you want to make a class where each object cannot change, provide it with the const constructors and ensure that every property is const or final, for example, the ImmutableSquare class in square_v1.dart:

```
class ImmutableSquare {
  final num length;
  static final ImmutableSquare ONE = const ImmutableSquare(1);
  const ImmutableSquare(this.length);
}
```

Objects are created with const instead of new, using the const constructor in the last line of the class to give length its value:

```
var s4 = const ImmutableSquare(4);
var s5 = const ImmutableSquare(4);
assert(identical(s4,s5));
```

Inheritance

Inheritance in Dart comes with no surprises if you know the concept from Java or .NET. Its main use is to reduce the codebase by factoring common code (properties, methods, and so on) into a common parent class. In square_v2.dart, the Square class inherits from the Rectangle class indicated by the extends keyword (line (4)). A Square object inherits the properties from its parent class (see line (1)), and you can refer to the constructors or methods from the parent class with the super keyword (like in line (5)):

```
main() {
  var s1 = new Square(2);
  print(s1.width);                        (1)
  print(s1.height);
  print('${s1.area()}'); // 4
  assert(s1 is Rectangle);                (2)
}

class Rectangle {
  num width, height;
  Rectangle(this.width, this.height);
  num area() => width * height;           (3)
}

class Square extends Rectangle {          (4)
```

```
  num length;
  Square(length): super(length, length) {          (5)
    this.length = length;
  }
  num area() => length * length;                    (6)
}
```

Methods from the parent class can be overridden in the derived class without special annotations, for example, the `area()` method (lines (3) and (6)). An object of a child class is also of the type of the parent class (see line (2)) and thus it can be used whenever a parent class object is needed. This is the basis of what is called the polymorphic behavior of objects. All classes inherit from `Object`, but a class can have only one direct parent class (single inheritance). Constructors are not inherited. An object, the class of this object, its parent class, and so on (until `Object`) are all searched for the method that is called on. A class can have many derived classes, so an application is typically structured as a class hierarchy tree.

In OO programming, the class composition (with properties representing components / objects of other classes) and inheritance are used to support a divide-and-conquer approach toward problem solving. Class A inherits from class B only when A is a subset of B, for example, a square is a rectangle, a manager is an employee; basically when class B is more generic and less specific than class A. It is recommended that inheritance be used with caution, because an inheritance hierarchy is more rigid in the maintenance of programs than a composition.

Abstract classes and methods

Looking for parent classes is an abstraction process and it can go so far that the parent class we have decided to work with can no longer be fully implemented. That is, it can contain methods that we cannot code at this point by the so-called **abstract methods**. Extending the previous example to `square_v3.dart`, we could easily abstract out a `Shape` parent class. This could contain methods to calculate the area and the perimeter, but they would be empty because we can't calculate them without knowing the exact shape. Other classes such as `Rectangle` and `Square` could inherit from `Shape` and provide the implementation for these methods:

```
main() {
  var s1 = new Square(2);
  print('${s1.area()}');          // 4
  print('${s1.perimeter()}');     // 8
  var r1 = new Rectangle(2, 3);
  print('${r1.area()}');          // 6
  print('${r1.perimeter()}');     // 10
  assert(s1 is Shape);
```

```
    assert(r1 is Shape);
    // warning + exception in checked mode: Cannot instantiate
    // abstract class Shape
    // var f = new Shape();
  }

  abstract class Shape {
    num perimeter();
    num area();
  }

  class Rectangle extends Shape {
    num width, height;
    Rectangle(this.width, this.height);
    num perimeter() => 2 * (height + width);
    num area() => height * width;
  }

  class Square extends Shape {
    num length;
    Square(this.length);
    num perimeter() => 4 * length;
    num area() => length * length;
  }
```

Also, making instances of Shape isn't very useful, so it is rightfully an abstract class.
An abstract class can also have properties and implemented methods, but you cannot
make objects from an abstract class unless it contains a factory constructor that
creates an object from another class. This can be useful as a default object creator for
this abstract class. A simple example can be seen in the factory_abstract.dart file:

```
  void main() {
    Animal an1 = new Animal();                    (1)
    print('${an1.makeNoise()}'); // Miauw
  }

  abstract class Animal {
    String makeNoise();
    factory Animal() => new Cat();                (2)
  }

  class Cat implements Animal {
    String makeNoise() => "Miauw";
  }
```

`Animal` is an abstract class and, because we need cats in our app, we decide to give it a factory constructor to make a cat (line (2)). Now, we can construct an object from the `Animal` class (line (1)) and it will behave like a cat. Note that we must use the `implements` keyword here to make the relationship between the class and the abstract class (which is also an interface, as we will discuss in the next section). Many of the core types in the Dart SDK are abstract classes (or interfaces), such as `num`, `int`, `String`, `List`, and `Map`. They often have factory constructors that redirect to a specific implementation class to make an object.

The interface of a class – implementing interfaces

In Java and .NET, an abstract class without any implementation in its methods is called an **interface** — a description of a collection of fields and methods — and classes can implement interfaces. Dart's interfaces work differently from Java / C# and there is no need for an explicit interface concept. Here, every class implicitly defines its own interface (also called API), containing all the public instance members of the class (and of any interfaces it implements). The abstract classes of the previous section are also interfaces in Dart. Interface is not a keyword in the Dart syntax, but both the words are used as synonyms. Class B can implement any other class C by providing the code for C's public methods. In fact, the previous example, `square_v3.dart`, continues to work when we change the `extends` keyword to `implements`:

```
class Rectangle implements Shape {
  num width, height;
  Rectangle(this.width, this.height);
  num perimeter() => 2 * (height + width);
  num area() => height * width;
}
```

This has the additional benefit that the `Rectangle` class could now inherit from another class if necessary. Every class that implements an interface is also of that type as is proven by the following line of code (when `r1` is an object of class `Rectangle`):

```
assert(r1 is Shape);
```

The `extends` keyword is much less used than `implements`, but it clearly has a different meaning too. While using `extends`, the inheritance chain is searched for a called method, not the implemented interfaces, as is the case while using `implements`.

Implementing an interface is not restricted to one interface. A class can implement many different interfaces, for example, `class Cat implements Mammal, Pet { ... }`. In this new vision, where every class defines its own interface, abstract classes (which could be called explicit interfaces) are of much less importance (in fact, the `abstract` keyword is optional; leaving it off only gives a warning of its unimplemented members). This interface concept is more flexible than the one in most OO languages, and it doesn't force us to define our interfaces right from the start of a project. The `dynamic` type, which we discussed briefly in the beginning of this chapter, is the base interface that every other class (also `Object`) implements. However, it is an interface without properties or methods and cannot be extended.

To summarize it, interfaces are used to describe functionality that is shared (implemented) by a number of classes. The implementing classes must fulfill the interface requirements. Coding against interfaces is an excellent way to provide more coherence and structure in your class hierarchy.

Polymorphism and the dynamic nature of Dart

Because Dart fully implements all the OO principles, we are able to write polymorphic code in which an object can be used wherever something of its type, the type of its parent classes, or the type of any of the interfaces it implements is needed. We will see this in action in `polymorphic.dart`:

```
main() {
  var duck1 = new Duck();
  var duck2 = new Duck('blue');
  var duck3 = new Duck.yellow();
  polytest(new Duck()); // Quack   I'm gone, quack!       (1)
  polytest(new Person());
    // human_quack  I am a person swimming                (2)
}

polytest(Duck duck) {                                     (3)
  print('${duck.sayQuack()}');
  print('${duck.swimAway()}');
}

abstract class Quackable {
  String sayQuack();
}

class Duck implements Quackable {
  var color;
  Duck([this.color='red']);
```

```
    Duck.yellow() { this.color = 'yellow';}

    String sayQuack() => 'Quack';
    String swimAway() => "I'm gone, quack!";
}

class Person implements Duck {                           (4)
    sayQuack() => 'human_quack';
    swimAway() => 'I am a person swimming';              (5)

    noSuchMethod(Invocation invocation) {                (6)
       if (invocation.memberName == new Symbol("swimAway"))
         print("I'm not really a duck!");
    }
}
```

The top-level `polytest` function in line (3) takes anything that is in `Duck` as an argument. In this case, this is not only a real duck, but also a person, because the `Person` class also implements `Duck` (line (4)). This is polymorphism. This property of a language permits us to write code that is generic in nature; using objects of interface types, our code can be valid for all the classes that implement the interface used.

Another property shows that Dart also resembles dynamic languages such as Ruby and Python; when a method is called on an object, its class, parent class, the parent class of the parent class, and so on (until the class `Object`), are searched for the method called. If it is found nowhere, Dart searches the class tree from the class to the `Object` class again for a method called `noSuchMethod()`.

The `Object` has this method and its effect is to throw `noSuchMethodError`. We can use it to our advantage by implementing the method in our class itself; see line (6) in the `Person` class (the argument mirror is of the `Invocation` type; its `memberName` property is the name of the method called and its `namedArguments` property supplies a Map with the method's arguments). If we now remove line (5) so that `Person` no longer implements the `swimAway()` method, the Editor will give us a warning:

```
Concrete class Person has unimplemented members from
   Duck: String swimAway().
```

However, if we now execute the code, the `I'm not really a duck!` message would be printed when `print('${duck.swimAway()}')` is called for the `Person` object. Because `swimAway()` didn't exist for the `Person` class or any of its parent classes, `noSuchMethod` is searched, found in the class itself, and executed. `noSuchMethod` can be used to do what is generally called **metaprogramming** in the dynamic languages arena, giving our applications greater flexibility to efficiently handle new situations.

Collection types and generics

In the *Built-in types and their methods* section in *Chapter 2, Getting to Work with Dart*, we saw that very powerful data structures such as List and Map are core to Dart, not something that were added afterwards in a separate library like in Java or .NET.

Typing collections and generics

How can we check the type of the items in a List or Map? A list created either as a literal or with the default constructor can contain items of any type, like the following code shows (refer to `generics.dart`):

```
var date = new DateTime.now();
// untyped List (or a list of type dynamic):
var lst1 = [7, "lucky number", 56.2, date];
print('$lst1'); // [7, lucky number, 56.2,
   // 2013-02-22 10:08:20.074]
var lst2 = new List();
lst2.add(7);
lst2.add("lucky number");
lst2.add(56.2);
lst2.add(date);
print('$lst2'); // [7, lucky number, 56.2,
   // 2013-02-22 10:08:20.074]
```

While this makes for very versatile lists most of the time, you know that the items will be of a certain type, such as int, `String`, BankAccount or even List, themselves. In this case, you can indicate the E type between < and > in this way: `<E>`. An example is shown in the following code:

```
var langs = <String>["Python","Ruby", "Dart"];
var langs2 = new List<String>();               (1)
langs2.add("Python");
langs2.add("Ruby");
langs2.add("Dart");
var lstOfString = new List<List<String>>();    (2)
```

> Don't forget `()` at the end of lines `(1)` and `(2)`, because this calls the constructor!

With this, Dart can control the items for us; `langs2.add(42);` gives us a warning and a `TypeErrorImplementation` exception when it is run in the checked mode:

```
type 'int' is not a subtype of type 'String' of 'value'
```

Here, value means 42. However, when we run in the production mode, this code runs just fine. Again, indicating the type helps us to prevent possible errors and, at the same time, document the code.

Why is the special `<>` notation also used as `List<E>` in the API documents for list? This is because all of the properties and methods of List work for any `E` type. This is why the `List<E>` type is called generic (or parameterized). The `E` formal type parameter stands for any possible type.

The same goes for Maps; a Map is, in fact, a generic `Map<K,V>` type, where K and V are formal type parameters for the types of the keys and values respectively, giving us the same benefits as the following code will demonstrate:

```
var map = new Map<int, String>();
map[1] = 'Dart';
map[2] = 'JavaScript';
map[3] = 'Java';
map[4] = 'C#';
print('$map'); // {1: Dart, 2: JavaScript, 3: Java, 4: C#}
map['five'] = 'Perl'; // String is not assignable to int   (3)
```

Again, line (3) gives us a `TypeError` exception in the checked mode, not in the production mode. We can test the generic types like this:

```
print('${langs2 is List}'); // true
print('${langs2 is List<String>}'); // true              (4)
print('${langs2 is List<double>}'); // false             (5)
```

We can see that, in line (5), the type of the List is checked; this check works even in the production mode! (Uncheck the **Run in Checked Mode** checkbox in **Run | Manage Launches** and click on **Apply** to see it in action.) This is because generic types in Dart (unlike in Java) are **reified**; their type information is preserved during runtime, so you can test the type of collection even in the production mode. Note, however, that this is the type of the collection only. While adding the `langs2.add(42);` statement (which executes fine in the production mode), the check in line (4) still gives us the `true` value. If you want to check the types of all the elements in a collection in the production mode, you will have to do it for each element, individually, as shown in the following code:

```
for (var s in langs2) {
  if (s is String) print('$s is a String');
  else            print ('$s is not a String!');
}
// output:
//   Python is a String
//   Ruby is a String
//   Dart is a String
//   42 is not a String!
```

Checking the types of generic Lists gives expected results mostly:

```
print(new List
<String>() is List<Object>);                    // true   (1)
print(new List<Object>() is List<String>);     // false  (2)
print(new List<String>() is List<int>);        // false  (3)
print(new List<String>() is List);             // true   (4)
print(new List() is List<String>);             // true   (5)
```

Line (1) is `true`, because Strings (as everything) are Objects. Line (2) is `false`, because not every Object is a String. Line (3) is `false`, because Strings are not integers. Line (4) is `true`, because Strings are also of the `dynamic` general type. Line (5) can be a surprise: `dynamic` is `String`. This is because those generic types without type parameters are considered to be substitutable (subtypes of) for any other version of the generic type.

The collection hierarchy and its functional nature

Apart from `List` and `Map`, there are other important collection classes, such as `Queue` and `Set`, among the others specified in the `dart:collection` library; most of them are generic. We can't review them all here, but the most important ones have the following relations (an arrow is UML notation for "is a subclass of" (`extends` in Dart)):

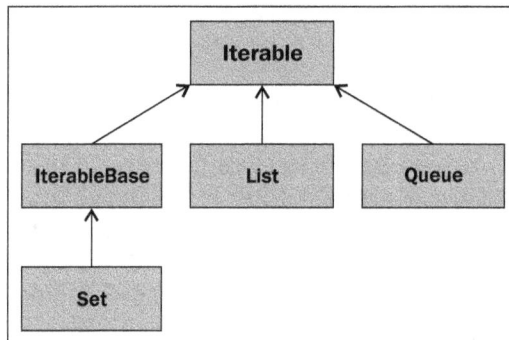

The collection hierarchy

`List` and `Queue` are classes that inherit from `Iterable`, and `Set` inherits from `IterableBase`; all these are abstract classes. The `Map` class is also abstract and forms on its own the root of a whole series of classes that implement the containers of values associated with keys, sometimes also called dictionaries. Put simply, the `Iterable` interface allows you to enumerate (or iterate, that is, read but not change) all the items of a collection one by one using what is called an **iterator**. As an example, you can make a collection of the numbers 0 to 9 by making an iterator with:

```
var digits = new Iterable.generate(10, (i) => i);
```

The iteration can be performed with the for (*item* in *collection*) statement:

```
for (var no in digits) {
    print(no);
} // prints 0 1 2 3 4 5 6 7 8 9 on successive lines
```

This prints all the numbers from 0 to 9, successively. Members such as isEmpty, length, and contains(), which we saw in action with list (refer to the lists.dart file), are already defined at this level, but there is a lot more. Iterable also defines very useful methods for filtering, searching, transforming, reducing, chaining, and so on. This shows that Dart has a lot of characteristics of a functional language: we see lots of functions taking functions as parameters or returning functions. Let's look at some of the examples applied to a list by applying toList() to our Iterable object digits:

```
var digList = digits.toList();
```

An even shorter and more functional version than for...in is forEach, which takes a function as a parameter that is applied to every i item of the collection in turn. In the following example, a function that simply prints the item is shown:

```
digList.forEach((i) => print('$i'));
```

It is called an anonymous function, because it has no name.

Use forEach, whenever you don't need the index of the item in the loop. This also works for Maps, for example, to print out all the keys in the following map:

```
Map webLinks =    { 'Dart': 'http://www.dartlang.org/',
    'HTML5': 'http://www.html5rocks.com/' };
webLinks.forEach((k,v) => print('$k')); // prints: Dart    HTML5
```

If you want the first or last element of a List, use the corresponding functions.

If you want to skip the first *n* items, use skip(n), or skip by testing on a condition with skipWhile(condition):

```
var skipL1 = digList.skip(4).toList();
print('$skipL1'); // [4, 5, 6, 7, 8, 9]
var skipL2 = digList.skipWhile((i) => i <= 6).toList();
print('$skipL2'); // [7, 8, 9]
```

The take and takeWhile functions do the opposite; they take the given number of items or the items that fulfill the condition:

```
var takeL1 = digList.take(4).toList();
print('$takeL1'); // [0, 1, 2, 3]
var takeL2 = digList.takeWhile((i) => i <= 6).toList();
print('$takeL2'); // [0, 1, 2, 3, 4, 5, 6]
```

If you want to test whether any of the items fulfill a condition, use any; to test whether all of the items do so, use every:

```
var test = digList.any((i) => i > 10);
print('$test');   // false
var test2 = digList.every((i) => i < 10);
print('$test2');   // true
```

Suppose you have a List and you want to filter out only the items that fulfill a certain condition (this is a function that returns a Boolean called a **predicate**), in our case, the even digits. Here, is how it's done:

```
var even = (i) => i.isEven;                         (1)
var evens = digList.where(even).toList();           (2)
print('$evens');   // [0, 2, 4, 6, 8]               (3)
evens = digList.where((i) => i.isEven).toList();    (4)
print('$evens');   // [0, 2, 4, 6, 8]
```

We use the isEven property of int to construct an anonymous function in line (1). It takes the i parameter to test its evenness, and we assign the anonymous function to a function variable called even. We then pass this function as a parameter to where and make a list of the result in line (2). The output in line (3) is what we expect.

It is important to note that where takes a function that, for each item, tests a certain condition and thus returns true or false. In line (4), we write it more tersely in one line, which makes it appropriate and elegant for short predicate functions. Why do we need the toList() function to be called in this and the previous functions? Because where (and the other Iterable methods) returns a so-called lazy Iterable method. Calling where alone does nothing; it is toList() that actually performs the iteration and stuffs the results in a list (try it out: if you leave out toList(), you will get an instance of WhereIterable).

If you want to apply a function to every item and form a new List with the results, you can use the map function; in the following example, we will triple each number:

```
var triples = digList.map((i) => 3 * i).toList();
print('$triples'); // [0, 3, 6, 9, 12, 15, 18, 21, 24, 27]
```

Another useful utility is to apply a given operation with each item in succession combined with a previously calculated value. Concretely say, we want to sum all the elements of our List. We can, of course, do this in a for loop, accumulating the sum in a temporary variable:

```
var sum = 0;
for (var i in digList) {
  sum += i;
}
print('$sum'); // 45
```

Dart provides a more succinct and functional way to do this kind of manipulation with the `reduce` function (eliminating the need for a temporary variable):

```
var sum2 = digList.reduce((prev, i) => prev + i);
print('$sum2'); // 45
```

We can apply `reduce` to obtain the minimum and maximum of a numeric List, as follows:

```
var min = digList.reduce(Math.min);
print('minimum: $min'); // 0
var max = digList.reduce(Math.max);
print('maximum: $max'); // 9
```

For this to work, we need to import the math library:

```
import 'dart:math' as Math;
```

We could do this because `min` and `max` are defined for numbers, but what about the other types? For this, we need to be able to compare the two List items: `i1` and `i2`. If `i2` is greater than `i1`, we will know the `min` and `max` values of the two and be able to sort them. Dart has this intrinsically defined for the basic `int`, `num`, `String`, `Duration`, and `Date` types. So, in our example with the `int` types, we can simply write:

```
var lst = [17, 3, -7, 42, 1000, 90];
lst.sort();
print('$lst'); // [-7, 3, 17, 42, 90, 1000]
```

If you look up the definition of `sort ()`, you will see that it takes, as an optional argument, a function of the `int` type, `compare(E a, E b)`, belonging to the `Comparable` interface. Generally, this will be implemented as follows:

- If `a < b`, return `-1`
- If `a > b`, return `1`
- If `a == b`, return `0`

In the following code, we will use the preceding logic to obtain the minimum and maximum of a List of Strings:

```
var lstS = ['heg', 'wyf', 'abc'];
var minS = lstS.reduce((s1,s2) =>
  s1.compareTo(s2) < 0 ? s1 : s2);
print('Minimum String: $minS'); // abc
```

In a general case, we need to implement compareTo ourselves for the element type of the list. It turns out that the preceding code lines can then be used to obtain the minimum and maximum of a List of a general type! To illustrate this, we will construct a list of persons; these are objects of a very simple Person class:

```
class Person {
    String name;
    Person(this.name);
}
```

We will make a List of the four Person objects and try to sort it, as shown in the following code:

```
var p1 = new Person('Peeters Kris');
var p2 = new Person('Obama Barak');
var p3 = new Person('Poetin Vladimir');
var p4 = new Person('Lincoln Abraham');
var pList = [p1, p2, p3, p4];
pList.sort();
```

We will then get the following exception:

```
type 'Person' is not a subtype of type 'Comparable'.
```

This means that the Person class must implement the Comparable interface by providing the code for the compareTo method. Because String already implements this interface, we can use the compareTo method for the person's name:

```
class Person implements Comparable{
    String name;
    Person(this.name);
    // many other properties and methods
    compareTo(Person p) => name.compareTo(p.name);
}
```

Then, we can get the min and max values and sort our Person list in place simply by:

```
var minP = pList.reduce((s1,s2) => s1.compareTo(s2)
    < 0 ? s1 : s2);
print('Minimum Person: ${minP.name}'); // Lincoln Abraham
var maxP = pList.reduce((s1,s2) => s1.compareTo(s2)
    < 0 ? s2 : s1);
print('Maximum Person: ${maxP.name}'); // Poetin Vladimir

pList.sort();
pList.forEach((p) => print('${p.name}'));
```

The preceding code will print the following output (on successive lines):

```
Lincoln Abraham    Obama Barak    Peeters Kris    Poetin Vladimir
```

To use Queue, your code must import the collection library by using `import 'dart:collection';`, because this is the library the class is defined in. It is another collection type differing from a List in a way that the first (head) or the last item (tail) are important. You can add an item to the head with `addFirst` or to the tail with `add` or `addLast`, or you can remove an item with `removeFirst` or `removeLast`:

```
var langsQ = new Queue();
langsQ.addFirst('Dart');
langsQ.addFirst('JavaScript');
print('${langsQ.elementAt(1)}'); // Dart
var lng = langsQ.removeFirst();
assert(lng=='JavaScript');
langsQ.addLast('C#');
langsQ.removeLast();
print('$langsQ'); // {Dart}
```

You have access to the items in a Queue by the index with `elementAt(index)` and `forEach` is also available. For this reason, Queues are ideal when you need a **first-in first-out (FIFO)** data structure or a **last-in first-out (LIFO,** which is called a **stack** in most languages) data structure.

Lists and Queues allow duplicate items. If you don't need ordering and your requirement is to only have unique items in a collection, use a Set type:

```
var langsS = new Set();
langsS.add('Java');
langsS.add('Dart');
langsS.add('Java');
langsS.length == 2;
print('$langsS'); // {Dart, Java}
```

Again, Sets allow for the same methods as List and Queue from their place in the collection hierarchy (see the following diagram). They also have the specific intersection method that returns the common elements between a Set and another collection.

Here is a handy flowchart to decide which data structure to use:

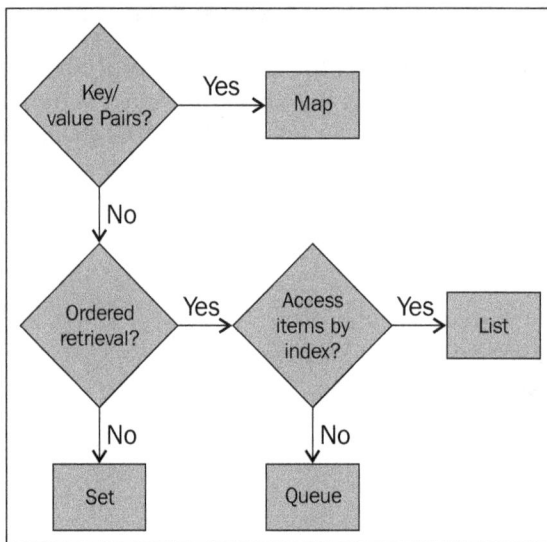

Choosing a collection type

> Maps have unique keys (but not values) and Sets have unique items, while Lists and Queues do not. Lists are ideal for arbitrary access to items anywhere in the collection (by index), but changing their size can be costly. Queues are the type to use if you mainly want to operate on the head or tail of the collection.

Structuring your code using libraries

Using classes, extending them, and implementing interfaces are the way to go to structure your Dart code. However, how do we group together a number of classes, interfaces, and top-level functions that are coupled together? To package an application or to create a shareable code base, we use a **library**. The Dart SDK already provides us with some 30 utility libraries, such as dart:core, dart:math, and dart:io. You can look them up in your Editor by going to **Help | API Reference** or via the http://api.dartlang.org URL. All the built-in libraries have the dart: prefix. We have seen them in use a few times and know that we have to import them in our code as import 'dart:math'; in prorabbits_v7.dart. Web applications will always import dart:html (dart:core is the most fundamental library and so is imported automatically). Likewise, we can create our own libraries and let other apps import them to use their functionality.

To illustrate this, let's make use of our rabbit breeding application (perhaps, there is a market for this app after all). For an app this simple, this is not needed, of course. However, every Dart app that contains a `main()` function is also a library, even when this is not indicated. We make a new app called `breeding` that could contain all kinds of breeding calculations. We group together all the constants that we will need in a file called `constants.dart` and move the function that calculates the rabbit breeding to a file named `rabbits.dart` in a subfolder called `rabbits`. All the files now have to declare how they are a part of the library. There is one code file (the library file in the `bin` subfolder; its file icon in the Editor is shown in bold) that contains the `library` keyword; in our example, it is `breeding.dart` in line (1):

```
library breeding;                               (1)

import 'dart:math';                             (2)

part 'constants.dart';                            (3)
part 'rabbits/rabbits.dart';

void main() {                                    (4)
  print("The number of rabbits increases as:\n");
  for (int years = 0; years <= NO_YEARS; years++) {
    print("${calculateRabbits(years)}");
  }
}
```

A library needs a name; here, it is `breeding` (all in lowercase and not in quotes). Other apps can import our library through this name. This file also contains all the necessary `import` statements (line (2)) and sums up (in no particular order) all the source files that together constitute of the library. This is done with the `part` keyword, followed by the quoted (relative) pathname to the source file, for example, when `rabbits.dart` resides in a subfolder called `rabbits`, this will be written as:

```
part 'rabbits/rabbits.dart';
```

However, everything is simple if all the files of a library reside in one folder. So, the library file presents an overview of all the part files it is split in; if needed, we can structure our library with subfolders, but Dart sees all this code as a single file. Furthermore, all the library source files need to indicate that they are a part of the library (we show only `rabbits.dart` here); again, the library name is not quoted (line (1)):

```
part of breeding;                               (1)

String calculateRabbits(int years) {
```

```
calc() => (2 * pow(E, log(GROWTH_FACTOR) *
    years)).round().toInt();

var out = "After $years years:\t ${calc()} rabbits";
return out;
}
```

> GROWTH_FACTOR is defined in the `constants.dart` file.

All these statements (`library`, `import`, `part`, and `part of`) need to appear at the top before any other code. The Dart compiler will import a specific source file only once, even when it is mentioned several times. If there is a main entry function in our library, it must be in the library file (line (4)); start the app to verify that we obtained the same breeding results as in our previous versions. A library that contains `main()` is also a runnable app in itself but, in general, a library does not need to contain a `main()` function. The `part of` annotation enforces that a file can only be a part of one library. Is this a restriction? No, because it strengthens the principle that the code must not be duplicated. If you have a collection of business classes in an app, group them in their own library and import them into your app; this way, these classes will be reusable.

> You can start coding your app (library) in a single file. Gradually, you will begin to discover units of the functionality of classes and/or the functions that belong together; then, you can move these into part files, while the library file, which contains the part statements, structures the whole.

Using a library in an app

To show how we can use our newly made library in another app, create a new `app_breeding` application. In its startup file (`app_breeding.dart`), we can call our library, as shown in the following code:

```
import '../../breeding/bin/breeding.dart';            (1)

int years;

void main() {
  years = 5;
  print("The number of rabbits has attained:");
  print("${calculateRabbits(years)}");
}
```

```
// Output:
//The number of rabbits has attained:
//After 5 years:    1518750 rabbits
```

The import statement in line (1) points to the main file of our library relative, in the file system, to the `.dart` file we are in (two folders level up with two periods (`..`) and then into the `bin` subfolder of `breeding`). As long as your libraries retain the same relative position to your client app (while deploying it in production), it will work. You can also import a library from a (remote) website using a URL in the following manner:

```
import 'http://www.breeding.org/breeding.dart';
```

Absolute file paths in `import` are not recommended, because they break too easily while deploying. In the next section, we will discuss the best way of importing a library by using the package manager called pub.

Resolving name conflicts

If you only want one or a few items (variables, functions, and classes) from a library, you will have the option of only importing these by enumerating them after `show`:

```
import 'library1.dart' show var1, func1, Class1;
```

The inverse can also be done; if you want to import everything from the library excluding these items, use `hide`:

```
import 'library1.dart' hide var1, func1, Class1;
```

We know that everything in a Dart app must have a unique name or, to put it another way, there can be no name conflicts in the app's namespace. What if we have to import into our app two libraries that have the same names for some of their objects? If you only need one of them, you can use `show` and/or `hide`. However, what if you need both? In such a case, you can give one of the libraries an alias and differentiate between the two using this alias as a prefix. Suppose `library1` and `library2` have an object A; you can differentiate between the two as follows:

```
import 'library1.dart';            // contains class A
import 'library2.dart' as libr2; // contains class A

var obj1 = new A();                // Use A from library1.
var obj2 = new libr2.A();          // Use A from library2.
```

Use this feature only when you really have to, for example, to solve name conflicts or aid readability. Finally, the `export` command (possibly combined with `show` or `hide`) gives you the ability to combine (parts of) libraries, refer to the `export` app.

Suppose `liba.dart` contains the following code:

```
library liba;
abc() => 'abc from liba';
xyz() => 'xyz from liba';
```

Additionally, suppose `libb.dart` contains the following code:

```
library libb;
import 'liba.dart';
export 'liba.dart' show abc;
```

Then, if `export.dart` imports `libb`, it will know the `abc` method but not the `xyz` method:

```
import 'libb.dart';
void main() {
  print('${abc()}'); // abc from liba
  // xyz();  // cannot resolve method 'xyz'
}
```

Visibility of objects outside a library

In the *A touch of class – how to use classes and objects* section, we mentioned that starting a file name with _ makes it private for the library (only known in the library itself). This is the case for all objects: variables, functions, classes, methods, and so on. Now, we will illustrate this in our `breeding` library.

Suppose `breeding.dart` contains two top-level variables:

```
String s1 = 'the breeding of cats';          (1)
var _s2    = 'the breeding of dogs';          (2)
```

We can use them both in `main()`, but also anywhere else in the library, for example, in `rabbits.dart`:

```
String calculateRabbits(int years) {
  print('$s1 and $_s2');
  //…
  return out;
}
```

However, if we try to use them in the `breeding.dart` app, which imports `breeding`, we will get a warning in line (3) of the following code in the Editor; it will say **cannot resolve _s2; s1 is visible but _s2 is not**:

```
void main() {
  years = 5;
  // …
  print('$s1 and $_s2');                        (3)
}
```

An exception occurs when the code is run (both in the checked and production modes). Note that, in lines (1) and (2), we typed the `s1` public variable as `String`, while the `_s2` private variable was left untyped. This is a general rule: give the publicly visible area of your library strong types and signatures. Privacy is an enhancement for developers used to JavaScript, but people coming from the OO arena will certainly ask why there is no class privacy. There are probably a number of reasons: classes are not that primordial in Dart as in OO languages, Dart has to compile to JavaScript, and so on. Class privacy is not needed to the extent usually imagined, and if you really want to have it in Dart, you can do it. Let the library only contain the class that has some private variables; these are visible only in this class, because other classes or functions are outside of this library.

Managing library dependencies with pub

Often, your app depends on libraries (packages) that are stored in the cloud (in the pub repository, or the GitHub repository, and so on). In this section, we will discuss how to install such packages and make them available to your code.

In the web version of our rabbits program (`prorabbits_v3.dart`) in *Chapter 1, Dart – A Modern Web Programming Language,* we discussed the use of the `pubspec. yaml` file. This file is present in every Dart project and contains the dependencies of our app on external packages. The **pub** tool takes care of installing (or updating) the necessary packages: right-click on the selected `pubspec.yaml` file and choose **Pub Get** (or **Upgrade** in case you need a more recent version of the packages). Alternatives are to select the folder name of the app, go to **Tools | Pub Get**, and double-click on the `.yaml` file (a screen called **Pubspec Details** appears and lets you change the contents of the file itself; this screen contains a section called **Pub Actions**, where you will find a link to **Run Pub get**). It even automatically installs the so-called transitive dependencies: if the package to install needs other packages, they will also be installed.

Let's prepare for the next section on unit testing by installing the `test` package with the pub tool. Create a new command-line application and call it `unittest_v1`. When you open the **Pubspec** screen, you see no dependencies. However, at the bottom, there is a tab called **Source** to go to the text file itself. This shows us:

```
name: unittest_v1
description: A sample command-line application
dependencies:
   test: any
```

We see that our app depends on the `test` package. If we now run **Pub Get**, we will see that a folder called `packages` will appear, containing in it a folder called `test` of the complete source of the requested package. The same subfolders appear under the `bin` folder. If needed, the `pub install` command can also be run outside the Editor from the command line. Pub installs the `test` package from its `https://pub.dartlang.org/` central repository, as you can see in the following screenshot. Another `pubspec.lock` file is also created (or updated); this file is used by the pub tool and contains the version info of the installed packages (don't change anything in here). In our example, this contains:

```
# Generated by pub. See: http://pub.dartlang.org/doc/glossary.
html#lockfile
        {"packages":{"test":{"version":"0.12.0","source":"hosted",
  "description":"test"},"meta":{"version":"0.12.0","source":
    "hosted","description":"meta"}}}
```

The following screenshot shows the configuration information for `pubspec.yaml`:

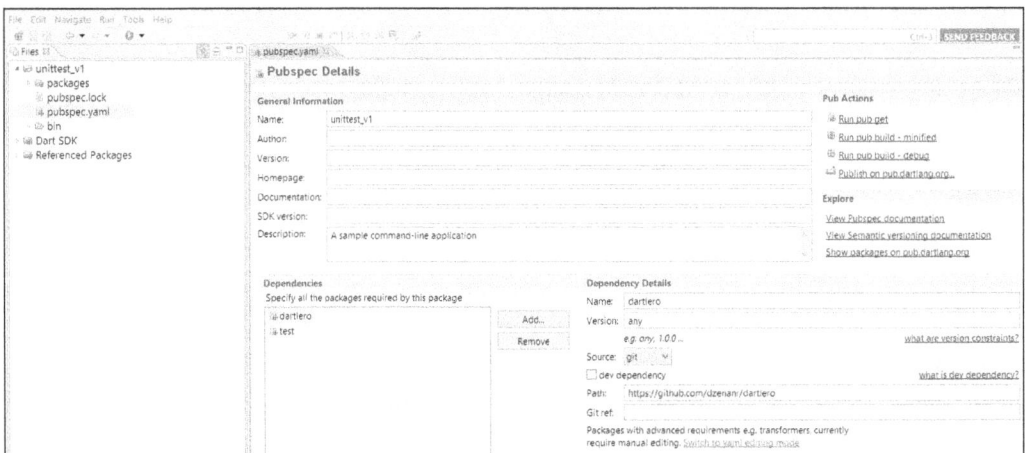

Configuring pub specifications for the app

The **Pubspec** screen, as you can see in the preceding screenshot, also gives you the ability to change or fill in the complementary app info such as **Name**, **Author**, **Version**, **Homepage**, **SDK version**, and **Description**. The **Version** field is of particular importance; with it, you can indicate that your app needs a specific version of a package (such as 2.1.0) or a major version number of 1 (>= 1.0.0 < 2.0.0); it locks your app to these versions of the dependencies. To use the installed test package, write the following code line at the top of test_v1.dart:

```
import 'package:test/unittest.dart';
```

The path to a Dart source file after package: is searched for in the packages folder. As a second example and in preparation for the next chapter, we will install the dartlero package from GitHub (although the unittest_v1.dart program will not use its specific functionality). We will then add a dependency called dartlero via the pubspec screen; any version would be good. Simply choose git from the source list and fill in https://github.com/dzenanr/dartlero for the path. Save this and then run **Pub Install**. Pub will clone the project from GitHub, install it in the packages folder, and update the pubspec.lock file. To make it known to your app, use the following import statement:

```
import 'package:dartlero/dartlero.dart';
```

The pub publish command checks whether your package conforms to certain conditions and uploads it to the pub's central repository at pub.dartlang.org.

> Dart Editor stores links to the installed packages for each app; these become invalid when you move or rename your code folders. If the Editor gives you the Cannot find referenced source: package: somepkg/pkg.dart error, close the app in the Editor and restart the Editor. In most cases, the problem would be solved. However, if not, clean out the Editor cache by deleting everything in C:\users\yourname\DartEditor. When you reopen the app in the Editor, the problem will be solved.

Here is a summary of how to install the packages:

1. Change pubspec.yaml and add dependencies through the **Details** screen.
2. Run the pub get command.
3. Add an import statement to your code for every installed package.

Unit testing in Dart

Dart has a built-in unit test framework. We learned how to import it in our app in the previous section. Every real app and, certainly, the ones that you're going to deploy somewhere should contain a sufficient amount of unit tests. Test programs will normally be separated from the main app code, residing in their own directory called `test`. Unit testing offers quite a lot of features; we will apply them in the forthcoming projects. Here, we want to show you the basics and we will do so by creating a `BankAccount` object, making some transactions on it and verifying the results, so we can trust that our `BankAccount` methods are doing fine (we will continue to work in `unittest_v1.dart`). Let's create a `BankAccount` constructor and do some transactions:

```
var bal = new BankAccount("John Gates","075-0623456-72", 1000.0);
bal.deposit(500.0);
bal.withdraw(300.0);
bal.deposit(136.0);
```

After this, `bal.balance` is equal to `1336.0` (because *1000 + 500 – 300 + 136 = 1336*). We can test whether our program calculated this correctly with the following statement:

```
test('Account Balance after deposit and withdrawal', () {
  expect(bal.balance, equals(1336.0));
});
```

Or, we can use a shorter statement as follows:

```
test('Account Balance after deposit and withdrawal', () =>
  expect(bal.balance, equals(1336.0)));
```

The `test` function from the `test` package takes two parameters:

- A test name (`String`); here, this is `Account Balance after deposit and withdrawal`

- A function (here, it is anonymous) that calls the `expect` function; this function also takes two parameters:

    ○ The value as given by the program

    ○ The expected value; here, given by `equals` (*expected value*)

Now, running the program will give the following output:

```
test-suite-wait-for-done
PASS: Account Balance after deposit and withdrawal
All 1 tests passed.
test-suite-success
```

Of course, here PASS indicates that our program is tested successfully. If this were not the case (suppose the balance had to be 1335.0, but the program produced 1336.0), we would get an exception with the Some tests failed message:

```
test-suite-wait-for-done
FAIL: Account Balance after deposit and withdrawal
  Expected: <1335.0>
       but: was <1336.0>
0 PASSED, 1 FAILED, 0 ERRORS
```

There would also be a screen output showing you which tests went wrong, the expected (correct) value, and the program value (it is important to note that the tests run after all the other statements in the method have been executed). Usually, you will have more than one test. You can then group them as follows using the same syntax as test:

```
group('Bank Account tests', () {
  test('Account Balance after deposit and withdrawal', () =>
    expect(ba1.balance, equals(1336.0)));
  test('Owner is correct', () => expect(ba1.owner, equals
    ("John Gates")));
  test('Account Number is correct', () => expect
    (ba1.number, equals("075-0623456-72")));
});
```

We can even prepare the tests in a setUp function (here, this would involve creating the account and doing the transactions) and clean up after the tests in a tearDown function (indicating that the test objects are no longer needed):

```
group('Bank Account tests', () {
  setUp(() {
    ba1 = new BankAccount("John Gates","075-0623456-72", 1000.0);
    ba1.deposit(500.0);
    ba1.withdraw(300.0);
    ba1.deposit(136.0);
  });
  tearDown(() {
    ba1 = null;
  });
```

```
    test('Account Balance after deposit and withdrawal', () =>
      expect(ba1.balance, equals(1336.0)));
    test('Owner is correct', () => expect(ba1.owner, equals
      ("John Gates")));
    test('Account Number is correct', () => expect
      (ba1.number, equals("075-0623456-72")));
});
```

The preceding code produces the following output:

```
test-suite-wait-for-done
PASS: Bank Account tests Account Balance after
  deposit and withdrawal
PASS: Bank Account tests Owner is correct
PASS: Bank Account tests Account Number is correct
All 3 tests passed.
test-suite-success
```

In general, the second parameter of `expect` is a so-called **matcher** that tests whether the value satisfies some constraint. Here are some matcher possibilities: `isNull, isNotNull, isTrue, isFalse, isEmpty, isPositive, hasLength(m), greaterThan(v), closeTo(value, delta), inInclusiveRange(low, high)`, and their variants. For a more detailed discussion of their use, see the documentation at `http://www.dartlang.org/articles/dart-unit-tests/#basic-synchronous-tests`. We'll apply unit testing in the coming projects, notably in the example that illustrates Dartlero in the next chapter.

Asynchronous programming with async and await

Dart has added new language features to support asynchronous programming in version 1.9: notably, the `async` functions and `await` expressions. The code is asynchronous when it calls a possibly time-consuming operation (such as I/O) and continues executing without waiting for the operation to complete.

In the following code snippet, `computeResult` represents an operation that could take some time to complete and we will wait for its result to return by calling it with `await`. We will wrap this call inside an `anasyncfunc` function, which is marked as `async`: the code that calls `anasyncfunc` will continue to execute immediately after this call:

```
anasyncfunc() async {
    var result = await computeResult();
    if (result > limit) {
      // Do something.
    } else {
      // Do something else.
    }
}
```

We can even use the normal `try`/`catch` mechanism for exception handling on the functions called with `await`, like this:

```
anasyncfunc() async {
    var result;
    try {
        result = await computeResult();
    }
    catch (e) {
        // react on possible exception e
    }
    // process result
}
```

If you want to call an asynchronous function inside your app's `main()` function, the body of `main()` must be marked as `async` as follows:

```
main() async {
    // call to asynchronous function:
    await computeResult();
}
```

These constructs enable us to write code much more elegantly than before so that asynchronous code looks like normal synchronous code. For a more detailed discussion, you can look up https://www.dartlang.org/docs/dart-up-and-running/ch03.html#dartasync---asynchronous-programming.

Project – word frequency

We will now develop systematically a small but useful web app that takes as input an ordinary text and produces as output an alphabetical listing of all the words appearing in the text, together with the number of times they appear (their frequency). For an idea of the typical output, see the following screenshot (word_frequency.dart):

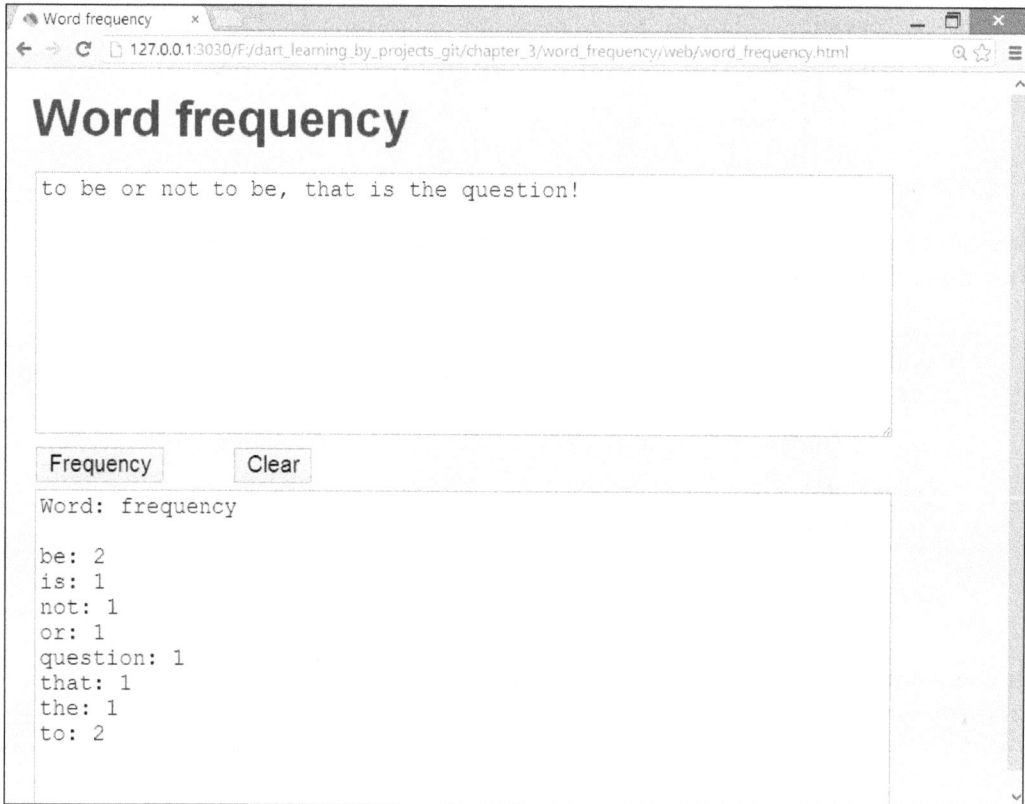

The Word frequency app

The user interface is easy: the text is taken from the textarea tag with the id text in the top half. Clicking on the frequency button sets the processing in motion and the result is shown in the bottom half with the id words. Here is the markup from word_frequency.html:

```
<!DOCTYPE html>
<html>
  <head>
    <meta charset="utf-8">
    <title>Word frequency</title>
```

```
    <link rel="stylesheet" href="word_frequency.css">
  </head>
  <body>
    <h1>Word frequency</h1>

    <section>
      <textarea id="text" rows=10 cols=80></textarea>
      <br/>
      <button id="frequency">Frequency</button>
             
      <button id="clear">Clear</button>
      <br/>
      <textarea id="words" rows=40 cols=80></textarea>
    </section>

    <script type="application/dart"
      src="word_frequency.dart"></script>
    <script src="packages/browser/dart.js"></script>
  </body>
</html>
```

In the last line, we will see that the special `dart.js` script (which checks for the existence of the Dart VM and starts the JavaScript version if it is not found) is also installed by pub. In *Chapter 1, Dart – A Modern Web Programming Language*, we learned how to connect variables with the HTML elements through the `query` function:

```
variable = query('#id')
```

So, this is what we will do first in `main()`:

```
// binding to the user interface:
var textArea = querySelector('#text');
var wordsArea = querySelector ('#words');
var wordsBtn = querySelector ('#frequency');
var clearBtn = querySelector ('#clear');
```

Our buttons listen to the click events with the mouse; this is translated into Dart as:

```
wordsBtn.onClick.listen((MouseEvent e) { ... }
```

Here is the processing we need to do in this click event handler:

1. The input text is a String; we need to clean it up (remove the spaces and special characters).

2. Then, we must translate the text into a list of words. This will be programmed in the following function:

    ```
    List fromTextToWords(String text)
    ```

3. Then, we traverse through the list and count the number of times each word occurs; this effectively constructs a map. We'll do this in the following function:

    ```
    Map analyzeWordFreq(List wordList)
    ```

4. From the map, we will then produce a sorted list for the output area:

    ```
    List sortWords(Map wordFreqMap)
    ```

With this design in mind, our event handler becomes:

```
wordsBtn.onClick.listen((MouseEvent e) {
  wordsArea.value = 'Word: frequency \n';
  var text = textArea.value.trim();
  if (text != '') {
    var wordsList = fromTextToWords(text);
    var wordsMap = analyzeWordFreq(wordsList);
    var sortedWordsList = sortWords(wordsMap);
    sortedWordsList.forEach((word) =>
    wordsArea.value = '${wordsArea.value} \n${word}');
  }
});
```

In the last line, we appended the output for each word to wordsArea.

Now, we will fill in the details. Removing unwanted characters can be done by chaining replaceAll() for each character, like this:

```
var textWithout = text.replaceAll(',', '').replaceAll
  (';', '').replaceAll('.', '').replaceAll('\n', ' ');
```

This is a very ugly code! We can do better by defining a regular expression that assembles all these characters. We can do this with the \W expression that represents all the noncharacters (letters, digits, or underscores). Then, we will only have to apply replaceAll once:

```
List fromTextToWords(String text) {
    var regexp = new RegExp('\W+');                    (1)
    var textWithout = text.replaceAll(regexp, '');
    return textWithout.split(' ');                     (2)
}
```

We used the RegExp class in line (1), which is more often used to detect pattern matches in a String. Then, we applied the split() method of String in line (2) to produce a list of wordsList. This list is transformed into a Map with the following function:

```
Map analyzeWordFreq(List wordList) {
    var wordFreqMap = new Map();
    for (var w in wordList) {
        var word = w.trim();
        wordFreqMap.putIfAbsent(word, () => 0);        (3)
        wordFreqMap[word] += 1;
    }
    return wordFreqMap;
}
```

Note the use of putIfAbsent instead of if...else in line (3).

Then, we will use the generated Map to produce the desired output in the sortWords method:

```
List sortWords(Map wordFreqMap) {
    var temp = new List<String>();
    wordFreqMap.forEach((k, v) => temp.add('${k}:
        ${v.toString()}'));
    temp.sort();
    return temp;
}
```

The resulting list is shown in the bottom text area. You can find the complete listing in the word_frequency.dart file.

The Observatory tool

Observatory is the Dart Virtual Machine's (VM) built-in profiling and debugging tool. It is a new class of development tools with a focus on live, immediate reporting of data. Observatory includes tools to profile memory and the CPU usage of Dart programs. Starting with Dart 1.9, Observatory includes a full debugger.

Observatory runs in your browser and allows you to peek inside the running Dart VM on demand while providing real-time reporting on your executing code. For standalone applications, execute your start up `<script>.dart` dart file from the command line with:

```
dart --enable-vm-service --pause-isolates-on-start <script>.dart
```

Then, open your browser with the `http://localhost:8181/` URL. The main screen of Observatory will now appear as follows:

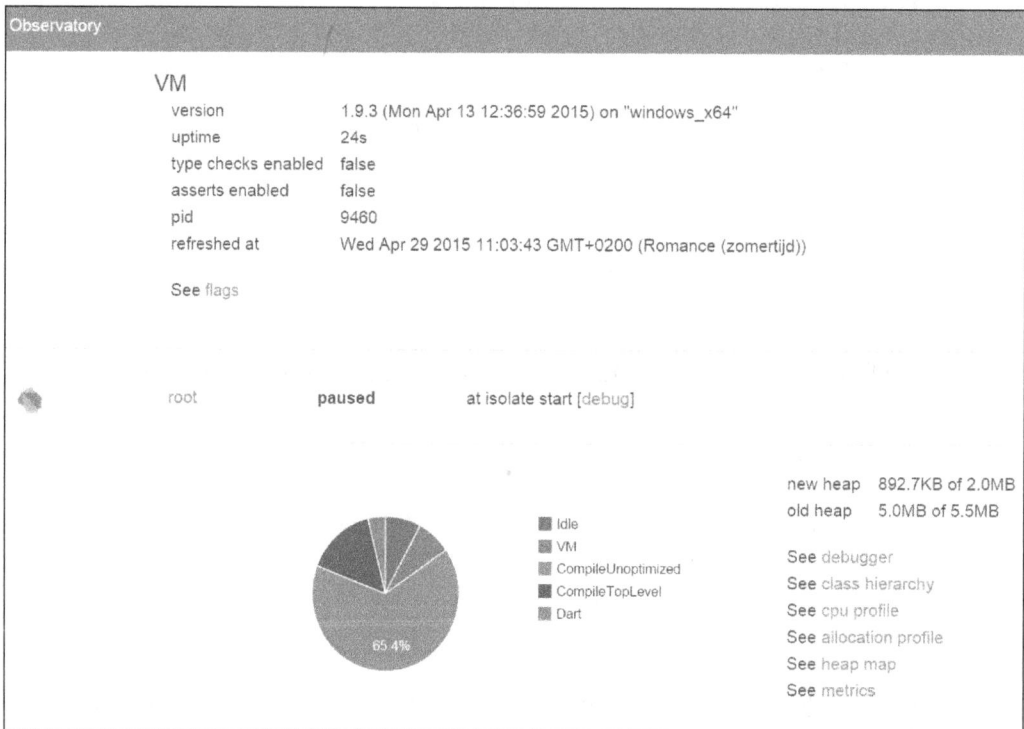

From this screen, follow the links to more detailed screens:

- To investigate in which code sections your code spends most of its time, use the **cpu profile**
- To take a look at the memory allocation of your data and possible memory fragmentation, use **allocation profile** and **heap map**
- To see which classes are used in your app, start **class hierarchy**

To start **Observatory** for a web app, launch chromium from the command line with the HTML start up page (here `script.html`) as an argument, like this:

```
<path to chromium>\chrome.exe script.html
```

The command-line output includes a line similar to the following:

```
Observatory listening on http://127.0.0.1:49621
```

Open this URL in any browser to bring up the **Observatory** main screen.

For more detailed information, consult `https://www.dartlang.org/tools/observatory/`.

Summary

Congratulations! You can call yourself a Dart programmer now. By working through this and the previous chapter, you have acquired a lot of technical skills and gained insights into how Dart works.

Modeling the data of your project in classes, perhaps extending another class or implementing the interface of some classes is certainly one of the main ideas to take away from this chapter. Then, there is the library concept, which allows you to structure your code at a higher level, using packages from other developers and eventually publishing your own app with pub. Finally, we have learned how to apply unit testing to our Dart app.

In the next chapter, we will graphically design a model for our app and base the code on a modeling framework, all in Dart.

4
Modeling Web Applications with Model Concepts and Dartlero

Up until now, the apps we discussed were quite simple; there was no real need to design a model. However, while developing more complex (web) applications, a good model to start from will lay a more stable foundation for the code. In this chapter, we will build a project from scratch, designing its model graphically and implementing it with a framework. The good thing is that we will use tools developed in Dart to do this. Because most of the projects we will develop are hosted on GitHub, we start by looking at how Git and GitHub work. We will cover the following topics:

- A short introduction to Git and GitHub
- What is a model and why we need it in programming
- Model concepts—a graphical design tool for our models
- Dartlero—a simple domain model framework
- The categories and links application

A short introduction to Git and GitHub

Git is an open source software tool that allows groups of people to work together harmoniously on the same code project at the same time. So, it's a **Distributed Version Control System (DVCS)**. The projects are published on the cloud, for example, in the GitHub repository `https://github.com/` (there are other websites that accept Git projects, for example, Bitbucket at `https://bitbucket.org/`). Git maintains local copies of these projects on your computer(s). For this to work, the Git tool must be installed locally as well. To get started, create an account on the GitHub website or sign in if you already have one. Go to the `https://help.github.com/articles/set-up-git` site and click on the **Download and install the latest version of Git** link. If necessary, choose your OS and let the wizard install Git on your machine with the default options. The code from this book resides in the `https://github.com/Ivo-Balbaert/learning_dart` GitHub repository. To create a local copy of the code examples, all you will need to do is:

1. Make a folder where you store your Git downloads (for example, `/home/git` or `d:\git`)

2. Start the Git Bash command-line tool and go to the folder:

   cd git

3. Clone the remote repository into your local repository by using the following command:

   git clone git://github.com/Ivo-Balbaert/learning_dart.git

A `learning_dart` subfolder is created and all the files are copied in it locally. Afterwards, if you want to get the latest changes from the remote repository, go to the local directory and use the following command:

git pull

Creating a repository on GitHub and a local version

This is easy; just follow the steps given here:

1. Sign in to GitHub, click on the **New Repository** button, and fill in a repository name, say `dart_projects`. Then, click on the **Create Repository** button (we follow the Dart style guidelines here and name it as a directory: `lowercase_with_underscores`). Now, your remote repository is created with the `https://github.com/your_name/dart_projects.git` URL.

2. Create a folder for your local version of this repository, say `git/dart_projects`. Start Git bash and go to the folder with `cd`.

3. Initialize an empty Git repository with the following command:

```
git init
```

4. Every project needs a readme file to provide minimal documentation; so create an empty README.md text file in a simple text editor and put some useful information in it with Dart Editor (or your favorite text editor).

5. We add this file to our local repository with the command:

```
git add README.md.
```

In general, the git add command will put all that is inside the directory into a waiting room (called staging area or index). The git status command will show these new changes that are yet to be committed to your project. This time, you can make these changes permanent by committing our project with the following command:

```
git commit -m 'created first version'
```

Here, -m provides a message. You can also provide a text file called .gitignore to contain files (or patterns of files) that are not to be included in the version control system.

6. To push your local changes to your remote GitHub repository, use the following commands:

```
git remote add origin https://github.com/your_name
  /dart_projects.git
```

```
git push -u origin master
```

You will be asked to authenticate with your GitHub username and password.

7. The next time you work on your project and want to store the changes in the repository (local and GitHub), you can simply use the following command:

```
git add .
```

```
git commit -m 'verb something'
```

```
git push
```

Collaborating on a GitHub project

If you want to invite someone else to join your project in order to make changes, select the repository of your project and use the **Settings** menu. Then, select the **Collaborators** option. Add that person by using his or her GitHub name. If you are not alone on your project, always start your working session with the `git pull` command to get the latest changes and avoid conflicts. Watch the videos at `http://git-scm.com/videos` to get a good introduction to Git. Also, the basic concepts are explained in this course at `http://www.codeschool.com/courses/try-git`.

What is a model and why we need it in programming

Most applications that go beyond simple exercises are too complex to be developed from the start; a model that describes the entities in the application domain and their relations is needed. To fully support such a domain-driven development, we need three things:

- A **graphical tool** for model design and the import/export of the model definitions; this is the **Model Concepts** tool

- A **domain model framework** — **Dartlero** for simple cases and **dartling** for more complicated business domains

- A **web component framework** for the rapid development of dynamic web applications: the `Polymer.dart` package

The first two were developed by *Dzenan Ridjanovic,* one of the authors, and the third was developed by the Google Dart team. All are written in Dart and are available as free, open source software. The remainder of this chapter will show how to use model concepts and Dartlero, and we will apply them in constructing a simple model of categories and links. Web components, which are essentially chunks of the reusable HTML5, are explained in *Chapter 9, Modeling More Complex Applications with dartling*. We will also build a web component application for the category links model. The dartling is discussed in depth in *Chapter 10, Local Data and Client-Server Communication*. Both of them will be used in the projects from *Chapter 10, Local Data and Client-Server Communication*, onwards. First, we will explore the model concepts.

Model Concepts – a graphical design tool for our models

This project is also hosted on GitHub. To get a local copy, open your Git bash terminal, go to the folder where you want to store the code, and issue the following command:

```
git clone git://github.com/dzenanr/model_concepts.git
```

After a few seconds, the `model_concepts` folder is created. It contains the whole project. Open the folder in Dart Editor to get a feel of how it is constructed. It is a web app containing the `<script type="application/dart" src="model_concepts.dart"></script>` script tag, and it starts the Dart VM with `model_concepts.dart`. When you run the app, the graphical designer appears in Chrome (Dartium). If you want to run it in another browser without Dart VM, first generate the JavaScript version through **Tools | Pub Build – Debug** and then paste the URL in the address window of your favorite browser (something like `http://127.0.0.1:3030/F:/git/model_concepts/web/model_concepts.html`) or simply run it with `pub serve`. The web folder contains the HTML file and the `model_concepts.dart` start up script, which contains the following code snippet:

```
import 'dart:html';
import 'package:model_concepts/model_concepts.dart';           (1)

void main() {
  // Get a reference to the canvas.
  CanvasElement canvas = document.querySelector('#canvas');    (2)
  Board board = new Board(canvas);                             (3)
}
```

Line (1) loads the `model_concepts` library from the `packages` folder; the original source code of the library resides in the `lib` directory. The `library` header file, also called `model_concepts.dart`, shows the dart libraries that we need (`html`, `async`, and `convert`) as well as all the part files:

```
library model_concepts;

import 'dart:html';
import 'dart:async';
import 'dart:convert';


part 'board.dart';
part 'box.dart';
```

```
part 'item.dart';
part 'json_panel.dart';
part 'line.dart';
part 'menu_bar.dart';
part 'png_panel.dart';
part 'tool_bar.dart';
```

This app uses canvas painting in HTML5 (we'll explore that bottom up in the coming chapters). In line (2), the <canvas> tag with the canvas ID is bound to a canvas object of the CanvasElement class. Then, in line (3), an object of the Board class (the board.dart file) is instantiated with a reference to this canvas to start up the program.

> We shall not provide further explanation on how the code works here. The app was built up in versions (called **spirals**, so far there are 14). On the *On Dart* blog (http://dzenanr.github.com/), under the **Magic Boxes** posts, you can find a detailed description of how the code evolved from **Spirals 00** to the current app (magic boxes grew into model concepts), along with a summary of the development on http://goo.gl/DqF7d. This is a truly great way to learn Dart!

When the app starts up, we will see the following screen:

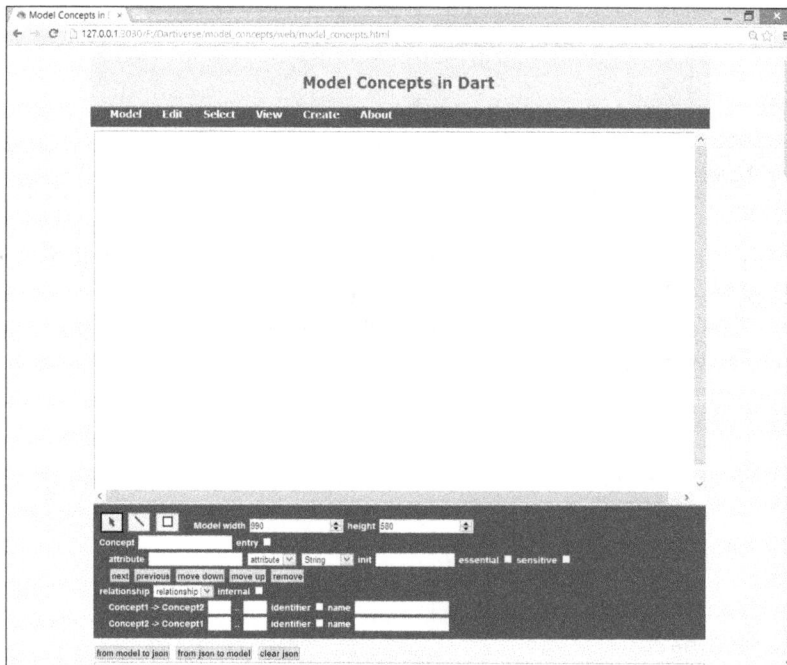

Model concepts start screen

Working with model concepts

The purpose of this tool is to graphically design a **domain model** of your app. Concepts or entities are drawn as rectangular boxes; these contain **items** that represent the **attributes**. The boxes are connected with the lines that represent the **relationships** between the entities; their multiplicity (that is, how many entities of kind B are associated with an entity of kind A, for example, many employees working in one department) can be indicated by **0..N** or **1..1**. The tool itself contains a (tiny) user guide, which is revealed by scrolling down the screen.

Explaining the model

We will learn how to work with this tool by designing the model for our next app: the category links application. This app is all about subjects (called categories here) such as HTML5; Dart; Apple; Google; Programming, the economic crisis; and the hyperlinks (called links here) to the web postings about these subjects. Here are some examples of the links for HTML5: www.html5rocks.com, http://diveintohtml5. info/ and http://animateyourhtml5.appspot.com/. Clearly, a category can have multiple links, but it may also have none; so, the relationship from category to link will be **0..N**.

Our app (that will be developed in *Chapter 8, Developing Business Applications with Polymer Web Components*) will show all the categories and the corresponding links for each category. Furthermore, we will be able to edit, remove, and add categories as well as links. However, first we will draw a model with two concepts (**Category**/**Link**) and one relationship (**links**). It will look like the following figure:

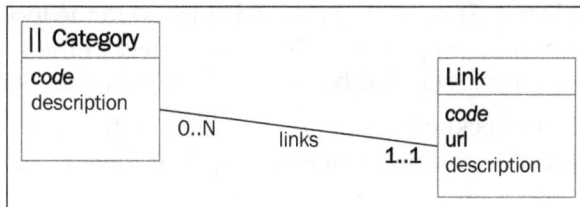

The graphical model of category-links

The category concept has two attributes: a code (name) like `Dart` and a description like `Web programming language`, `tools`, and `how to`. The **code** attribute is drawn in italics because it is an identifier, and in bold because its value is required. The link concept has the code identifier, the required URL attribute, and an optional description attribute. For example, the URL for `Dart` could be `http://www.dartlang.org/` and the description could be *Official Google site for Dart*. In our model, a link has exactly one category, so a **1..1** relation is applied (this is, a simplification of a more realistic situation, where a link could belong to many categories). A relationship between two concepts has two directions (**neighbors**). The category link direction, where **Link** is a neighbor of **Category**, has a min cardinality of **0** (a category need not have any link) and a max cardinality of **N** (many). In addition, it has the link's name. The link category direction has no name. Hence, it will not be represented explicitly in Dart; its min and max cardinalities are in bold and italics. Together with the code, it is the identifier of the link (note that **1..1** is in italics and bold). Within the same category, all the links must have a unique code value. **Category** is the only entry (| | as a door) into the model. This means that the model will have a collection of categories and each category will have a collection of links.

Drawing the model

The steps to draw a model are given as follows:

1. Click on the box tool icon in the tool bar (brown background, refer to the model concepts' start screen) and create a box for the category concept by clicking on the empty space in the board.

2. Click on the box to select it (four squares appear in the corners) and click again to deselect it. The selected box is displayed in the tool bar and you can enter the name `Category` for it in the concept field of the tool bar. The name will not appear in the selected box until you use the *Enter* key.

3. Check the entry checkbox; **Category** is marked with | |. To move a box, select it and keep the mouse down while moving it. If there are connecting lines, they will follow.

   The size of selected boxes may be changed by the menu items in the **View** menu. If you want to create several boxes, double-click on the box tool to stay active. To return to the **Select** mode, double-click on the **Select tool**.

   A box item (an attribute of a concept) may be created by entering its name in the attribute field of the toolbar and using the *Enter* key.

4. Select the identifier from the drop-down list; the default `String` type is ok. Enter `code` and the item will appear in the **Category** box. Repeat the steps for the `description` item, but select an attribute from the list.

5. Now, design the link concept with its attributes and mark the URL attribute from the list as per your requirements.

6. Click on the line tool to create a line between the last two clicked boxes by clicking on the empty space in the board.

The first box is a parent and the second box is a child. By default, the parent box has **0..N** cardinalities. The min is **0** and the max is **N**. By default, the child box has **1..1** cardinalities. For more details, see the tiny user guide in the program screen beneath the brown toolbar.

1. To make a PNG image from our model, scroll down to the **To Image** button above the PNG panel and click on the button. The created image will become visible in the panel. Right-click to save it as a file (**Save Image as**), or copy (**Copy Image**) and paste it into another file (for example, as documentation).

2. Name the current model in the **Model** menu as `Category_Links` and save it in the local storage of your browser. In a later session, simply enter the model name (it is case-sensitive!) and open it.

Exporting the model

Drawing the model clarifies our thoughts about it, but it wouldn't be of much use if we can't get to code from it. We can export the semantics of a model (only the nonhidden boxes and lines) in the JSON format by clicking on the **From model to json** button above the JSON panel. After doing this, the JSON text will appear in the JSON panel; copy and save it into a local `category_links.json` text file. It will also work the other way around: the JSON text may be used to recreate the graphical model in magic boxes. Paste the JSON text from a previous model into the JSON panel and click on the **From json to model** button to visualize the model. For a pretty JSON version of the model, click on the **Pretty json** button, but only after you click on the **From model to json** button. Then, open the `.json` file in a text editor to see how the information about our model is contained in it:

```
{
    "width":990,
    "lines":[
        {
```

```
            "box2box1Max":"1",
            "box1Name":"Category",
            "box1box2Min":"0",
            "box2Name":"Link",
            "box1box2Id":false,
            "box2box1Id":false,
            "box2box1Name":"",
            "box1box2Max":"N",
            "box1box2Name":"",
            "box2box1Min":"1",
            "category":"relationship",
            "internal":true
        }
    ],
    "height":580,
    "boxes":[
        {
            "width":120,
            "entry":true,
            "name":"Category",
            "x":125,
            "height":80,
            "y":63,
            "items":[
                {
                    "sequence":10,
                    "name":"code",
                    "category":"identifier",
                    "type":"String",
                    "init":""
                },
                {
                    "sequence":20,
                    "name":"description",
                    "category":"attribute",
                    "type":"String",
                    "init":""
                }
            ]
        },
// omitted analogous entry for link
    ]
}
```

What is JSON?

JavaScript Object Notation (JSON) is a simple text format (easy to be read and written by humans and machines) to represent structured objects and collections, and exchange data between applications or computers. For example, when a client sends data to or receives data from a server through a web service, it is often in the JSON format. It arose from the open source world, more or less as a competitor to the *heavier* XML format; but it is used everywhere now. Any production language has special functions (in the `dart:convert` library) to make it easy to use, Dart being no exception. Let's examine a simple JSON example and see how it connects to List and Map: look at the `BankAccount` object from `banking_v3.dart` (*Chapter 2, Getting to Work with Dart*):

```
var bal = new BankAccount("John Gates","075-0623456-72", 1000.0);
```

It contains three data items: the owner, the number, and the balance of the account. The JSON representation of this data (object) is:

```
{
    "owner": "John Gates",
    "number": "075-0623456-72",
    "balance": 1000.0
}
```

In a Dart app, this could be typed as a multiline string (see line (1) in `json.dart` at `code\chapter_3`). Looking at it from the Dart perspective, it is a Map where the names of the object's properties are the keys and the values are the Map's values; there is a close relationship between the objects and JSON (hence, the name). This object notation can be nested (for example, the owner could be an object in itself with a name, an address, and a telephone number). To express that there are many of these objects, you can use the [ ] notation, as in the following code snippet:

```
[
  {
    "owner": "John Gates",
    "number": "075-0623456-72",
    "balance": 1000.0
  },
  {
    "owner": "Bill O'Connor",
    "number": "081-0731645-91",
    "balance": 2500.0
  }
]
```

This effectively corresponds to a List of Maps in Dart.

You can encode a Dart object into a JSON string with the `JSON.encode()` function from the `dart:convert` library, for example, the `bankAccounts` variable in line (2). The resulting JSON can be sent over the network or it could be the return value of a call to a web service. The Dart object to encode needs to be of the `null`, `bool`, `int`, `double`, `String`, `List`, or `Map` type; any other object needs to have a `toJson()` method that is called while encoding. The other way around, decoding a JSON string into a Dart object, is done with the `JSON.decode` method (see line (3) in `json.dart`):

```dart
import 'dart:convert';

var jsonStr1 = '''                                          (1)
{
    "owner": "John Gates",
    "number": "075-0623456-72",
    "balance": 1000.0
}
''';
var jsonStr2 = '''
[
  {
      "owner": "John Gates",
      "number": "075-0623456-72",
      "balance": 1000.0
  },
  {
      "owner": "Bill O'Connor",
      "number": "081-0731645-91",
      "balance": 2500.0
  }
]
''';
var bankAccounts = [{ "owner": "John Gates","number": "075-0623456-
72",
                    "balance": 1000.0 },
                  { "owner": "Bill O'Connor", "number": "081-
0731645-91",
                    "balance": 2500.0 }];
main() {
  // encoding a Dart object (here a List of Maps) to a JSON
  // string:
  var jsonText = JSON.encode(bankAccounts);                 (2)
  print('$jsonText'); // all white space is removed
  // decoding a JSON string into a Dart object:
  var obj = JSON.decode(jsonText);                          (3)
```

```
    assert(obj is List);
    assert(obj[0] is Map);
    assert(obj[0]['number']=="075-0623456-72");

    var ba1 = new BankAccount("John Gates","075-0623456-72", 1000.0);
    var json = JSON.encode(ba1);
}

class BankAccount {
  // other properties and methods ...
  String toJson() {
    return '{"owner":"$owner", "number":"$number", "balance:
      "$balance"}';
  }
}
```

In the previous section, data were exported from model concepts in the JSON format. This data can be imported in the domain model framework, dartling (see *Chapter 9, Modeling More Complex Applications with dartling*), to generate the code for it. We will use JSON again as the format to store data in or to send data to the server in some of the forthcoming projects. In the `dartlero_tasks` project of *Chapter 11, Data-Driven Web Applications with MySQL and MongoDB*, we will read and write the JSON files. For an in-depth look, refer to `http://en.wikipedia.org/wiki/JSON`.

Dartlero – a simple domain model framework

We will now discuss Dartlero to get an idea of what a domain model framework is all about and how you can build upon it. **Dartlero** is a limited model framework used in teaching and learning basic data structures in Dart. It will give you a better understanding of the more encompassing dartling framework. How dartling works together with model concepts is explained in detail in *Chapter 9, Modeling More Complex Applications with dartling*.

Get your copy of Dartlero with the following command:

```
git clone git://github.com/dzenanr/dartlero.git
```

Open the `dartlero` folder in your Dart Editor. Dartlero's code sits in the `lib` folder and the `dartlero.dart` library file, referencing three part files in the `model` subdirectory (lines (2) to (5)):

```
library dartlero;

part 'model/action_reactions.dart';                          (2)
part 'model/concept_model.dart';                             (3)
part 'model/concept_entities.dart';                          (4)
part 'model/concept_errors.dart';                            (5)
```

Dartlero is just a library; it cannot be started by itself. We see that the central concepts are entities and models, and it builds heavily on the built-in `List` and `Map` classes. The code is quite *abstract*, but it is instructive to dig into it (use the Editor to see the code in its entirety). In the `concept_entities.dart` file, the `ConceptEntityApi` abstract class is defined. It describes the properties and methods of an entity in this framework. We see that an entity has only one property named `code` (with get and set), and there are abstract methods to create (`newEntity`), copy, and transform an entity into a Map (`toJson`) and vice versa (`fromJson`):

```
abstract class ConceptEntityApi<T extends ConceptEntityApi<T>>
    implements Comparable, ActionReaction {

  String get code;
  set code(String code);
  ConceptEntityApi<T> newEntity();                           (1)
  T copy();
  Map<String, Object> toJson();                              (2)
  void fromJson(Map<String, Object> entityMap);              (3)
}
```

The `newEntity` method (line (1)) is used to provide a specific object within the generic code of the `ConceptEntity` class. The `toJson` and `fromJson` methods (lines (2) and (3)) provide for the export and import of entities, which will be used in the saving and loading of data.

This class is implemented by `ConceptEntity`, which also contains the methods to display an entity and compare two entities. Although all the methods contain code, this class is meant as an interface to be implemented by concrete entity classes (this is why it is called `ConceptEntity`):

```
abstract class ConceptEntity<T extends ConceptEntity<T>>
    implements ConceptEntityApi {
    // code left out
}
```

The `ConceptEntitiesApi` abstract class defines a number of properties and methods such as `length`, `forEach`, `add`, `toList`, and `toJson` for a collection of entities; in fact, it contains a List and a Map of entities:

```
abstract class ConceptEntitiesApi<T extends ConceptEntityApi<T>>
implements ActionReaction {
    int get length;
    bool get isEmpty;
    Iterator<T> get iterator;
    ConceptEntitiesApi<T> newEntities();
    ConceptEntityApi<T> newEntity();
    void forEach(Function f);
// other code left out
}
```

Again, this class is implemented by the `ConceptEntities` class:

```
abstract class ConceptEntities<T extends ConceptEntity<T>>
    implements ConceptEntitiesApi {
    // code left out
}
```

All of the above classes are defined for a generic `T` type, for example:

```
abstract class ConceptEntity<T extends ConceptEntity<T>>
```

When the framework is applied in a concrete domain, `T` will be replaced by a concrete type. This type has to be a child class of `ConceptEntity<T>`. This will become clearer when we discuss the example in the next section.

In the `concept_model.dart` file, a `ConceptModelApi` abstract class is defined, which is implemented by `ConceptModel`. This is essentially a Map connecting names to `ConceptEntities`:

```
abstract class ConceptModelApi {
  Map<String, ConceptEntitiesApi> newEntries();
  ConceptEntitiesApi getEntry(String entryConcept);
}

abstract class ConceptModel implements ConceptModelApi {
  Map<String, ConceptEntities> _entryMap;
  ConceptModel() {
    _entryMap = newEntries();
}

  ConceptEntities getEntry(String entryConcept) => _
entryMap[entryConcept];
}
```

The third `concept_errors.dart` file defines some specific `Error` classes:

```
class DartleroError extends Error {
  final String msg;
  DartleroError(this.msg);
  toString() => '*** $msg ***';
}

class JsonError extends DartleroError {
  JsonError(String msg) : super(msg);
}
```

Dartlero mostly hides the use of the List and Map data structures (by looking at the code, you can see how List and Map are used internally). It does not support identifiers and relationships, and it doesn't have a code generator.

An example of using Dartlero

To get a better feeling of what using a framework entails, let's examine the project that exists as the example folder in the `dartlero` project, and as a separate project called `dartlero_example` at GitHub (there are slight differences due to the pub specifications). Get your copy in a separate folder with:

```
git clone git://github.com/dzenanr/dartlero_example.git
```

Then, open the `dartlero_example` folder in Dart Editor.

This app defines the simplest possible model: a project model with only one concept, `Project`. We will now use the Dartlero framework. The dependency on this package is indicated in the `pubspec.yaml` file so that it can be managed by pub:

```
name: dartlero_example
version: 1.0.0
author: Dzenan Ridjanovic <dzenanr@gmail.com>
description: An example how to use Dartlero, a model framework
  for educational purposes.
homepage: http://ondart.me/
dependencies:
  dartlero:
  git: git://github.com/dzenanr/dartlero.git
```

The `dartlero_example.dart` library file in the `lib` folder imports Dartlero and references two files in a subfolder model:

```
library dartlero_example;
import 'package:dartlero/dartlero.dart';

part 'model/project_entities.dart';
part 'model/project_model.dart';
```

In the `project_entities.dart` file, we will see a `Project` class that extends the `ConceptEntity<Project>` framework class, and the `Projects` collection class that extends the `ConceptEntities<Project>` class:

```
class Project extends ConceptEntity<Project> { ... }
class Projects extends ConceptEntities<Project> { ... }
```

What has happened here? The `<Project>` type argument is passed to the `ConceptEntity` class (or `ConceptEntities`) and its `T` parameter is replaced by `Project`. If we replace this, the `signature` class in the `ConceptEntity<T extends, ConceptEntity<T>>` abstract class will become more specific: `abstract class ConceptEntity<Project extends ConceptEntity<Project>>`.

After this, wherever we will see `T`, Dart (or Dart Editor) will see project; the same is true for the `ConceptEntities` class. This means that a collection of entities will contain only projects. Thus, if we want to add a task to projects (let's say of the `Task` type), Dart Editor will complain. Without generics, Dart Editor would happily accept a new task in the projects collection. Using generics makes a framework more general. It can be used with all kinds of concrete types, constraining data so that the model is valid. The following is the complete code of `project_entities.dart`:

```
part of dartlero_example;

class Project extends ConceptEntity<Project> {

  String _name;
  String description;

  String get name => _name;
  set name(String name) {
    _name = name;
    if (code == null) {
      code = name;
    }
  }
}
```

```dart
    Project newEntity() => new Project();

    Project copy() {
      var project = super.copy();
      project.name = name;
      project.description = description;
      return project;
    }

    String toString() {
      return '  {\n '
             '    ${super.toString()}, \n '
             '    name: ${name}, \n '
             '    description: ${description}\n'
             '  }';
    }

    Map<String, Object> toJson() {
      Map<String, Object> entityMap = super.toJson();
      entityMap['name'] = name;
      entityMap['description'] = description;
      return entityMap;
    }

    fromJson(Map<String, Object> entityMap) {
      super.fromJson(entityMap);
      name = entityMap['name'];
      description = entityMap['description'];
    }

    bool get onProgramming =>
        description.contains('Programming') ? true : false;

    int compareTo(Project other) {
      return name.compareTo(other.name);
    }
}

class Projects extends ConceptEntities<Project> {
  Projects newEntities() => new Projects();
  Project newEntity() => new Project();
}
```

The `Project` and `Projects` classes also contain the `newEntity` and `newEntities` methods to create concrete objects, implementing the abstract methods of their parent classes. A project has a name and a description, and some of its methods (such as `copy`, `toString`, `toJson`, and `fromJson`) extend the methods inherited from `ConceptEntity` by using the `super` keyword. The inherited `compareTo` method gets a new implementation in the project: it is completely overridden. Furthermore, `Project` adds a new `onProgramming` method, which is a get-only property to see from the description whether the project has something do to with programming.

The `subfolder` model also contains `project_model.dart` with a `ProjectModel` class that extends the `ConceptModel` class from the Dartlero framework. Three projects are created in the `init()` method. The `display()` method on the model delegates work to the inherited (from `ConceptEntities`) `display()` method on the projects object. The following is the code from `project_model.dart`:

```
part of dartlero_example;

class ProjectModel extends ConceptModel {

  static final String project = 'Project';

  Map<String, ConceptEntities> newEntries() {
    var projects = new Projects();
    var map = new Map<String, ConceptEntities>();
    map[project] = projects;
    return map;
  }

  Projects get projects => getEntry(project);

  init() {
    var design = new Project();
    design.name = 'Dartling Design';
    design.description =
        'Creating a model of Dartling concepts based on
          MagicBoxes.';
    projects.add(design);

    var prototype = new Project();
    prototype.name = 'Dartling Prototype';
    prototype.description =
        'Programming the meta model and the generic model.';
```

```
      projects.add(prototype);

      var production = new Project();
      production.name = 'Dartling';
      production.description =
          'Programming Dartling.';
      projects.add(production);
    }

  display() {
    print('Project Model');
    print('=============');
    projects.display('Projects');
    print(
      '============= ============= ============= '
      '============= ============= ============= '
    );
  }
}
```

In the `packages` folder, we will see not only `dartlero`, but also `unittest`, because Dartlero needs this library. This project model is exercised in the accompanying `project_model_test.dart` test program in the test/model. It contains the following code:

```
import 'package:unittest/unittest.dart';
import 'package:dartlero/dartlero.dart';
import 'package:dartlero_example/dartlero_example.dart';

testProjects(Projects projects) {
  group("Testing Projects", () {
    setUp(() { ...    });
    tearDown(() { ... });
    test('Add Project', () { ... });
    // various other tests
    });
}

initDisplayModel() {
  ProjectModel projectModel = new ProjectModel();
  projectModel.init();
  projectModel.display();
}

testModel() {
```

```
    ProjectModel projectModel = new ProjectModel();
    Projects projects = projectModel.projects;
    testProjects(projects);
}

main() {
  // initDisplayModel();
  testModel();
}
```

The `main()` method calls `testModel()`, which in turn calls `testProjects()` that uses the `unittest` framework. It contains one `group ("Testing Projects", ()` `{...}` method with `setUp`, `tearDown`, and a number of test methods. In the `setUp()` function, some projects and a collection containing them are created and displayed. Running this test program will give the following output:

```
Project Model
=============

Projects
[
  {
     code: Dartling Design,
     name: Dartling Design,
     description: Creating a model of Dartling concepts based on
                 MagicBoxes.
  }
]
// some output omitted for brevity //
unittest-suite-wait-for-done
PASS: Testing Projects Add Project
// some output omitted for brevity //
PASS: Testing Projects From JSON to Project Model

All 13 tests passed.
unittest-suite-success
```

Some of the applied tests are given as follows:

- While instantiating an object:

```
var design = new Project();
expect(design, isNotNull);
```

- While adding a project to projects, to count the number of projects:

```
expect(projects.length,equals(++projectCount));
    var added = projects.add(project);
    expect(added, isTrue);
```

- When projects are cleared:

```
expect(projects.isEmpty, isTrue);
```

- While searching for a project:

```
var project = projects.find(searchName); expect(project.name,
equals(searchName));
```

- Testing that every project has a name:

```
expect(projects.every((p) => p.name != null), isTrue);
```

So, what are the advantages of using a domain model framework? Clearly, by inheriting from the model classes, we get a (lot of) code that we don't have to write ourselves. So, we get a head start in the functionality of our app. For the simple Dartlero framework, there are methods such as `copy`, `toJson`, `fromJson`, `contains`, `find`, and `display`.

The categories and links application

Let's now apply Dartlero to a model with two concepts and one relationship, our category links model. Once again, we will clone the project from GitHub with:

```
git clone git://github.com/dzenanr/dartling_category_links.git
```

The model is implemented in the `lib` folder of the `dartlero_category_links` application (refer to the following screenshot):

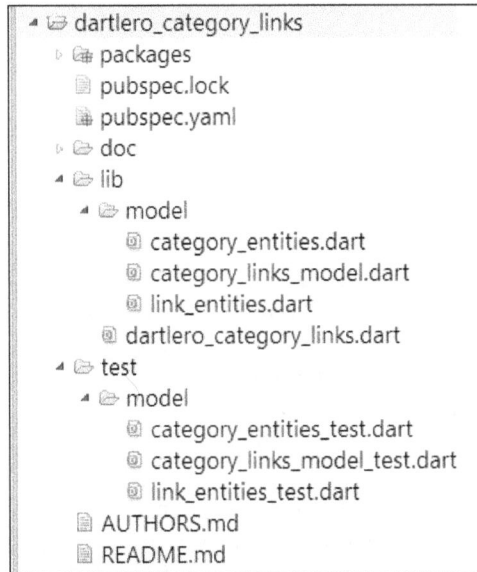

The code structure of categories-links

There are three dart files in the `model` folder, one for the model and two for the two entities. The `dartlero_category_links` library is defined in the `dartlero_category_links.dart` file:

```
library dartlero_category_links;

import 'package:dartlero/dartlero.dart';

part 'model/category_entities.dart';
part 'model/category_links_model.dart';
part 'model/link_entities.dart';
```

There are two classes in the `category_entities.dart` file, one for the entity definition and the other for a collection of entities. The `Category` class of the model extends the `ConceptEntity` class of `Dartlero` (line (1)), while the `Categories` class inherits its properties and methods from the `ConceptEntities` class (line (2)):

```
part of dartlero_category_links;
class Category extends ConceptEntity<Category> {   (1)

    String description;
```

```dart
  Links links = new Links();

  Category newEntity() => new Category();

  String toString() {
    return '  {\n '
            '    ${super.toString()}, \n '
            '    description: ${description}\n'
            '  }\n';
  }

  Map<String, Object> toJson() {
    Map<String, Object> entityMap = super.toJson();
    entityMap['description'] = description;
    entityMap['links'] = links.toJson();
    return entityMap;
  }

  fromJson(Map<String, Object> entityMap) {
    super.fromJson(entityMap);
    description = entityMap['description'];
    links.fromJson(entityMap['links']);
  }

  bool get onProgramming =>
      description.contains('programming') ? true : false;
}

class Categories extends ConceptEntities<Category> {     (2)
  Categories newEntities() => new Categories();
  Category newEntity() => new Category();
}
```

The Category class inherits the code property from the ConceptEntity class; it has its own description and links properties. Note that a parent-child relationship direction is represented as the links property in the Category class. In addition, the Category class inherits the public application interface of the ConceptEntityApi class. The Categories class (line (2)) is simple because most of its behavior is defined in the ConceptEntities class of Dartlero. The Link and Links classes are created in a similar way (refer to link_entities.dart).

The CategoryLinksModel class extends the ConceptModel class of Dartlero (refer category_links_model.dart). The newEntries method in the CategoryLinksModel class provides the only entry into the model. The init method creates a few categories and links. The display method shows the data of the model in the console. To see the model in action, run the these programs in the test folder: category_links_model_test.dart, category_entities_test.dart, or link_entities_test.dart. They will exercise the same methods and tests we saw in the first Dartlero example. For example, the model test program will call the init and display methods:

```
import 'package:unittest/unittest.dart';
import 'package:dartlero_category_links/dartlero_category_links.dart';

testModel() {
  CategoryLinksModel categoryLinksModel;
  Categories categories;
  group("Testing Model: ", () {
    setUp(() {
      categoryLinksModel = new CategoryLinksModel();
      categoryLinksModel.init();
      categories = categoryLinksModel.categories;
    });
    tearDown(() {
      categories.clear();
      expect(categories.isEmpty, isTrue);
    });
    test('Display model', () {
      categoryLinksModel.display();
    });
  });
}

main() {
  testModel();
}
```

This code produces a similar output as the previous code snippet.

Summary

In this chapter, we acknowledged the importance of defining a domain model before starting the development of an app. We used a graphical tool (model concepts) to design a model for categories and links, which can be exported in the JSON format. Also, we saw how JSON can be used in Dart. A simple domain model framework, Dartlero, was explored and we implemented it in two models: a project model and a category links model. By doing this, we exercised the knowledge of classes, interfaces, generics, Lists, Maps, and unit testing that we acquired in *Chapter 2, Getting to Work with Dart*.

The next few chapters are more practical in nature. We will learn how to work with the **Document Object Model (DOM)** in the HTML pages, how to build forms, how to draw, and how to use audio and video in the web pages.

5
Handling DOM in a New Way

A web application runs inside the browser that hosts the app; a single-page web app has become more and more common these days. This page may already contain some HTML elements or nodes, such as `<div>` and `<input>`, and your Dart code will manipulate and change them, but it can also create new elements. The user interface may even be entirely built up through the code. Besides this, Dart is responsible for implementing interactivity with the user (the handling of events, such as button clicks) and the dynamic behavior of the program, for example, fetching data from a server and showing it on the screen. In the previous chapters, we explored some simple examples of these techniques. Compared to JavaScript, Dart has simplified the way in which the code interacts with the collection of elements on a web page (called the DOM tree). This chapter teaches you this new method using a number of simple examples, culminating with a Ping Pong game. The following are the topics:

- Finding elements and changing their attributes
- Creating and removing elements
- Handling events
- Manipulating the style of page elements
- Animating a game
- Ping Pong using style(s)
- How to draw on a canvas — Ping Pong revisited

Finding elements and changing their attributes

All web applications import the `dart:html` Dart library; this is a huge collection of functions and classes needed to program the DOM (look it up at `api.dartlang.org`). Let's discuss the base classes, which are as follows:

- The `Navigator` class contains information about the browser running the app, such as the product (the name of the browser), its vendor, the MIME type supports the installed plugins, and also the geolocation object.

- Every browser window corresponds to an object of the `Window` class, which contains, among many others, a `navigator` object, the `close`, `print`, `scroll`, and `moveTo` methods, and a whole bunch of event handlers, such as `onLoad`, `onClick`, `onKeyUp`, `onMouseOver`, `onTouchStart`, and `onSubmit`. Use an alert to get a pop-up message in the web page, such as in `todo_v2.dart`:

  ```
  window.onLoad.listen( (e) =>
    window.alert("I am at your disposal") );
  ```

- If your browser has tabs, each tab will open in a separate window. From the `Window` class, you can access local storage or `IndexedDB` to store app data on the client.

- The `Window` object also contains an object document of the `Document` class, which corresponds to the HTML document. It is used to query for, create, and manipulate elements within the document. The document also has a list of stylesheets (objects of the `StyleSheet` class) — we will use this in our first version of the Ping Pong game.

- Everything that appears on a web page can be represented by an object of the `Node` class; so, not only are the tags and their attributes nodes, so are text, comments, and so on. The `Document` object in a `Window` class contains a `List<Node>` element of the nodes in the document tree (DOM) called `childNodes`.

- The `Element` class, being a subclass of `Node`, represents the web page elements (tags such as `<p>`, `<div>`, and so on); it has subclasses, such as `ButtonElement`, `InputElement`, `TableElement`, and so on, each corresponding to a specific HTML tag, such as `<button>`, `<input>`, `<table>`, and so on (for examples, see `prorabbits_v3.dart` and `todo_v1.dart` in *Chapter 1, Dart – A Modern Web Programming Language*). Every element can have embedded tags, so it contains a `List<Element>` element called children.

Let's make this more concrete by looking at `todo_v2.dart` (which is a modified version of `todo_v1.dart` from *Chapter 1, Dart – A Modern Web Programming Language;* see the next screenshot) (solely for didactic purposes) — the HTML file contains an `<input>` tag with the `id` value `task`, and a `<ul>` tag with the `id` value `list`:

```
<div><input id="task" type="text" placeholder="What do you want to
do?"/>
    <p id="para">Initial paragraph text</p>
</div>
<div id="btns">
    <button class="backgr">Toggle background color of header</button>
    <button class="backgr">Change text of paragraph</button>
    <button class="backgr">Change text of placeholder in input
field and the background color of the buttons</button>
</div>
<div><ul id="list"/>
</div>
```

In our Dart code, we will declare the following objects representing the:

```
InputElement task;
UListElement list;
```

The following list object contains the objects of the `LIElement` class, which are made in `addItem()`:

```
var newTask = new LIElement();
```

You can see the different elements and their layout in the following screenshot:

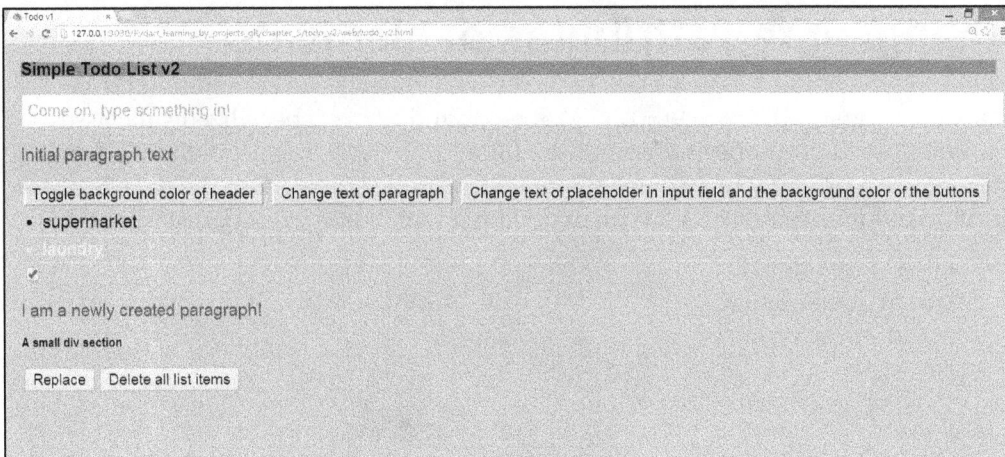

The screen of todo_v2

Finding elements

Now, we must bind these objects to the corresponding HTML elements. For this, we will use the top-level `querySelector` and `querySelectorAll` functions; for example, the `InputElement` task is bound to the `<input>` tag with the `id` value `task` using: **`task = querySelector('#task');`**.

Both functions take a string (a CSS selector) that identifies the element; where the `id` value `task` will be preceded by #. CSS selectors are patterns that are used in the `.css` files to select elements that you want to style. There are a number of them; but, generally, we only need a few basic selectors (for an overview, visit `http://www.w3schools.com/cssref/css_selectors.asp`). They are as follows:

- If the element has an `id` attribute with the `abc` value, use `querySelector('#abc')`.

- If the element has a `class` attribute with the `abc` value, use `querySelector('.abc')`.

- To get a list of all the elements with the `<button>` tag, use `querySelectorAll('button')`.

- To get a list of all the text elements, use `querySelectorAll('input[type="text"]')` together with all the sorts of combinations of selectors. For example, `querySelectorAll('#btns .backgr')` will get a list of all the elements with the `backgr` class that are inside a tag with the `id` value `btns`.

These functions are defined on the document object of the web page. So, in the code, you will also see `document.querySelector()` and `document.querySelectorAll()`.

Changing the attributes of elements

All the objects of the `Element` class have several properties in common, such as `classes`, `hidden`, `id`, `innerHtml`, `style`, `text`, and `title`; specialized subclasses have additional properties such as `value` for a `ProgressElement` method. Changing the value of a property in an element makes the browser re-render the page to show the changed user interface. You can experiment with `todo_v2.dart` as follows:

```dart
import 'dart:html';
InputElement task;
UListElement list;
Element header;
List<ButtonElement> btns;
main() {
  task = querySelector('#task');
  list = querySelector('#list');
```

```
    task.onChange.listen( (e) => addItem() );
    // find the h2 header element:
    header = querySelector('.header');                            (1)
    // find the buttons:
    btns = querySelectorAll('button') as List<ButtonElement>; (2)
    // attach event handler to 1st and 2nd buttons:
    btns[0].onClick.listen( (e) => changeColorHeader() );         (3)
    btns[1].onDoubleClick.listen( (e) => changeTextPara() );   (4)
    // another way to get the same buttons with class backgr:
    var btns2 = querySelectorAll('#btns .backgr');            (5)
    btns2[2].onMouseOver.listen( (e) => changePlaceHolder() );(6)
    btns2[2].onClick.listen((e) => changeBtnsBackColor() );   (7)
    addElements();
}
changeColorHeader() => header.classes.toggle('header2');    (8)
changeTextPara() => querySelector('#para').text = "You changed my
    text!";                                                      (9)
changePlaceHolder() => task.placeholder = 'Come on, type something
    in!';                                                       (10)
changeBtnsBackColor() => btns.forEach( (b) =>
    b.classes.add('btns_backgr'));                              (11)
void addItem() {
    var newTask = new LIElement();                              (12)
    newTask.text = task.value;                                  (13)
    newTask.onClick.listen( (e) => newTask.remove());
    task.value = '';
    list.children.add(newTask);                                 (14)
}
addElements() {
    var ch1 = new CheckboxInputElement();                      (15)
    ch1.checked = true;
    document.body.children.add(ch1);                           (16)
    var par = new Element.tag('p');                            (17)
    par.text = 'I am a newly created paragraph!';
    document.body.children.add(par);
    var el = new Element.html('<div><h4><b>A small div
    section</b></h4></div>');                                  (18)
    document.body.children.add(el);
    var btn = new ButtonElement();
    btn.text = 'Replace';
    btn.onClick.listen(replacePar);
    document.body.children.add(btn);
    var btn2 = new ButtonElement();
    btn2.text = 'Delete all list items';
```

```
    btn2.onClick.listen( (e) => list.children.clear() );    (19)
    document.body.children.add(btn2);
}
replacePar(Event e) {
    var el2 = new Element.html('<div><h4><b>I replaced this
      div!</b></h4></div>');
    el.replaceWith(el2);                                      (20)
}
```

Comments for the numbered lines are as follows:

1. We find the `<h2>` element via its class.

2. We get a list of all the buttons via their tags.

3. We attach an event handler to the `Click` event of the first button, which toggles the class of the `<h2>` element, changing its background color on each click (line (8)).

4. We attach an event handler to the `DoubleClick` event of the second button, which changes the text in the `<p>` element (line (9)).

5. We get the same list of buttons via a combination of CSS selectors.

6. We attach an event handler to the `MouseOver` event of the third button, which changes the placeholder in the input field (line (10)).

7. We attach a second event handler to the third button, clicking it changes the background color of all the buttons by adding a new CSS class to their classes' collection (line (11)).

Every HTML element also has an attribute Map, where the keys are the attribute names; you can use this Map to change an attribute, for example:

```
    btn.attributes['disabled'] = 'true';
```

Please refer to `https://developer.mozilla.org/en-US/docs/HTML/Attributes` to see which attributes apply to which element.

Creating and removing elements

The structure of a web page is represented as a tree of nodes in the DOM. A web page can start its life with an initial DOM tree, marked up in its HTML file, and the tree can be changed using the code; or it can start off with an empty tree, which is then entirely created using the code in the app: every element is created through a constructor and its properties are set in the code. Elements are subclasses of `Node`; they take up a rectangular space on the web page (with a width and height). They have, at most, one parent element in which they are enclosed and can contain a list of elements—their children (you can check this with the `hasChildNodes()` function that returns a `bool` function). Furthermore, they can receive events. Elements must first be created before they can be added to the list of a parent element. Elements can also be removed from a node. When elements are added or removed, the DOM tree changes and the browser has to re-render the web page.

An element object is either bound to an existing node with the `querySelector` method of the `document` object or it can be created with its specific constructor, such as the one in line (12) (where `newTask` belongs to the `LIElement` class—the List Item element) or line (15). If useful, we could also specify `id` in the code, such as in `newTask.id = 'newTask';`.

> If you need a DOM element in different places in your code, you can improve the performance of your app by querying it only once, binding it to a variable, and then working with that variable.

After being created, the element properties can be given a value such as the one in line (13). Then, the object (let's name it `elem`) will be added to an existing node, for example, to the body node with `document.body.children.add(elem)` like in line (16), or to an existing node like `list` in line (14). Elements can also be created with two named constructors from the `Element` class:

1. Like `Element.tag('tagName')` in line (17), where `tagName` is any valid HTML tag, such as `<p>`, `<div>`, `<input>`, `<select>`, and so on.

2. Like `Element.html('htmlSnippet')` in line (18), where `htmlSnippet` is any valid combination of the HTML tags.

Use the first constructor if you want to create everything dynamically at runtime. Use the second constructor, when you know what the HTML for the element would be like and you won't need to reference its child elements in your code (but, by using the `querySelector` method, you will always find them if needed).

> You can leave the type of the created object open using `var`, the `Element` type, or the specific class name (such as `InputElement`) — use the latter if you want your IDE to give you more specific code completions and warnings/errors against the possible misuse of the types.

While hovering over a list item, the item changes color and the cursor becomes a hand icon; it could be done in the code, but it is easier to do in the CSS file:

```css
#list li:hover {
  color: aqua;
  font-size:20 px;
  font-weight: bold;
  cursor: pointer;
   }
```

To delete an `elem` element from the DOM tree, use `elem.remove()`. We can delete list items by clicking on them, which is coded with only one line:

```
newTask.onClick.listen( (e) => newTask.remove() );
```

To remove all the list items, use the `clear()` List function, such as in line (19). Replace `elem` with another `elem2` element using `elem.replaceWith(elem2)`, such as in line (20).

Handling events

When the user interacts with the web form, such as while clicking on a button or filling in a text field, an event fires; any element on the page can have events. The DOM contains hooks for these events and the developer can write the code (an event handler) that the browser must execute when the event fires. How do we add an event handler to an element (which is also called registering an event handler)? The general format is (the spaces are not needed, but can be used to make the code more readable):

```
element.onEvent.listen( event_handler )
```

Examples of events are `Click`, `Change`, `Focus`, `Drag`, `MouseDown`, `Load`, `KeyUp`, and so on. View this as the browser listening to the events on the elements. When they occur, the indicated event handler can be executed. The argument that is passed to the `listen()` method is a callback function and it has to be of the `EventListener` type; it has the `void EventListener(Event e)` signature.

The event handler gets passed via an `Event` parameter, succinctly called e or ev, that contains more specific information on the event, such as which mouse button has been pressed in case of a mouse event, which object the event took place on using `e.target`, and so on. If an event is not handled on the target object itself, you can still write the event handler in its parent, or its parent's parent, and so on up the DOM tree, where it will also get executed; in such a situation, the target property can be useful to determine the original event object. In `todo_v2.dart`, we will examine the various event coding styles. Using the general format, the `Click` event on `btns2[2]` can be handled using the following code:

```
btns2[2].onClick.listen( changeBtnsBackColor );
```

Here, `changeBtnsBackColor` is either the event handler or the callback function. This function is written as:

```
changeBtnsBackColor(Event e) => btns.forEach( (b) =>
b.classes.add('btns_backgr'));
```

Another way to write this (such as in line (7)) is as:

```
btns2[2].onClick.listen( (e) => changeBtnsBackColor() );
changeBtnsBackColor() => btns.forEach( (b) =>
b.classes.add('btns_backgr'));
```

When a `Click` event occurs on `btns2[2]`, the `changeBtnsBackColor` handler is called.

In case the event handler needs more code lines, use the brace syntax as follows:

```
changeBtnsBackColor(Event e) {
        btns.forEach( (b) => b.classes.add('btns_backgr'));
   // possibly other code
}
```

Familiarize yourself with these different ways of writing event handlers.

Of course, when the handler needs only one line of code, there is no need for a separate method, as in the following code:

```
newTask.onClick.listen( (e) => newTask.remove() );
```

For clarity, we will use the `=>` function expression syntax whenever possible. However, you can inline the event handler and use the brace syntax along with an anonymous function, thus avoiding a separate method. So, instead of executing the following code:

```
task.onChange.listen( (e) => addItem() );
```

We could have executed:

```
task.onChange.listen( (e) {
   var newTask = new LIElement();
   newTask.text = task.value;
   newTask.onClick.listen( (e) => newTask.remove());
   task.value = '';
   list.children.add(newTask);
} );
```

JavaScript developers will find the preceding code very familiar, but it is also used frequently in the Dart code, so make yourself acquainted with the `( (e) {...} );` code pattern. The following code is an example of how you can respond to key events (in this case, on the `window` object) using the `keyCode` and `ctrlKey` properties of the `e` event:

```
window.onKeyPress.listen( (e) {
  if (e.keyCode == KeyCode.ENTER) {
    window.alert("You pressed ENTER");
  }
  if (e.ctrlKey && e.keyCode == CTRL_ENTER) {
    window.alert("You pressed CTRL + ENTER");
  }
});
```

In this code, the `const int CTRL_ENTER = 10;` constant is used.

> The list of `keyCodes` can be found at `http://www.cambiaresearch.com/articles/15/javascript-char-codes-key-codes`.

Manipulating the style of page elements

CSS style properties can be changed in the code as well: every `elem` element has a `classes` property, which is a set of CSS classes. You can add a CSS class as we did in `changeBtnsBackColor` (line (11)):

```
elem.classes.add('cssclass');
```

On adding this class, the new style is immediately applied to the element. Or, we can remove it to take away the style:

```
elem.classes.remove('cssclass');
```

The `elem.classes.toggle('cssclass');` toggle method (line (8)) is a combination of both: first `cssclass` is applied (added), next it is removed. The time after that, it is applied again, and so on.

Working with CSS classes is the best way to change the style, because the CSS definition is separated from the HTML markup. If you want to change the style of an element directly, use its `elem.style` style property, where the cascade style of coding (see *Chapter 2, Getting to Work with Dart*) is very appropriate, for example:

```
newTask.style
      ..fontWeight = 'bold'
      ..fontSize = '3em'
      ..color = 'red';
```

Animating a game

We people like motion in games and a movie is nothing but a quick succession of image frames. So, we need to be able to redraw our screen periodically to get this effect; with Dart screen frame rates of 60 fps or higher, this becomes possible. A certain time interval is represented in Dart as an object of the `Duration` type. To do something periodically in Dart, we use the `Timer` class from the `dart:async` library and its `periodic` method. To execute a `moveBall()` function at every `INTERVAL` ms (you could call it a periodic event), use the following method:

```
new Timer.periodic( const Duration(milliseconds: INTERVAL),
           (t) => moveBall()  );
```

The first parameter is the time period, the second is the callback function that has to be periodically executed, and `t` is the `Timer` object. If the callback function has to be executed only once, just write a new `Timer(.,.)` method omitting the `periodic` function. While drawing on the canvas, the first thing that the periodically called function will have to do is to erase the previous drawing. To stop a `Timer` object (usually in a game over situation), use the `cancel()` function.

Another way of doing this is by using the `animationFrame` method from the `window` class, as we will demonstrate in the `ping_pong_dom` game in the next section and in the memory game in *Chapter 7, Building Games with HTML5 and Dart*. With this technique, we will start `gameLoop` in the `main()` method and let it call itself recursively, as in the following code:

```
main() {
  // code left out
  // redraw
  window.animationFrame.then(gameLoop);
}

gameLoop(num delta) {
  moveBall();
  window.animationFrame.then(gameLoop);
}
```

Ping Pong using style(s)

To show these DOM possibilities, here is a Ping Pong game using styles, based on a similar JavaScript project described in the book at `http://www.packtpub.com/html5-games-development-using-css-javascript-beginners-guide/book`. Normally, you would write an HTML Dart game using canvas, as we would do in the next section. However, it is interesting to see what is possible just by manipulating the styles. Download the project from GitHub with `git clone git://github.com/dzenanr/ping_pong_dom.git`.

This project was developed in spirals; if you want to see how the code was developed, explore the seven stages in the `spirals` subfolder (spiral `s07`, especially, contains a `examineCSS()` function that shows you how to read the rules in the stylesheet of the Dart code; also, the game screen contains some useful links to learn more about reading and changing CSS rules).

The following is the Dart code of the master version; we have commented on it using line numbers:

```
import 'dart:html';
const int increment= 20; // move increment in pixels
CssStyleSheet styleSheet;                    (1)

var pingPong = {                             (2)
  'ball': {
    'speed': 3,
    'x'    : 195,
    'y'    : 100,
```

```
      'dx'    : 1,
      'dy'    : 1
    },
      'key': {
              'w'     : KeyCode.W,
              's'     : KeyCode.S,
              'up'    : KeyCode.UP,
              'down' : KeyCode.DOWN
    },
    'paddleA' : {
      'width'  : 20,
      'height' : 80,
      'left'   : 20,
      'top'    : 60,
      'score'  : 0
    },
    'paddleB' : {
      'width'  : 20,
      'height' : 80,
      'left'   : 360,
      'top'    : 80,
      'score'  : 0
    },
    'table' : {
      'width'      : 400,
      'height'     : 200
    }
};

main() {
  styleSheet = document.styleSheets[0];          (3)
  document.onKeyDown.listen(onKeyDown);          (4)
          // redraw
  window.animationFrame.then(gameLoop);          (5)
}

gameLoop(num delta) {
    moveBall();
    window.animationFrame.then(gameLoop);
}
String ballRule(int x, int y) {
  String rule = '''
    #ball {
      background: #fbbfbb;
```

```
        position: absolute;
        width: 20px;
        height: 20px;
        left: ${x.toString()}px;
        top: ${y.toString()}px;
        border-radius: 10px;
      }
    ''';
    return rule;
}


String paddleARule(int top) {
    String rule = '''
      #paddleA {
        background: #bbbbff;
        position: absolute;
        width: 20px;
        height: 80px;
        left: 20px;
        top: ${top.toString()}px;
      }
    ''';
    return rule;
}


String paddleBRule(int top) {
    String rule = '''
      #paddleB {
        background: #bbbbff;
        position: absolute;
        width: 20px;
        height: 80px;
        left: 360px;
        top: ${top.toString()}px;
      }
    ''';
    return rule;
}


updateBallRule(int left, int top) {
    styleSheet.removeRule(1);
```

```
    styleSheet.insertRule(ballRule(left, top), 1);
  }

  updatePaddleARule(int top) {
    styleSheet.removeRule(2);
    styleSheet.insertRule(paddleARule(pingPong['paddleA']['top']),
      2);
  }

  updatePaddleBRule(int top) {
    styleSheet.removeRule(3);
    styleSheet.insertRule(paddleBRule(pingPong['paddleB']['top']),
      3);
  }


  onKeyDown(e) {
    var paddleA = pingPong['paddleA'];
    var paddleB = pingPong['paddleB'];
    var key = pingPong['key'];
    if (e.keyCode == key['w']) {                    (6)
      paddleA['top'] = paddleA['top'] - increment;
      updatePaddleARule(paddleA['top']);
    } else if (e.keyCode == key['s']) {
      paddleA['top'] = paddleA['top'] + increment;
      updatePaddleARule(paddleA['top']);
    } else if (e.keyCode == key['up']) {
      paddleB['top'] = paddleB['top'] - increment;
      updatePaddleBRule(paddleB['top']);
    } else if (e.keyCode == key['down']) {
      paddleB['top'] = paddleB['top'] + increment;
      updatePaddleBRule(paddleB['top']);
    }
  }

  moveBall() {
    var ball = pingPong['ball'];
    var table = pingPong['table'];
    var paddleA = pingPong['paddleA'];
    var paddleB = pingPong['paddleB'];
    // check the table boundary
    // check the bottom edge
```

```
if (ball['y'] + ball['speed'] * ball['dy'] > table['height']) {
  ball['dy'] = -1;                              (7)
}
// check the top edge
if (ball['y'] + ball['speed'] * ball['dy'] < 0) {
  ball['dy'] = 1;
}
// check the right edge
if (ball['x'] + ball['speed'] * ball['dx'] > table['width']) {
  // player B lost                              (8)
  paddleA['score']++;
  querySelector('#scoreA').innerHtml
  paddleA['score'].toString();
  // reset the ball;
  ball['x'] = 250;
  ball['y'] = 100;
  ball['dx'] = -1;
}
// check the left edge
if (ball['x'] + ball['speed'] * ball['dx'] < 0) {
  // player A lost                              (9)
  paddleB['score']++;
  querySelector('#scoreB').innerHtml =
    paddleB['score'].toString();
  // reset the ball;
  ball['x'] = 150;
  ball['y'] = 100;
  ball['dx'] = 1;
}
ball['x'] += ball['speed'] * ball['dx'];
ball['y'] += ball['speed'] * ball['dy'];
// check the moving paddles
// check the left paddle
if (ball['x'] + ball['speed'] * ball['dx'] <        (10)
    paddleA['left'] + paddleA['width']) {
  if (ball['y'] + ball['speed'] * ball['dy'] <=
      paddleA['top'] + paddleA['height'] &&
      ball['y'] + ball['speed'] * ball['dy'] >= paddleA['top']) {
    ball['dx'] = 1;
  }
}
// check the right paddle
```

```
if (ball['x'] + ball['speed'] * ball['dx'] >= paddleB['left']) {
  if (ball['y'] + ball['speed'] * ball['dy'] <=
      paddleB['top'] + paddleB['height'] &&
      ball['y'] + ball['speed'] * ball['dy'] >= paddleB['top']) {
    ball['dx'] = -1;                          (11)
  }
}
// update the ball rule
updateBallRule(ball['x'], ball['y']);
}
```

The screen will look as shown in the following screenshot:

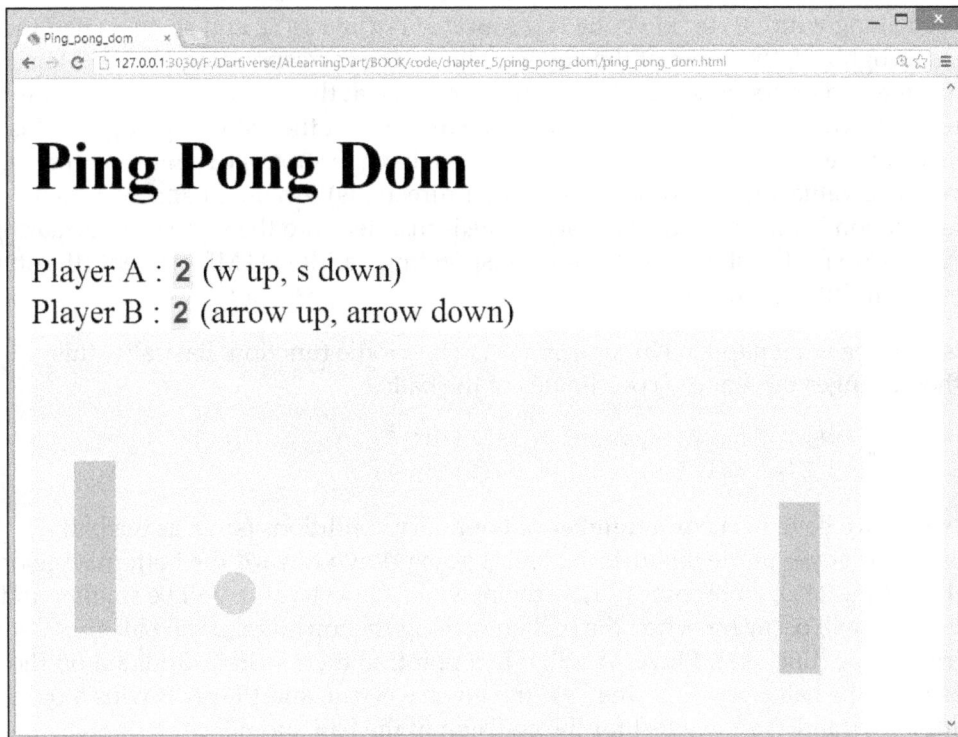

The screen of Ping Pong DOM

Basically, the mechanism is that we change the left and top property values in the style rules for the ball, and both the paddles in the function `ballRule` and `paddlARule`, and so on. When this new style rule is attached to our document, the HTML element moves on the screen. In line (1), we declare a stylesheet that we append to our document in line (3). The `pingPong` variable in line (2) is a Map with the `ball`, `key`, `paddleA`, `paddleB`, and `table` keys (these correspond to the HTML element IDs), and their values are, themselves, maps containing variables and their values (for example, `top` has the value 60). These maps are further referenced using variables, as follows:

```
var paddleA = pingPong['paddleA'];
```

In line (4), an `onKeyDown` event handler is defined. This tests the key that was pressed along with if (e.keyCode == key['w']) (line (6)), and so on. When the key is recognized, the value of the `top` variable in the corresponding paddle Map is incremented or decremented (the value of `Top` is 0 at the top of the screen and it increases towards the bottom of the screen. `w` means that the value is going up; this means that the value of `top` is decreasing, so we have to subtract `increment` from the current `top` value and, likewise, for the other directions). An `updatePaddle(A-B)` `Rule` function is called; in it, a new style rule is inserted into the stylesheet, updating the `top` value for the style rule of the corresponding paddle HTML element (the style rules are multiline strings).

Let's then see what happens in the `moveBall()` periodic function. Basically, this method changes the `x` and `y` coordinates of the ball:

```
ball['x'] += ball['speed'] * ball['dx'];
ball['y'] += ball['speed'] * ball['dy'];
```

However, we have to check a number of boundary conditions (such as the ball crossing the edges of the table); if the ball is going down toward the bottom edge of the table (line (7)), `dy` becomes -1, so the new `ball['y']` value will be smaller and the inverse will occur for when the ball goes along the top edge. If the ball goes over the right edge (line (8)), **Player A** will win a point, so their score is updated on the screen and the ball is reset. In line (9), the inverse is true and **Player B** wins a point. In lines (10) and (11), we test for the collision of the ball and `paddleA` or `paddleB`, respectively; using `paddleA`, we want to send the ball to the right, so dx = 1; with `paddleB`, we want to send it to the left, so dx = -1. Then, in the same way as for the paddles, we will update the style rule for the ball.

How to draw on a canvas – Ping Pong revisited

Canvas is a way to draw graphics on a web page in a straightforward manner. It is an important part of HTML5 and it provides apps with a resolution-dependent bitmap canvas, which can be used to render graphs, game graphics, art, or other visual images on the fly. We will rewrite our Ping Pong game using the canvas drawing technique (this project is based on the Dart port of the canvas tutorial at `http://billmill.org/static/canvastutorial/` by Chris Buckett (`https://github.com/chrisbu/Bounce`)). Download the project from GitHub using `git clone git://github.com/dzenanr/ping_pong`.

When you open the project in Dart Editor, you will see the latest master version and you can run and play it immediately. In the `spirals` subfolder, you will see how the project has grown in 11 stages and we will learn about canvas drawing by exploring this evolution. The spiral approach to learning is used to advance step by step from simple spirals at the beginning to more complex ones close to the last version of the project. This is also an excellent development approach that encourages refactoring and, thus, produces clear, understandable code.

Spiral 1 – drawing a circle and a rectangle

Open the `spirals/ping_pong_01` project. The goal of this spiral is to display a small, black circle and a small, white rectangle with a black border; in other words, to learn how to draw. Take a look at the HTML file—all the drawing is done within the `<canvas>` tag:

```
<canvas id="canvas" width="300" height="300">
  Canvas is not supported in your browser.
</canvas>
```

You can adjust the `width` and `height` values to the app's needs and also include text, which will be displayed in the older browsers that do not support canvas (it is widely supported, but only in Internet Explorer from 9.0 onwards). Now, we will look at the code of `ping_pong.dart` in the `lib` folder of the spiral:

```
library ping_pong;                    (1)

import 'dart:html';
import 'dart:math';

part 'board.dart';                    (2)
```

The `ping_pong.dart` file in the web folder contains the startup code:

```
import 'dart:html';
import 'package:ping_pong/ping_pong.dart';

void main() {
  //get a reference to the canvas
  CanvasElement canvas = querySelector('#canvas');   (3)
  Board board = new Board(canvas);                    (4)
  board.circle(75, 75, 10);                           (5)
  board.rectangle(95, 95, 20, 20);                    (6)
}
```

Following good practices, we made our app a library in line (1); all the other code resides in the other parts (see line (2)). In line (3), we made a reference to <canvas> using an object of the CanvasElement (in dart:html) type. Now, we have to make a context object (which can be either 2d or webgl (3d)) to draw on:

```
CanvasRenderingContext2D context = canvas.getContext('2d');
```

In this app, we will draw on a Board object made in line (4); this object has the circle and rectangle methods that contain the details to draw these shapes and they are called in lines (5) and (6). Line (4) passes the canvas object to the Board constructor (line (7)) in the board.dart part file, where the context object is created:

```
part of ping_pong;

class Board {
  CanvasRenderingContext2D context;
  Board(CanvasElement canvas) {                       (7)
    context = canvas.getContext('2d');
  }

  //draw a circle
  void circle(x, y, r) {
    context.beginPath();                              (8)
    context.arc(x, y, r, 0, PI*2, true);              (9)
    context.closePath();                              (10)
    context.fill();                                   (11)
  }

  //draw a rectangle
  void rectangle(x, y, w, h) {
    context.beginPath();
    context.rect(x,y,w,h);                            (12)
```

```
      context.closePath();
      context.stroke();                              (13)
    }
  }
```

While drawing an arbitrary shape, we draw, in fact, a path. This usually involves a number of steps enclosed within a call to `beginPath()` (line (8)) and a call to `closePath()` (line (10)). This also closes the shape; while drawing basic shapes, such as lines, rectangles, and circles, like in this example, they can be left out. A black line or an open figure is drawn using `context.stroke()`, such as in line (13); for a filled-in shape, you need to use `context.fill()`, such as in line (11). When we run this script, it shows:

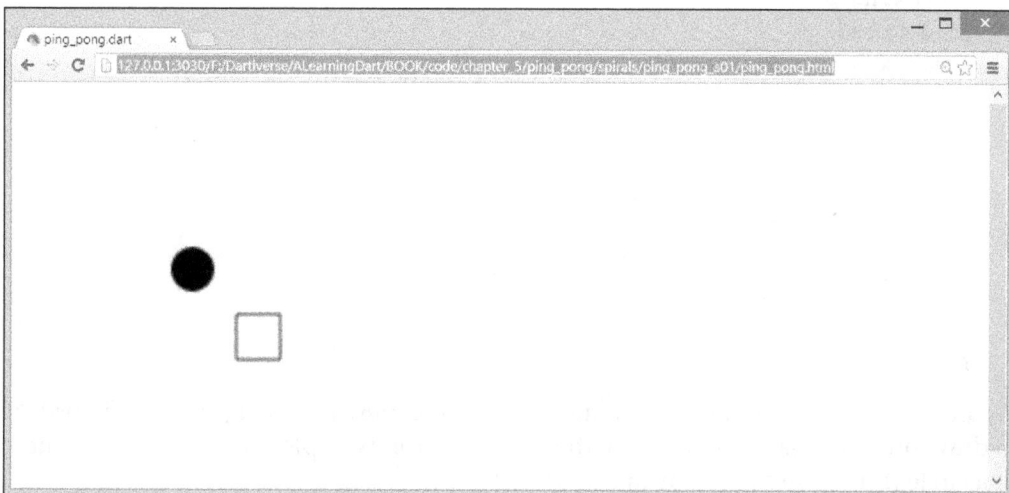

The screen of Ping Pong spiral 1

To further explore how the lines and arcs are drawn, we will create an additional `canvas_1` web app:

```
import 'dart:html';
import 'dart:math';

CanvasRenderingContext2D context;
var width, height;

void main() {
  //get a reference to the canvas
  CanvasElement canvas = querySelector('#canvas');
  width = canvas.width;                              (1)
  height = canvas.height;
  context = canvas.getContext('2d');
```

```
        lines();
        arcs();
    }
//drawing lines
void lines() {
    context.moveTo(100, 150);
    context.lineTo(450, 50);
    context.lineWidth = 2;
    context.lineCap = 'round'; // other values: 'square' or 'butt'
    context.stroke();
}

//drawing arcs
void arcs() {
    var x = width / 2;                                          (2)
    var y = height / 2;
    var radius = 75;
    var startAngle = 1.1 * PI;
    var endAngle = 1.9 * PI;
    var antiClockWise = false;
    context.arc(x, y, radius, startAngle, endAngle, antiClockWise);
    context.lineWidth = 8;
    context.stroke();
}
```

We obtain the `width` and `height` parameters of the `canvas` object (line (1)) in order to draw proportionally to the space that we have, for example, in choosing the center of a circle (for our arc), such as in line (2).

Canvas uses an (x, y) coordinate system, measured in pixels to locate points: the origin (0,0) is the upper-left corner of the drawing area, the x axis goes from left to right, and the y axis from top to bottom. `moveTo(x, y)` positions the drawing cursor at the `point (x, y)` method and the `lineTo(x', y')` method draws a straight line from (x, y) to (x', y') when the `stroke` or `fill` methods are called; `lineWidth` is an obvious property. To draw a circular arc, you use the method with the same name `arc`. This method takes no less than six parameters: `context.arc(x, y, radius, startAngle, endAngle, antiClockWise);` x and y are the coordinates of the circle's center; the third parameter is the circle's radius; the `startAngle` and `endAngle` parameters are the start and end angles (in radians); the `antiClockWise` parameter is `true` or `false` (the default value is `anticlockwise`, that is, from end to start) and defines the direction of the arc between its two end points. See the next figure for clarification and the example in the `arcs()` method (comment out the call to `lines()`). Now, we will see how a circle can be drawn by going from a 0 PI angle to a 2 PI angle, such as in `board.dart` in line (9), which is called using line (5).

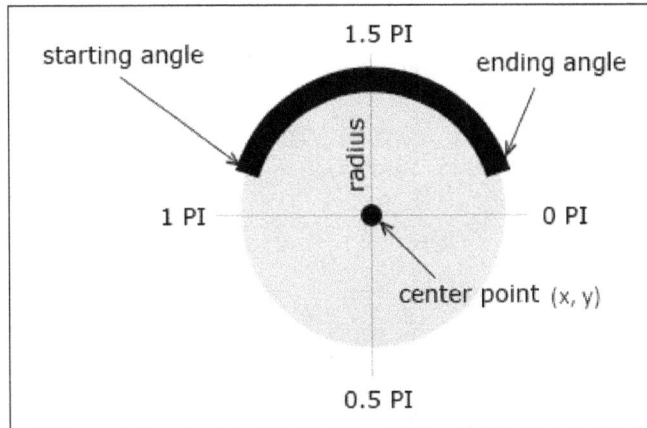

Drawing an arc

Using the lineTo method, it takes three calls to draw a triangle and four for a rectangle. The latter case was considered common enough to provide a rect(x,y,w,h) method (line (12) in board.dart), where x and y are the coordinates of the upper-left corner, w is the width, and h is the height of the rectangle; this is applied in the rectangle() method called on board (line (6)). To erase all the drawing in a rectangular area, use the context.clearRect(x,y,w,h) method (first used in *Spiral 3 – moving a ball*).

Spiral 2 – colored circles and rectangles

In the spirals/ping_pong_02 project, the goal is to display two circles and two rectangles in different colors; that is, how we can get some color in our drawing? For this, we need two new properties: context: strokeStyle sets the drawing color for the border and fillStyle sets the fill color. If you do not use these, black will be the default color. The color itself is given as a String, containing:

- A predefined color name, such as context.strokeStyle = 'red';
- A hexadecimal number, such as context.strokeStyle = '#ff0000';
- An rgba string containing the red, green, and blue values (between 0 and 255) and an alpha value (the opacity of the color having a value between 0 and 1), such as context.fillStyle ="rgba(55, 55, 0, .75)"

For example, a rectangle method can be given a border color and an inside color by calling:

```
board.rectangle(15, 150, 120, 120,
      "rgba(55, 55, 0, .75)", "rgba(155, 155, 0, .5)");
```

While the rectangle method will now be changed to:

```
void rectangle(x, y, w, h, strokeStyle, fillStyle) {
    context.beginPath();
    context.strokeStyle = strokeStyle;
    context.fillStyle = fillStyle;
    context.rect(x,y,w,h);
    context.stroke();
    context.fill();
    context.closePath();
}
```

Do experiment with the possibilities. We now know everything we need to draw our Ping Pong game; we'll do it and develop the game logic in the next spiral. However, often, you need other techniques in drawing applications: you'll find more of them in `canvas_2.dart` To see clearly what each code section does, comment on all the code and uncomment on only the sections you want to run. In this code file, you can find the methods to draw quadratic curves and Bezier curves, combining them in paths, custom shapes, linear and radial gradients, and drawing images and text. For more details on the different parameters, refer to `http://www.html5canvastutorials.com/tutorials`. You can find a lot more code examples in the GitHub repository at `https://github.com/dzenanr/ondart_examples`, especially in the `ondart_dom`, `ondart_html5`, and `ondart_canvas` folders; these accompany the course presentations found at `http://ondart.me/web_programming.md`.

Spiral 3 – moving a ball

In the `spirals/ping_pong_03` project, the goal is to position the small black circle (a ball) in a straight line using the subsequent calls of the `move()` method.

On running the app, we see a ball moving down diagonally from the upper-left corner to the right and then disappearing out of sight. In the main `ping_pong.dart` file, nothing much has changed; a new `ball.dart` part file has appeared (line (1)). To describe the ball and its behavior in the `Ball` class and in line (2), the `ball` object is created, giving it a reference to the `board` object.

The `ping_pong.dart` file in the `lib` folder contains the following code:

```
library ping_pong;
import 'dart:html';
import 'dart:math';

part 'board.dart';
part 'ball.dart';                                    (1)
```

While `ping_pong.dart` in the web folder contains:

```
import 'dart:async';
import 'dart:html';
import 'package:ping_pong/ping_pong.dart';

void main() {
  CanvasElement canvas = querySelector('#canvas');
  Board board = new Board(canvas);
  Ball ball = new Ball(board, 0, 0, 10);              (2)
  new Timer.periodic(const Duration(milliseconds: 10),
    (t) => ball.move());                              (3)
}
```

In `ball.dart`, we will see that in the constructor (line (4)), our ball is drawn by calling `context.arc` on the `board` object:

```
part of ping_pong;

class Ball {
  Board board;
  int x, y, r;
  int dx = 2;
  int dy = 4;
  Ball(this.board, this.x, this.y, this.r) {          (4)
    draw();
  }

  void draw() {
    board.context.beginPath();
    board.context.arc(x, y, r, 0, PI*2, true);
    board.context.closePath();
    board.context.fill();
  }

  void move() {
    board.clear();                                    (5)
    x += dx;                                          (6)
    y += dy;                                          (7)
    board.context.beginPath();
    board.context.arc(x, y, r, 0, PI*2, true);
    board.context.closePath();
    board.context.fill();
  }
}
```

In the `main()` method (line (3)) of the preceding code, `Timer` invoked periodically the `move()` method on the ball. In the `move()` method, the board was first cleared (line (5)). Within the `clear()` method, this was done through a new `clearRect()` method on the `context` object:

```
void clear() {
    context.clearRect(0, 0, width, height);
}
```

In lines (6) and (7), the values of the x and y coordinates of the center of the ball were increased using `dx` and `dy`, respectively. As these remained the same, the ball ran from left to right and top to bottom; it disappeared when it left the canvas area determined by the `width` and `height` parameters. We will improve this in *Spiral 5 – a bouncing ball* section; for now, let's give the `board` object the same dimensions as the `canvas` element:

```
Board(CanvasElement canvas) {
    context = canvas.getContext("2d");
    width = canvas.width;
    height = canvas.height;
}
```

Spiral 4 – reorganizing the code

In this spiral, we will pause and re-organize (refactor) our code a bit (we wrote the duplicate code in `draw()` and `move()` —horror!). In our `main()` method, we will only create the `board` object and call a new `init()` method on it:

```
void main() {
    CanvasElement canvas = querySelector('#canvas');
    Board board = new Board(canvas);
    board.init();
}
```

This method in `board.dart` creates the `ball` object, passing it a reference to the `board` object using the `this` parameter:

```
void init() {
    Ball ball = new Ball(this, 0, 0, 10);
    //move() called every 10ms:
    new Timer.periodic(const Duration(milliseconds: 10),
        (t) => ball.move());
}
```

The common code in `draw()` and `move()` from the *Spiral 3 – moving a ball* section is eliminated by letting `move()` call `draw()` from `ball.dart`:

```
void draw() {
  board.context.beginPath();
  board.context.arc(x, y, r, 0, PI*2, true);
  board.context.closePath();
  board.context.fill();
}

void move() {
  board.clear();
  draw();
  x += dx;
  y += dy;
}
```

We have applied a fundamental principle called DRY (don't repeat yourself, at least not in the code).

Spiral 5 – a bouncing ball

In most games, the ball has to stay on the board, so let's try to bounce the ball on the board's edges. The code that lets the ball move is the `move()` method, so only this code will have to expand. For both the coordinates, we will now have to check the boundary that the ball will cross on the board's edge lines.

- For x, this means that `(x + dx)` must be greater than `board.width` (right border) or less than 0 (left border); if any of these situations do occur (this is why we use or: `||`), for example, `if (x + dx > board.width || x + dx < 0)`, the ball must change its direction (the value of x must decrease instead of increase and vice versa). This we can obtain by reversing the sign of dx: `dx = -dx;`.

- For y, this means that `(y + dy)` must be greater than `board.height` (bottom border) and must be less than 0 (top border); if it does, for example, `if (y + dy > board.height || y + dy < 0)`, the ball must change its direction (y must decrease instead of increase and vice versa). This we can obtain by reversing the sign of dy: `dy = -dy;`.

Verify that this procedure works (although the movement is rather boring at this stage).

Spiral 6 – displaying the racket

In this spiral, we add a racket, which is displayed as a small, black rectangle. From the beginning of the code, we represent it through its own class in `lib\racket.dart`. In it, we provide a constructor and the `draw` method, which uses `context.rect`; the racket also has a reference to the `board` object:

```
part of ping_pong;

class Racket {
  Board board;
  num x, y, w, h;
  Racket(this.board, this.x, this.y, this.w, this.h) {
    draw();
  }

  void draw() {
    board.context.beginPath();
    board.context.rect(x, y, w, h);
    board.context.closePath();
    board.context.fill();
  }
}
```

To enhance the adaptability of the game, we will start by defining a number of constant values upfront in the `Board` class:

```
static const num START_X = 0;
static const num START_Y = 0;
static const num BALL_R = 10;
static const num RACKET_W = 75;
static const num RACKET_H = 10;
```

These are used in the `init()` method to construct the `ball` and `racket` objects:

```
void init() {
  ball = new Ball(this, START_X, START_Y, BALL_R);
  racket = new Racket(this, width/2, height-RACKET_H, RACKET_W,
  RACKET_H);
      // redraw every 10 ms:
  timer = new Timer.periodic(const Duration(milliseconds: 10),
          (t) => redraw());
  }
```

Since we now have to draw two objects, we will rename the `periodic` function to `redraw()` and give the responsibility to the `board` object, which will call the `draw` methods on the `ball` and `racket` objects (lines (1) and (2)):

```
void redraw() {
    clear();
    ball.draw();                                              (1)
    racket.draw();                                            (2)
    if (ball.x + dx > width || ball.x + dx < 0) {
        dx = -dx;
    }
    if (ball.y + dy > height || ball.y + dy < 0) {
        dy = -dy;
    } else if (ball.y + dy > height) {                        (3)
        if (ball.x > racket.x && ball.x < racket.x + racket.w) {
            dy = -dy;
        } else {
            timer.cancel();
        }
    }
    ball.x += dx;
    ball.y += dy;
}
```

It also does all the checks for the boundary conditions. We added in line (3) that the ball is bounced (`dy = -dy`) only when it touches the (`ball.x > racket.x &&` `ball.x < racket.x + racket.w`) racket. If it falls outside the racket, the game will be over. We will then cancel the timer, stopping the animation (line (4)). Due to the start location of the ball, the game over condition does not occur in this spiral.

Spiral 7 – moving the racket using keys

Here, the goal is to move the racket using the left and right keys of the keyboard. To this end, the racket will have to listen to key events. The following is the code of `racket.dart`:

```
part of ping_pong;

class Racket {
    Board board;
    num x, y, w, h;
    bool rightDown = false;                                   (1)
    bool leftDown = false;

    Racket(this.board, this.x, this.y, this.w, this.h) {
```

```
        draw();
        document.onKeyDown.listen(_onKeyDown);            (2)
        document.onKeyUp.listen(_onKeyUp);
    }

    void draw() { ... } // see Spiral 6
    _onKeyDown(event) {                                   (3)
        if (event.keyCode == 39) rightDown = true;
        else if (event.keyCode == 37) leftDown = true;
    }
    _onKeyUp(event) {                                     (4)
        if (event.keyCode == 39) rightDown = false;
        else if (event.keyCode == 37) leftDown = false;
    }
}
```

In line (2), we register for the KeyDown event and attach the _onKeyDown handler, which is also done in the following line for the KeyUp event. _onKeyDown and _onKeyUp are private methods that could have been used anonymously in the event definition. In these handlers, we test for keyCode of the pressed key: the keyCode for the left arrow is 37 and the right arrow is 39. We catch their state in two Boolean variables leftDown and rightDown: if the left arrow is pressed, we set leftDown to true, when the right arrow is pressed, we set rightDown to true (line (3)). In the KeyUp event handler in line (4) that fires when the key is released, Boolean value is reset to false. As long as the arrow key is pressed, its corresponding Boolean value is true. This is tested in the redraw() method of the Board class, where the following lines are added before racket.draw():

```
        if (racket.rightDown)      racket.x += 5;
        else if (racket.leftDown)  racket.x -= 5;
```

When the right arrow is pressed, the racket moves to the right and vice versa.

This is the first playable version of our game; but, we see that our racket can disappear and, perhaps, we want to be able to move the racket using the mouse as well.

Spiral 8 – moving the racket using the mouse

To accomplish moving the racket using the mouse, we will listen for a MouseMove event and attach the event handler to the racket constructor: document. onMouseMove.listen(_onMouseMove).

We will also define two variables that define the canvas width:

```
canvasMinX = 0;
 canvasMaxX = canvasMinX + board.width;
```

We use the preceding code statements to perform a test in the mouse event handler: if the x coordinate of the mouse pointer (given by `event.pageX`) is situated in our canvas, we will set the x coordinate of our `racket` object to the same value:

```
_onMouseMove(event) {
    if (event.pageX > canvasMinX && event.pageX < canvasMaxX)
  x = event.pageX;
  }
```

Spiral 9 – a real game

The goals for this spiral are as follows:

- The board should have a border
- We want two rackets
- The rackets cannot be moved outside the border

The border is easy; call the `border()` method from `init()` to draw a rectangle around the canvas:

```
void border() {
      context.beginPath();
      context.rect(X, Y, width, height);
      context.closePath();
      context.stroke();
  }
```

We add a second racket to the top of the screen, which moves synchronously with the bottom racket. Our `board` object will now contain two racket objects: `racketNorth` and `racketSouth`, both of which are created in the `init()` method:

```
racketNorth = new Racket(this, width/2, 0, RACKET_W, RACKET_H);
racketSouth = new Racket(this, width/2, height-RACKET_H, RACKET_W,
RACKET_H);
```

The code from *Spiral 7 – moving the racket with keys* is applied to both the objects.

The third goal is accomplished by adding a test to the MouseMove event handler:

```
_onMouseMove(event) {
    if (event.pageX > board.X && event.pageX < board.width) {
        x = event.pageX - board.X - w/2;
        if (x < board.X) x = board.X;
        if (x > board.width - w) x = board.width - w;
    }
}
```

By introducing an X constant for board, we have simplified the condition we saw in the *Spiral 8 – moving the racket with the mouse* section. The racket movements are now more synchronous with the mouse movement, and the last two if tests have made it impossible for the rackets to go outside of the borders of the board. Now, we have a minimally decent game.

Spiral 10 – title and replay

In this spiral, we will add a title and a button to restart the game; both are done in HTML. The button is placed in a <div> tag outside the canvas:

```
<button type="button" id="play">Play</button>
```

We will now change the constructor of board to only start init() when the button with the play id is clicked: querySelector('#play').onClick.listen((e) => init());

This is it!

Spiral 11 and the master version

No new Dart code is added here, but we will improve the display using CSS. Additionally, some relevant web links are added along with a section for each new spiral to indicate what is new. Take a look at ping_pong.html (in both the source and the browser) to learn how to use the document features of HTML5:

- The title within the screen is displayed in a <header> tag.

- The different parts of the document are placed in their own <section> tag with an appropriate ID, such as side or main; these sections can be nested. The two columns' layout design style is applied using the float property in layout2.css. The side section is the playground and it contains a <button> tag to start the game placed within a <footer> tag. The hyperlinks beneath it are placed within a <nav> tag; the design from link.css uses a background image to better display the links.

- The <footer> tags are used to separate the different spirals; at the bottom of the screen.

The preceding points are shown in the following screenshot:

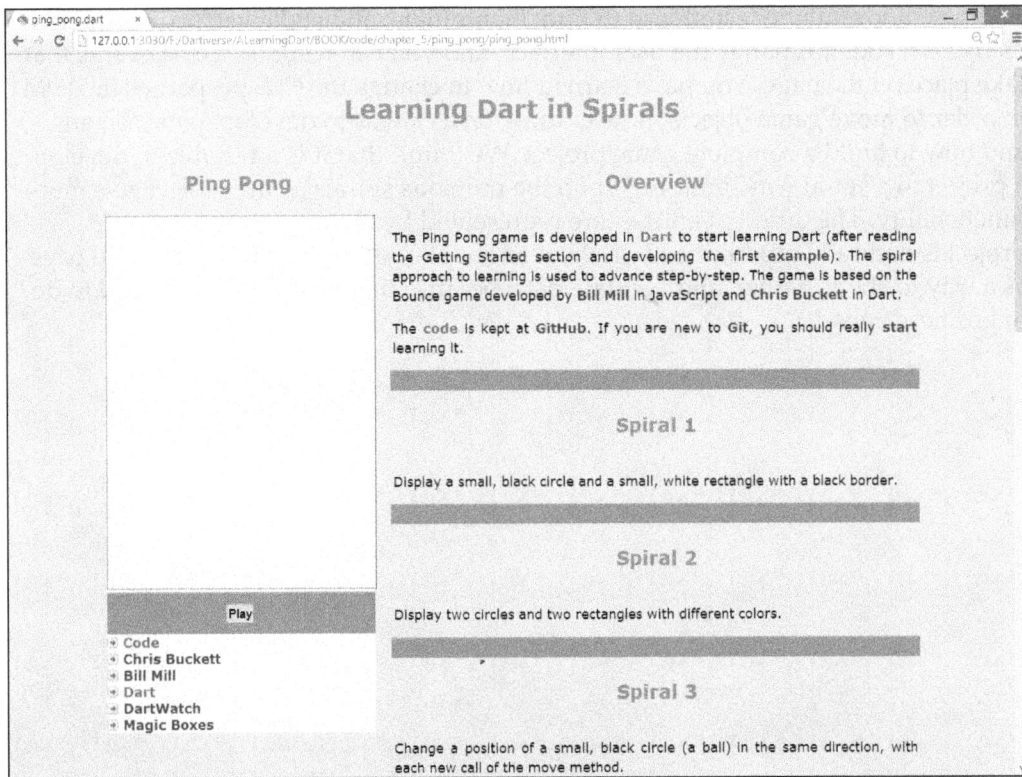

Ping Pong, the master version

As an exercise, you could decouple the rackets so that we have two independent players and keep score of the game (see the DOM version of the game for inspiration). Also, place the timer interval in a variable if you want to change the game's difficulty level.

Summary

You now know all the techniques to find, manipulate, and style web page elements using Dart code to change the user interface, and you can respond to the events that take place on the page. You have learned how to change the CSS properties in DOM in order to move game objects, how to draw on a canvas to develop game screens, and how to build a complete game project. We found that it is advisable to develop a project in a spiral way, building upon the previous spirals as the project gets more functionality. The different entities are represented by classes; in this way, our project is naturally modularized. In the next chapter, we will focus on the web page as a way to show, gather, and validate data, because this is what we will need to do in business apps.

6
Combining HTML5 Forms with Dart

In business applications, data is structured through model classes and stored permanently. However, the first step, controlling the input of data, is essential. In this chapter, the new input and validation functionalities of HTML5 are explored. You will learn how to:

- Process input data by validating them through HTML5 and Dart
- Store and retrieve data in the browser's local storage
- Show data in the HTML5 forms

We will expand on our bank account example to show these features; gradually, building it up in iterations.

Spiral 1 – the power of HTML5 forms

We will make a form that will enable us to create objects for the BankAccount class that we encountered in the code examples in *Chapter 1, Dart – A Modern Web Programming Language*, and *Chapter 2, Getting to Work with Dart*. Moreover, we will be able to deposit or withdraw money from these accounts, calculating and adding interest to them.

> For the code files of this section, refer to chapter 6\bank_terminal_s1 in the code bundle.

In this first spiral, we will construct our model classes and lay out a form to create and update a bank account using the new specialized input fields of HTML5. The code for the classes is kept in the web\model subfolder and these are a part of our application, as shown in the initial code of bank_terminal_s1.dart:

```
library bank_terminal;
import 'dart:html';
part 'model/bank_account.dart';
part 'model/person.dart';
void main() {
```

A bank account is owned by a person, as we see in the starting code of bank_account.dart:

```
part of bank_terminal;
class BankAccount {
  String number;
  Person owner;
  double balance;
  int pin_code;
  final DateTime date_created;
  DateTime date_modified;
  // constructors:
  BankAccount(this.owner, this.number, this.balance,
    this.pin_code): date_created = new DateTime.now();
  // rest of code omitted
}
```

The final item date_created is initialized to the current date in the initializer list of the constructor. The person's data is kept in the objects of a separate Person class in person.dart:

```
part of bank_terminal;
class Person {
  // Person properties and methods
  String name, address, email, gender;
  DateTime date_birth;
  // constructor:
  Person(this.name, this.address, this.email, this.gender,
  this.date_birth);
  // methods:
  String toString() => 'Person: $name, $gender'';
}
```

After applying some CSS3 to the form attribute, our input screen will look like the following screenshot:

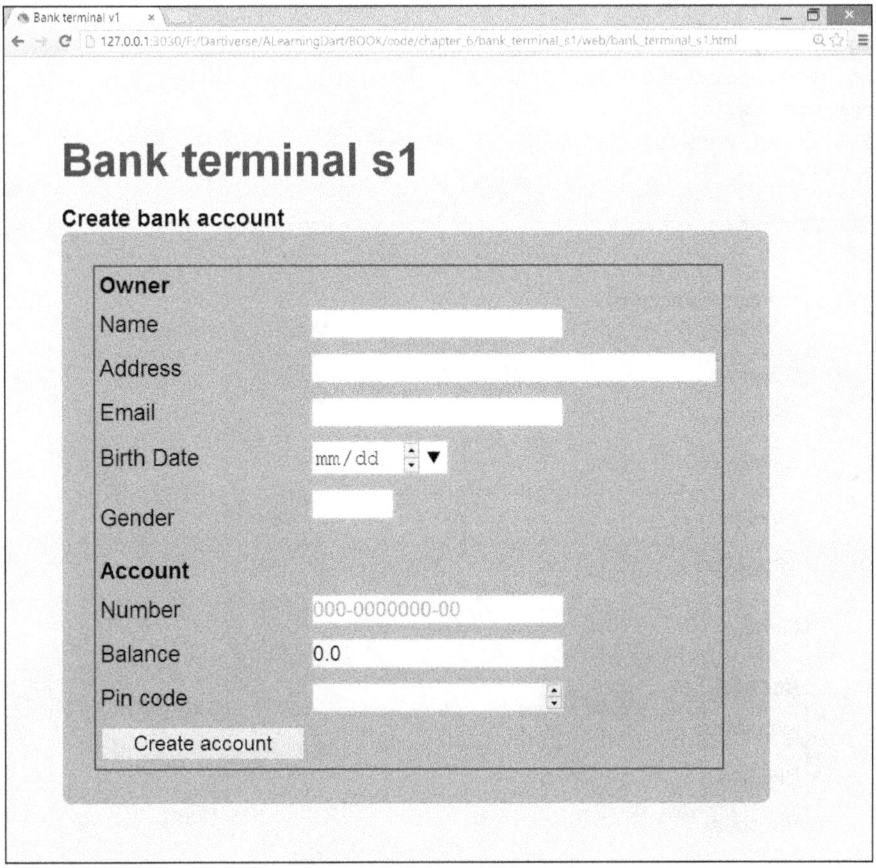

The Bank Account input screen

We surround all the input fields in this `<form name="account" autocomplete>` form tag. The `autocomplete` attribute makes sure that the browser shows a list based on values that the user has entered before. When all the data is filled in, clicking on the button **Create account** will create the objects and store them. The name of the owner certainly is a required field, but how do we enforce this in HTML5? Take a look at the source code in `bank_terminal_s1.html`:

```
<input id="name" type="text" required autofocus/>
```

The `required` attribute does exactly this: clicking on the button with an empty name field shows a popup with the **Please fill out this field** text. This is achieved by using the corresponding `:required` CSS3 pseudo-class:

```
:required {
  border-color: #1be032;
  box-shadow:
    0 0 5px rgba(57, 237, 78, .5);
      }
```

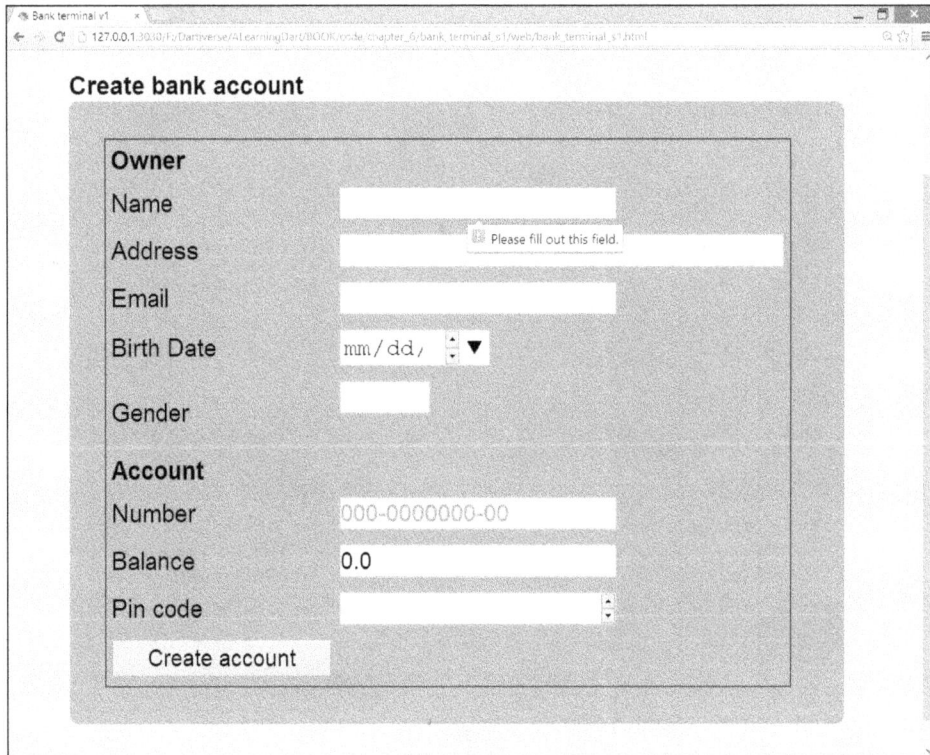

The required field pop-up screen

To automatically focus on the **Name** input field when the screen loads, use the **autofocus** attribute. The **Email** input field is required, but it is also of the **email** type:

```
<input id="email" type="email" required/>
```

This will check whether the value conforms to a standard e-mail address pattern of the "*@-.-" form; likewise, there is also a field of the url type. The **Birth Date** field is of HTML5 date type. You can type in the date by filling it in the mm/dd/yyyy pattern and use the spinner buttons to choose the year. The big down button will show all the days in the selected month, and allow you to change the month and day. The **Gender** field shows a pre-populated list of values, this can be attached to the field through the list attribute and the <datalist> tag. The **Account Number** and **Balance** fields use the placeholder attribute to give the user a hint of what the input should be; this value, however, is not taken as the default input value, hence you should use the value attribute instead. To control the input format, use the pattern attribute; for example, pattern="[0-9]{3}-[0-9]{7}-[0-9]{2}", where the string can be any valid regular expression. For a HTML5 url field type, use the "https?://.+" pattern. The **Pin code** field is of the number type, which checks the integer numerical input, possibly indicating a minimum and maximum value. Try out the validations by using different input values. Other valid HTML5 input types include color, date, datetime, datetime-local, month, search, tel (for a telephone number, use it with a pattern), time, week, range, and url.

Spiral 2 – how to validate data with Dart

If you have tested the *Spiral 1 – the power of HTML5 forms* version thoroughly, you would have come across some things that could be improved:

1. The HTML5 control only does its checks when the **Create Account** button is clicked; it would be better if the user is alerted earlier, preferably after filling in each field.

2. The **Birth Date** value is checked to be a correct DateTime value, but a value in the future is accepted.

3. The **Gender** field will gladly accept other values than M or F.

4. The **Balance** field accepts a negative number.

So, HTML5 doesn't give us full validation possibilities. To remedy and supplement this, we must add code validation, see bank_terminal_s2.dart:

> For the code files of this section, refer to chapter 6\bank_terminal_s2 in the code bundle.

```dart
InputElement name, address, email, birth_date, gender;
InputElement number, balance, pin_code;
void main() {
  // bind variables to DOM elements:
```

```
      name = querySelector('#name');
      address = querySelector('#address');
      email = querySelector('#email');
      birth_date = querySelector('#birth_date');
      gender = querySelector('#gender');
      number = querySelector('#number');
      balance = querySelector('#balance');
      pin_code = querySelector('#pin_code');
      lbl_error = querySelector('#error');
      lbl_error.text = "";
      lbl_error.style..color = "red";
      // attach event handlers:
      // checks for not empty in onBlur event:
      name.onBlur.listen(notEmpty);                    (1)
      email.onBlur.listen(notEmpty);
      number.onBlur.listen(notEmpty);
      pin_code.onBlur.listen(notEmpty);
      // other checks:
      birth_date.onChange.listen(notInFuture);         (2)
      birth_date.onBlur.listen(notInFuture);           (3)
      gender.onChange.listen(wrongGender);             (4)
      balance.onChange.listen(nonNegative);            (5)
      balance.onBlur.listen(nonNegative);              (6)
    }
  notEmpty(Event e) {
    InputElement inel = e.currentTarget as InputElement;
    var input = inel.value;
    if (input == null || input.isEmpty) {
      lbl_error.text = "You must fill in the field ${inel.id}!";
      inel.focus();
    }
  }
  notInFuture(Event e) {
    DateTime birthDate;
    try {
      birthDate = DateTime.parse(birth_date.value);
    } on ArgumentError catch(e) {                      (7)
      lbl_error.text = "This is not a valid date!";
      birth_date.focus();
      return;
    }
    DateTime now = new DateTime.now();
    if (!birthDate.isBefore(now)) {
      lbl_error.text = "The birth date cannot be in the future!";
```

```
      birth_date.focus();
    }
  }
  wrongGender(Event e) {
    var sex = gender.value;
    if (sex != 'M'' && sex != 'F'') {
      lbl_error.text = "The gender must be either M (male) or F
      (female)!";
      gender.focus();
    }
  }
  nonNegative(Event e) {
    num input;
    try {
      input = int.parse(balance.value);
    } on ArgumentError catch(e) {
      lbl_error.text = "This is not a valid balance!";
      balance.focus();
      return;
    }
    if (input < 0) {
      lbl_error.text = "The balance cannot be negative!";
      balance.focus();
    }
  }
}
```

When the user leaves a field, the `blur` event fires. So, to check whether a value was given in the field, we use the `onBlur` event handler. For example, for the `name` field in line (1), we show an alert window and use the `focus` method to put the cursor back in the field. Notice that the `notEmpty` method can be used for any input field. Controlling a given value is best done in the `onChange` event handler, as we do for `birth_date` in line (2); we use a `try` construct to `catch` the `ArgumentError` exception that occurs in line (7) when no date is given or selected (leave the method with return in the error case so that no further processing is done). To ensure that the user cannot leave the field, call the same method in `onBlur` (in line (3)). For checking gender and balance, we also use the `onChange` handlers (lines (4) and (5)). Check the e-mail address with a regular expression pattern in an `onChange` event handler as an exercise. Now, we are ready to store the data; we will add the following line after line (6):

```
    btn_create.onClick.listen(storeData);
```

In the `storeData` method, we will first create the objects:

```
storeData(Event e) {
  // creating the objects:
    Person p = new Person(name.value, address.value,
      email.value,gender.value, DateTime.parse(birth_date.value));
    BankAccount bac = new BankAccount(p, number.value,
      double.parse(balance.value), int.parse(pin_code.value));    }
```

Notice that we have to perform data conversions here, the value from the `balance` and `pin_code` element objects is always a string!

Validation in the model

For a more robust application, we should also include validations in the model classes themselves. This way, they are independent of the front-end graphical interface and could be reused in another application (provided we place them in their own library to import in this application, instead of using the part construct). We illustrate this with the `number` field in `BankAccount` (the class code in this spiral also contains the validations for the other fields). First, we will make the field private by prefixing it with an _:

```
String _number;
```

Then, we will make a `get` and `set` method for this property; it is in the setter that we can validate using the incoming value:

```
String get number => _number;
set number(value) {
  if (value == null || value.isEmpty)
    throw new ArgumentError("No number value is given");    (1)
  var exp = new RegExp(r"[0-9]{3}-[0-9]{7}-[0-9]{2}");      (2)
  if (exp.hasMatch(value)) _number = value;                (3)
}
```

In the model classes, we don't have the possibility of showing an error window, but we can throw an error or exception in line (1). To catch this error, we will have to change the code in `storeData`, where the `BankAccount` object is created:

```
try {
  BankAccount bac = new BankAccount(p, number.value,
    double.parse(balance.value),
  int.parse(pin_code.value));
}
  catch(e) {
    window.alert(e.toString());
}
```

To test the particular format, we make use of the `RegExp` class in the built-in `dart:core` library. We construct an exp object of this class by passing the regular expression as a raw string in line (2). Then, we use `hasMatch` to test whether the value conforms to the format of `exp` (line (3)).

Using this mechanism, it turns out that we cannot use the short version of the constructors anymore, because a setter can only be called from within the constructor body. So, the `BankAccount` constructor will change to:

```
BankAccount(this.owner, number, balance, pin_code) :        date_
created   = new DateTime.now() {
    this.number = number;
    this.balance = balance;
    this.pin_code = pin_code;
}
```

Spiral 3 – how to store data in a local storage

When a fully validated bank account object is created, we can store it in a local storage, also called the Web Storage API (see https://developer.mozilla.org/en-US/docs/Web/API/Web_Storage_API), which is widely supported in modern browsers. In this mechanism, the application's data is persisted locally (on the client-side) as a Map-like structure: a dictionary of key/value pairs. This is yet another example of the universal use of JSON for the storage and transportation of data (see *Chapter 4, Modeling Web Applications with Model Concepts and Dartlero*). Unlike cookies, local storage does not expire, but every application can only access its own data up to a certain limit depending on the browser. With it, our application can also have an offline mode of functioning, when the server is not available to store the data in a database. Web Storage also has another way of storing data called sessionStorage, but this limits the persistence of the data to only the current browser session. So, data is lost when the browser is closed or another application is started in the same browser window. In the localStorage mechanism, which we will use here, JSON strings are stored and retrieved, so we need a two-way mechanism to convert our objects to and from JSON and the corresponding toJson and fromJson methods in our classes, for example, in person.dart:

> For the code files of this section, refer to chapter 6\bank_terminal_s3 in the code bundle.

```
Map<String, Object> toJson() {
  var per = new Map<String, Object>();
  per["name"] = name;
  per["address"] = address;
  per["email"] = email;
  per["gender"] = gender;
  per["birthdate"] = date_birth.toString();
  return per;
}
```

The preceding method is called from the `toJson` method in the following `BankAccount` class (see `bank_terminal_s3\bank_account.dart`):

```
String toJson() {
    var acc = new Map<String, Object>();
    acc["number"] = number;
    acc["owner"] = owner.toJson();
    acc["balance"] = balance;
    acc["pin_code"] = pin_code;
    acc["creation_date"] = date_created.toString();
    acc["modified_date"] = date_modified.toString();
    var accs = JSON.encode(acc); // use only once for the root
            // object (here a bank account)
    return accs;
}
```

We will store our `bac` bank account object in `localStorage` using its number as the key:

```
window.localStorage["Bankaccount:${bac.number}"] = bac.toJson();
```

Now, we can create bank accounts and store them in the browser's machine. In Chrome, we can verify this by navigating to **Tools | Developer | Tools | Resources | Local Storage | http:127.0.0.1:port** (where port is the port number, usually 3030).

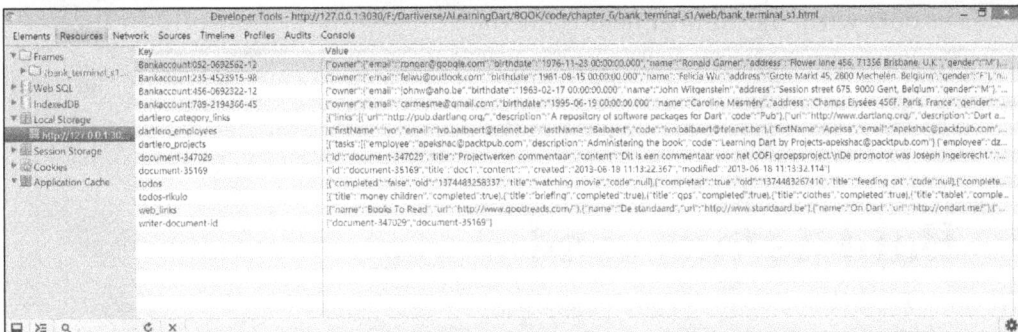

Viewing local storage screen

Local storage can be disabled (by user action, or via an installed plug-in or extension), so we must alert the user when this needs to be changed. We can do it by catching the exception that occurs in this case:

```
try {
    window.localStorage["Bankaccount:${bac.number}"] =
      bac.toJson();
} on Exception catch (ex) {
    window.alert("Data not stored: Local storage has been
    deactivated!");
}
```

Local storage is, in fact, of the `Map<String, String>` type; so it has a `length` property. You can query whether it contains something with `isEmpty` and loop through all the stored values with:

```
for (var key in window.localStorage.keys) {
    String value = window.localStorage[key];
}
```

Spiral 4 – reading and showing data

Having stored our data in local storage, it is just as easy to read this data from a local storage. Here is a simple screen that takes a bank account number as an input, and reads its data when the number field is filled in:

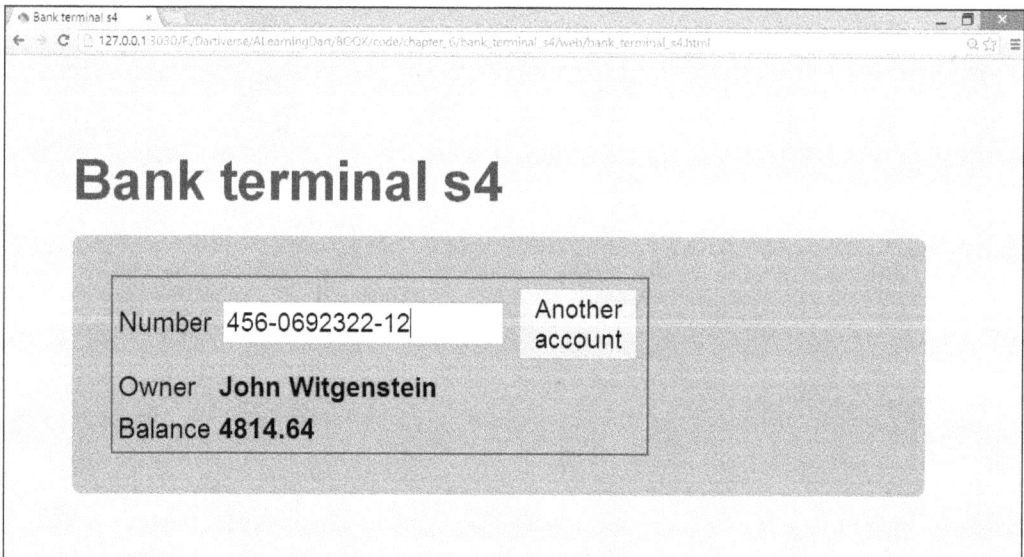

Bank terminal screen

> For the code files of this section, refer to `chapter 6\bank_terminal_s4` in the code bundle.

We clean up our code, making `main()` shorter by calling the methods:

```
void main() {
  bind_elements();
  attach_event_handlers();
}
bind_elements() {
  owner = querySelector('#owner'');
  balance = querySelector('#balance'');
  number = querySelector('#number'');
  btn_other = querySelector('#btn_other'');
  error = querySelector('#error'');
}
attach_event_handlers() {
  number.onInput.listen(readData);
  btn_other.onClick.listen(clearData);
}
```

Apply this refactoring from now on while coding a form. When the number is filled in, its input event listener is triggered:

```
number.onInput.listen(readData);
```

In the `readData` handler, the value is read from the local storage where the key contains the bank account number (line (2)). However, first, we will check whether our input sits in the local storage; if not, an error label will be shown. The field will get focus and we will leave the method with return (line (1) and following):

```
readData(Event e) {
  // show data:
  var key = 'Bankaccount:${number.value}'';
  if (!window.localStorage.containsKey(key)) {          (1)
    error.innerHtml = "Unknown bank account!";
    owner.innerHtml = "----------";
    balance.innerHtml = "0.0";
    number.focus();
    return;
  }
  error.innerHtml = "";
  // read data from local storage:
  String acc_json = window.localStorage[key];           (2)
```

```
    bac = new BankAccount.fromJson(JSON.decode(acc_json));    (3)
    // show owner and balance:
    owner.innerHtml = "<b>${bac.owner.name}</b>";              (4)
    balance.innerHtml = "<b>${bac.balance.toStringAsFixed(2)}</b>";
}
```

The `bac` bank account object is now created in line (3), the `owner` and `balance` labels can then be filled in line (4). Let's examine this in some detail. The resulting `acc_json` string has the structure of a map, and the `JSON.decode` method of the convert package transforms this string into a map. We will enhance our model classes with the functionality to convert this map into an object. The best way to do this is with a named constructor (called `fromJson` appropriately) that takes this map and makes a new object from it. So, in the `person` class, we add the following named constructor:

```
Person.fromJson(Map json) {
    this.name = json["name"];
    this.address = json["address"];
    this.email = json["email"];
    this.gender = json["gender"];
    this.date_birth = DateTime.parse(json["birthdate"]);
}
```

This is used by the `fromJson` constructor in the `BankAccount` class:

```
BankAccount.fromJson(Map json):  date_created =
  DateTime.parse(json["creation_date"]) {
    this.number = json["number"];
    this.owner = new Person.fromJson(json["owner"]);
    this.balance = json["balance"];
    this.pin_code = json["pin_code"];
    this.date_modified = DateTime.parse(json["modified_date"]);
}
```

Spiral 5 – changing and updating data

Now that we have our bank account back on screen, we will add an input field with the `#number` id (and of the `number` type) that captures the amount of money we want to deposit or withdraw from our account. We add a **Deposit-Withdrawal** button to initiate this action, and also an **Add interest** button to calculate and add interest to our account. Our screen now looks like the following screenshot:

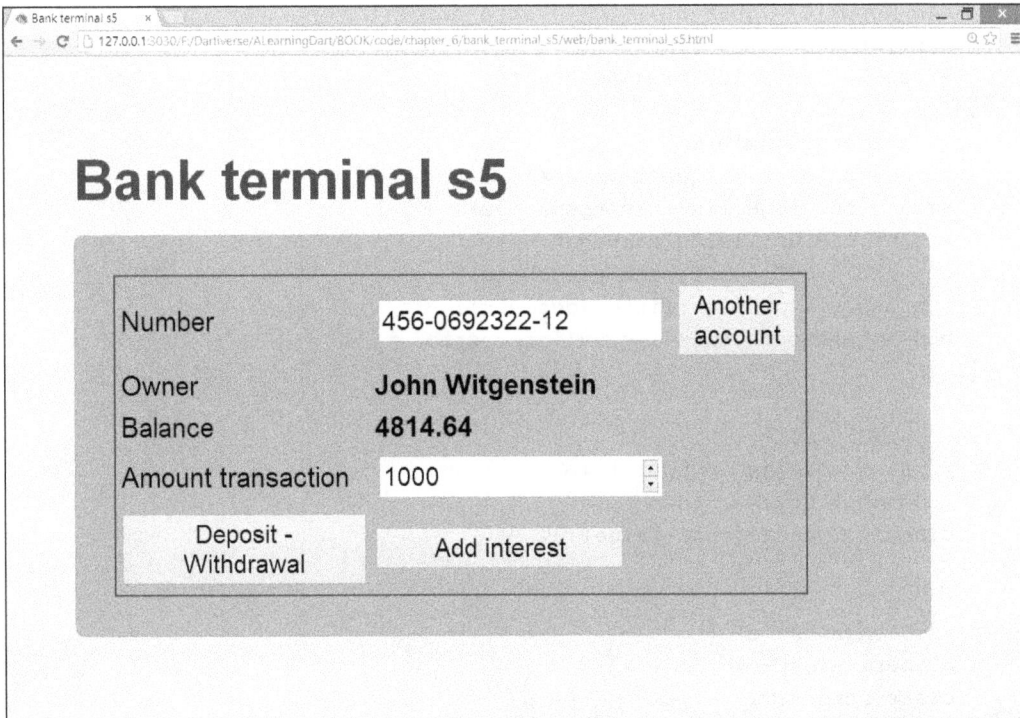

Changing data screen

> For the code files of this section, refer to chapter 6\bank_
> terminal_s5 in the code bundle.

Here is the code of bank_terminal_s5.dart (declarations are left out for brevity):

```
void main() {
  bind_elements();                              (1)
  attach_event_handlers();                      (2)
  disable_transactions(true);                   (3)
}
bind_elements() {
  owner = querySelector('#owner'');
  balance = querySelector ('#balance'');
  number = querySelector ('#number'');
  btn_other = querySelector ('#btn_other'');
  amount = querySelector ('#amount'');
```

```
    btn_deposit = querySelector ('#btn_deposit'');
    btn_interest = querySelector ('#btn_interest'');
    error = querySelector ('#error'');
  }
  attach_event_handlers() {
    number.onInput.listen(readData);
    amount.onChange.listen(nonNegative);
    amount.onBlur.listen(nonNegative);
    btn_other.onClick.listen(clearData);
    btn_deposit.onClick.listen(deposit);
    btn_interest.onClick.listen(interest);
  }

  readData(Event e) {
    // same code as in Spiral 4
    // enable transactions part:
    disable_transactions(false);                          (4)
  }

  clearData(Event e) {
    number.value = "";
    owner.innerHtml = "----------";
    balance.innerHtml = "0.0";
    number.focus();
    disable_transactions(true);
  }

  disable_transactions(bool off) {
    amount.disabled = off;
    btn_deposit.disabled = off;
    btn_interest.disabled = off;
  }

  changeBalance(Event e) {
    // read amount:
    double money_amount = double.parse(amount.value);      (5)
    // call deposit on BankAccount object:
    if (money_amount >= 0) bac.deposit(money_amount);      (6)
    else bac.withdraw(money_amount);
    window.localStorage["Bankaccount:${bac.number}"] = bac.toJson();
    // show new amount:
```

```
    balance.innerHtml = "<b>${bac.balance.toStringAsFixed(2)}</b>";
    // disable refresh screen:
    e.preventDefault();                                          (7)
    e.stopPropagation();
  }
  interest(Event e) {
    bac.interest();
    window.localStorage["Bankaccount:${bac.number}"] =
      bac.toJson(); (8)
    balance.innerHtml = "<b>${bac.balance.toStringAsFixed(2)}</b>";
    e.preventDefault();
    e.stopPropagation();
  }
```

The `main()` method in lines ((1) and (2)) calls the methods to create objects for the DOM elements, and creates the event handlers. When the screen displays for the first time, the **Amount transaction** field and the buttons are best shown as disabled; this is accomplished by line (3), which calls a handy `disable_transactions` method to disable or enable DOM elements by passing a Boolean value. When the data is shown, the `readData` method performs as in *Spiral 4, reading and showing data*, and the second part of the screen is enabled (line (5)). The **Deposit-Withdrawal** button can perform both the functions, whether the amount is greater or less than 0. The `double.parse` method in line (5) will not throw an exception, because we checked the number input. The corresponding methods on the object are called to change its balance in line (6), for example, the `deposit` method in the `BankAccount` class:

```
deposit(double amount) {
    balance += amount;
    date_modified = new DateTime.now();
}
```

The changed object is again stored in the local storage in line (8). The two lines, starting at line (7), are necessary to stop the event from propagating; if they are not used, the change will not be visible because the screen is refreshed immediately. The interest calculation will follow the same pattern.

Spiral 6 – working with a list of bank accounts

In this spiral, we will read all our Bank Account data from the local storage and display the numbers in a dropdown list. Upon selection, all the details of the bank account will be shown in a table. This is how our page will look like, at the start, upon opening the selection list:

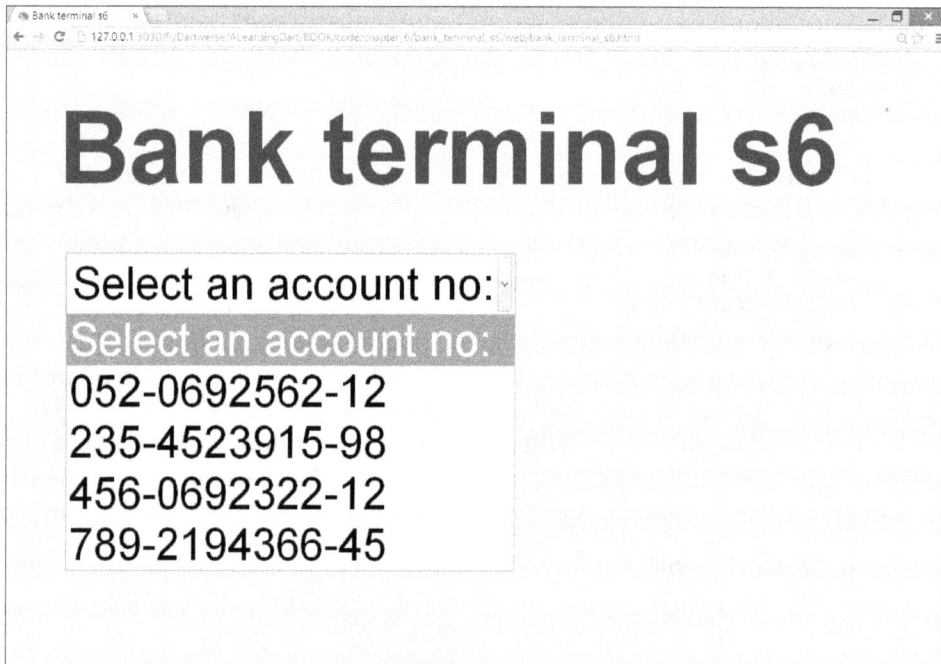

Selecting a bank account number screen

> [For the code files of this section, refer to chapter 6\bank_ terminal_s6 in the code bundle.]

In this spiral, we will let the code construct the web page:

```
void main() {
    readLocalStorage();                               (1)
    constructPage();                                  (2)
    sel.onChange.listen(showAccount);                 (3)
}
```

In line (1), the account numbers are read from the local storage, extracted, and put into a list:

```
readLocalStorage() {
  account_nos = [];
  for (var key in window.localStorage.keys) {
    account_nos.add(key.substring(12)); // extract account number
  }
}
```

The method in line (2) calls two other methods, constructSelect (line (4)) and constructTable (line (5)), to build up the select list and the empty table, respectively:

```
constructPage() {
// make dropdown list and fill with data:
  var el = new Element.html(constructSelect());        (4)
  document.body.children.add(el);
// prepare html table for account data:
  var el1 = new Element.html(constructTable());        (5)
  document.body.children.add(el1);
  sel = querySelector('#accounts');
  table = querySelector('#accdata');
  table.classes.remove('border');
}
String constructSelect() {
  var sb = new StringBuffer();                         (6)
  sb.write('<select id="accounts">');
  sb.write('<option selected>Select an account no:</option>');
  account_nos.forEach( (acc) =>
    sb.write('<option>$acc</option>'));                (7)
  sb.write('</select>');
  return sb.toString();
}
String constructTable() {
  var sb = new StringBuffer();
  sb.write('<table id="accdata" class="border">');
  sb.write('</table>');
  return sb.toString();
}
```

Both the `constructSelect` and `constructTable` methods use a `StringBuffer` method for efficiency (line (6)). We use string interpolation (line (7)) to merge the data with the HTML. Upon selection, using the `onChange` event (line (3)), the following method will be called:

```
showAccount(Event e) {
  // remove previous data:
  table.children.clear();                                    (8)
  table.classes.remove('border'');                           (9)
  // get selected number:
  sel = e.currentTarget;
  if (sel.selectedIndex >= 1) { // an account was chosen    (10)
    var accountno = account_nos[sel.selectedIndex - 1];
    var key = 'Bankaccount:$accountno';
    String acc_json = window.localStorage[key];
    bac = new BankAccount.fromJson(JSON.decode(acc_json));
    // show data:
    table.classes.add('border');
    constructTrows();
  }
}
```

To make sure no previous data is shown, the table is cleared in lines (8) and (9), and we also make sure that we select one of the accounts with line (10). The rest of the code is straightforward, using `constructRows` to fill in the table. We inserted all the `<tr>` tags in one `Element.html`; because of this, we are forced to include a `<p>` tag to surround all the table rows, because the HTML method needs a surrounding tag. The following screenshot shows the detail screen:

Detailed information of a selected bank account screen

Summary

You have now gained experience with the techniques to build HTML5 screens with input fields that know how to validate data, further controlling data through Dart and storing them in the browser's local storage for offline use. This is not a replacement for server side validation: data sent from a client should still be validated on the server.

Along the way, we perfected our skills to work with JSON, and learned how to (de) construct Dart objects to/from JSON. All these can be used at the front-end of your business application. If you need a more complex user interface, web components are the way to go. We will explore them in detail in *Chapter 8, Developing Business Applications with Polymer Web Components*. In the next chapter, we will sharpen our modeling and game building skills, adding multimedia functionality to our applications.

7
Building Games with HTML5 and Dart

In this chapter, you will use the knowledge of the previous chapters to create a well-known memory game. However, instead of presenting and explaining the code completed in the previous chapters, you will design a model first and work your way up from a modest beginning to a completely functional game, step by step. You will also learn how to enhance the attractiveness of web games with audio and video techniques. The following topics will be covered in this chapter:

- The model for the memory game
- Spiral 1 – drawing the board
- Spiral 2 – drawing cells
- Spiral 3 – coloring the cells
- Spiral 4 – implementing the rules
- Spiral 5 – game logic (bringing in the time element)
- Spiral 6 – some finishing touches
- Spiral 7 – using images
- Adding audio to a web page
- The Collision Clones game
- Adding video to a web page

The model for the memory game

When started, the game presents a board with square cells. Every cell hides an image that can be seen by clicking on the cell, but this disappears quickly. You must remember where the images are, because they come in pairs. If you quickly click on two cells that hide the same picture, the cells will "flip over" and the pictures will stay visible. The objective of the game is to turn over all the pairs of matching images in a very short time.

> The code for this project can be downloaded from GitHub using the following command:
>
> `git clone git://github.com/dzenanr/educ_memory_game.git`

After some thinking we came up with the following model, which describes the data handled by the application. In our game, we have a number of pictures, which could belong to a **Catalog**. For example, a travel catalog with a collection of photos from our trips or something similar. Furthermore, we have a collection of cells and each cell is hiding a picture. Also, we have a structure that we will call memory, and this contains the cells in a grid of rows and columns. Using our Model Concepts graphical design tool from *Chapter 4, Modeling Web Applications with Model Concepts and Dartlero*, we could draw it up as shown in the following figure. You can import the model from the `game_memory_json.txt` file that contains its JSON representation:

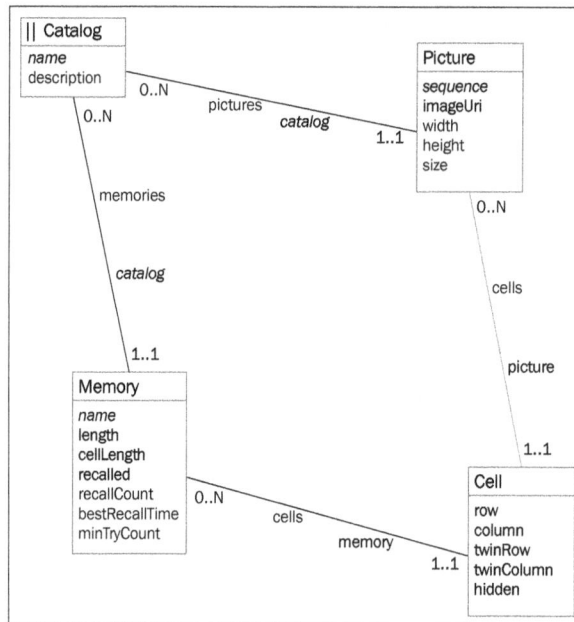

A conceptual model of the memory game

The **Catalog** ID is its name, which is mandatory, but the description is optional. The **Picture** ID consists of the sequence number within the Catalog. The imageUri field stores the location of the image file. width and height are optional properties, since they may be derived from the image file. The size may be small, medium, or large to help select an image. The ID of a **Memory** is its name within the Catalog, the collection of cells is determined by the memory length, for example, four cells per side. Each cell is of the same length cellLength, which is a property of the memory. A memory is recalled when all the image pairs are discovered. Some statistics must be kept, such as recall count, the best recall time in seconds, and the number of cell clicks to recover the whole image (minTryCount). The **Cell** has the row and column coordinates and also the coordinates of its twin with the same image. Once the model is discussed and improved, model views may be created: a **Board** would be a view of the Memory concept and a Box would be a view of the Cell concept. The application would be based on the Catalog concept. If there is no need to browse photos of a catalog and display them within a page, there would not be a corresponding view. Now, we can start developing this game from scratch.

Spiral 1 – drawing the board

The app starts with main() in educ_memory_game.dart:

```
library memory;

import 'dart:html';

part 'board.dart';

void main() {
  // Get a reference to the canvas.
  CanvasElement canvas = querySelector('#canvas');      (1)
  new Board(canvas);                                    (2)
}
```

> For the code files of this section refer to Chapter 7\code\ educ_memory_game\spirals\s01 in the code bundle.

As we did in *Chapter 5, Handling DOM in a New Way*, we'll draw a board on a canvas element. So, we need a reference that is given in line (1). The Board view is represented in code as its own Board class in the board.dart file. Since everything happens on this board, we construct its object with canvas as an argument (line (2)). Our game board will be periodically drawn as a rectangle in line (4) by using the animationFrame method from the Window class in line (3):

```dart
part of memory;

class Board {

  CanvasElement canvas;
  CanvasRenderingContext2D context;
  num width, height;

  Board(this.canvas) {
    context = canvas.getContext('2d');
    width = canvas.width;
    height = canvas.height;
    window.animationFrame.then(gameLoop);                    (3)
  }

  void gameLoop(num delta) {
    draw();
    window.animationFrame.then(gameLoop);
  }

  void draw() {
    clear();
    border();
  }

  void clear() {
    context.clearRect(0, 0, width, height);
  }

  void border() {
    context..rect(0, 0, width, height)..stroke();            (4)
  }
}
```

This is our first result:

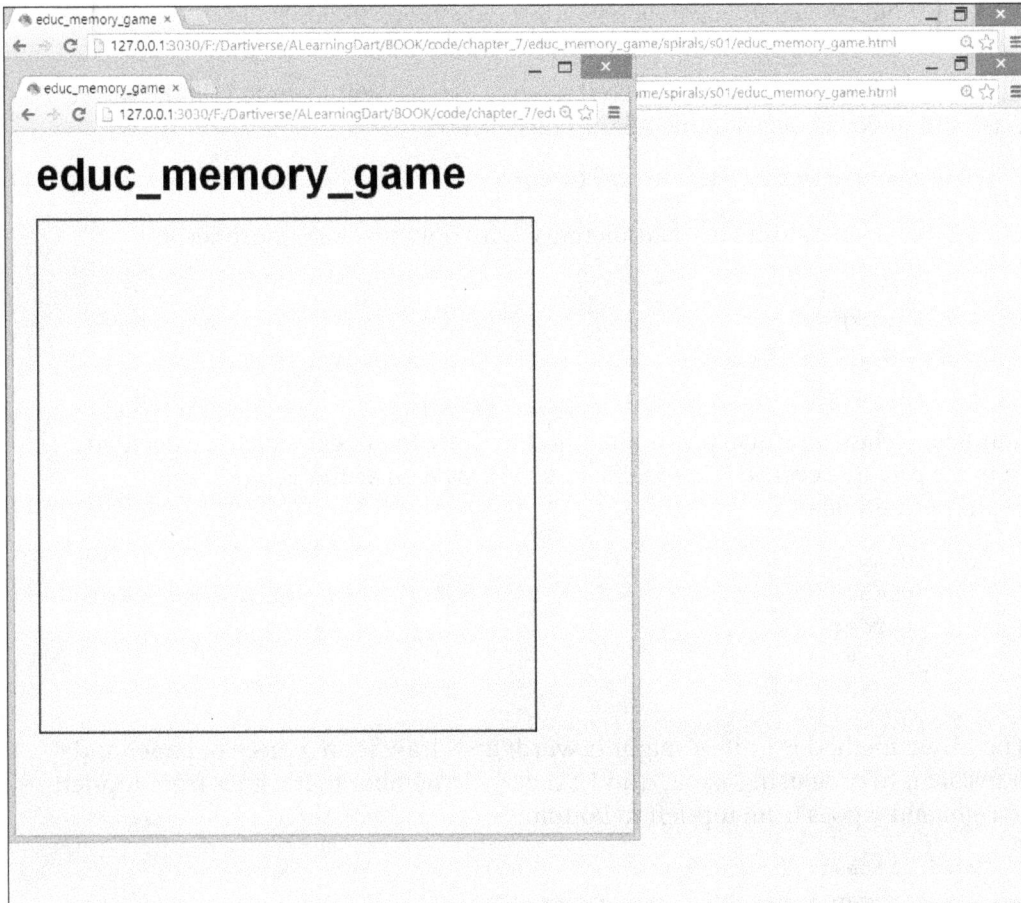

The game board

Spiral 2 – drawing cells

In this spiral, we will give our app code some structure: Board is a view, so board. dart is moved to the view folder. We will also introduce here the Memory class from our model in its own code memory.dart file in the model folder. So, we will have to change the part statements to the following:

```
part 'model/memory.dart';
part 'view/board.dart';
```

For the code file of this section, refer to `Chapter 7\code\educ_memory_game\spirals\s02`.

The `Board` view needs to know about `Memory`. So, we will include it in the `Board` class and make its object in the `Board` constructor:

```
new Board(canvas, new Memory(4));
```

The `Memory` class is still very rudimentary with only its `length` property:

```
class Memory {
  num length;
  Memory(this.length);
}
```

Our `Board` class now also needs a method to draw the lines, which we decided to make private because it is specific to `Board`, as well as the `clear()` and `border()` methods:

```
void draw() {
    _clear();
    _border();
    _lines();
}
```

The `lines` method is quite straightforward; first draw it on a piece of paper and translate it to code using `moveTo` and `lineTo`. Remember that x goes from top-left to right and y goes from top-left to bottom:

```
void _lines() {
    var gap = height / memory.length;
    var x, y;
    for (var i = 1; i < memory.length; i++) {
      x = gap * i;
      y = x;
      context
        ..moveTo(x, 0)
        ..lineTo(x, height)
        ..moveTo(0, y)
        ..lineTo(width, y);
    }
}
```

The result is a nice grid:

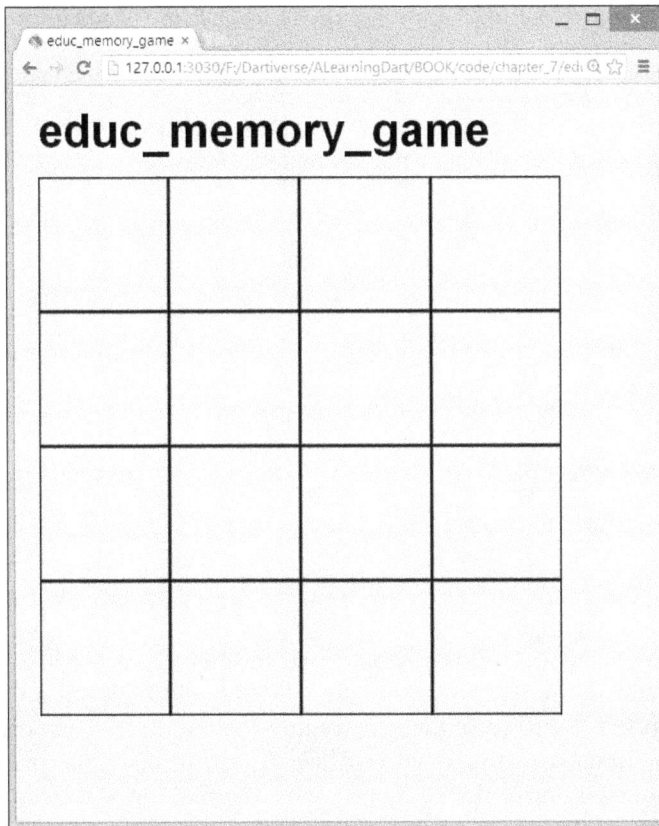

Board with cells

Spiral 3 – coloring the cells

To simplify, we will start using colors instead of pictures to be shown in the grid. Up until now, we didn't implement the cell from the model. Let's do that in model\ cell.dart. We start simple by saying that the Cell class has the row, column, and color properties, and it belongs to a Memory object passed in its constructor:

```
class Cell {
    int row, column;
    String color;
    Memory memory;
    Cell(this.memory, this.row, this.column);
}
```

[For the code files of this section, refer to `Chapter 7\code\`
`educ_memory_game\spirals\s03` in the code bundle.]

Because we need a collection of cells, it is a good idea to make a `Cells` class, which contains `List`. We give it an `add` method and also an iterator so that we are able to use a `for...in` statement to loop over the collection:

```
class Cells {
  List _list;

  Cells() {
    _list = new List();
  }

  void add(Cell cell) {
    _list.add(cell);
  }

  Iterator get iterator => _list.iterator;
}
```

We will need colors that are randomly assigned to the cells. We will also need some utility variables and methods that do not specifically belong to the model and don't need a class. Hence, we will code them in a folder called `util`. To specify the colors for the cells, we will use two utility variables: a `List` variable of colors (`colorList`), which has the name colors, and a `colorMap` variable that maps the names to their RGB values. Refer to `util\color.dart`; later on, we can choose some fancier colors:

```
var colorList = ['black', 'blue', //other colors  ];
var colorMap = {'black': '#000000', 'blue': '#0000ff', //... };
```

To generate (pseudo) random values (integers, doubles, or Booleans), Dart has the `Random` class from `dart:math`. We will use the `nextInt` method, which takes an integer (the maximum value) and returns a positive random integer in the range from 0 (inclusive) to `max` (exclusive). We will build upon this in `util\random.dart` to make methods that give us a random color:

```
int randomInt(int max) => new Random().nextInt(max);
randomListElement(List list) => list[randomInt(list.length - 1)];
String randomColor() => randomListElement(colorList);
String randomColorCode() => colorMap[randomColor()];
```

Our `Memory` class now contains an instance of the `Cells` class:

```
Cells cells;
```

We build this in the `Memory` constructor in a nested `for` loop, where each cell is successively instantiated with a row and column, given a random color, and added to `cells`:

```
Memory(this.length) {
  cells = new Cells();
  var cell;
  for (var x = 0; x < length; x++) {
    for (var y = 0; y < length; y++) {
      cell = new Cell(this, x, y);
      cell.color = randomColor();
      cells.add(cell);
    }
  }
}
```

We know from *Chapter 5, Handling DOM in a New Way*, that we can draw a rectangle and fill it with a color at the same time. So, we realize that we don't need to draw lines as we did in the previous spiral! The _boxes method is called from the draw animation: with a `for...in` statement, we loop over the collection of cells and call the _colorBox method that will draw and color the cell for each cell:

```
void _boxes() {
  for (Cell cell in memory.cells) {
    _colorBox(cell);
  }
}

void _colorBox(Cell cell) {
  var gap = height / memory.length;
  var x = cell.row * gap;
  var y = cell.column * gap;
  context
    ..beginPath()
    ..fillStyle = colorMap[cell.color]
    ..rect(x, y, gap, gap)
    ..fill()
    ..stroke()
    ..closePath();
}
```

Now, we have a colored board:

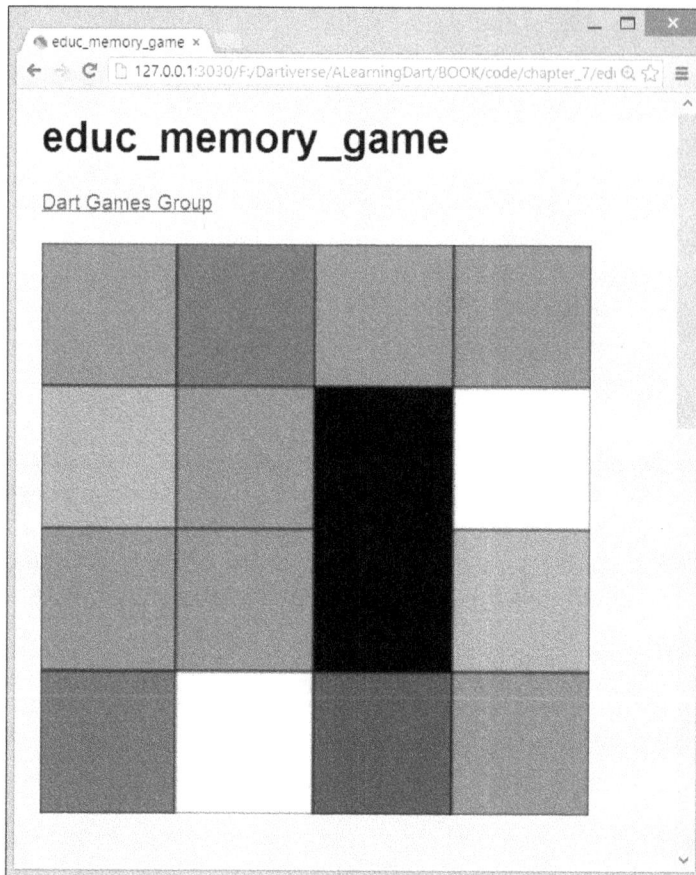

The colored board

Spiral 4 – implementing the rules

However, wait! Our game can only work if the same color appears in only two cells: a cell and its twin cell. Moreover, a cell can be hidden or not: can the color be seen or not? To take care of this, the Cell class gets two new attributes:

```
Cell twin;
bool hidden = true;
```

> For the code files of this section, refer to Chapter 7\code\
> educ_memory_game\spirals\s04 in the code bundle.

The `_colorBox` method in the `Board` class can now show the color of the cell when `hidden` is `false` (line (2)); when `hidden` = `true` (the default state), a neutral gray color will be used for the cell (line (1)):

```
static const String COLOR_CODE = '#f0f0f0';
```

We also gave the `gap` variable a better name, `boxSize`:

```
void _colorBox(Cell cell) {
    var x = cell.column * boxSize;
    var y = cell.row * boxSize;
    context.beginPath();
    if (cell.hidden) {
      context.fillStyle = COLOR_CODE;                      (1)
    } else {
      context.fillStyle = colorMap[cell.color];            (2)
    }
// same code as in Spiral 3
}
```

The lines (1) and (2) can also be stated more succinctly with the ? ternary operator. Remember that the drawing changes because the `_colorBox` method is called via drawing at 60 frames per second and the board can react to a mouse click. In this spiral, we will show a cell when it is clicked together with its twin cell and then they will stay visible. Attaching an event handler for this is easy. We add the following line to the `Board` constructor:

```
querySelector('#canvas').onMouseDown.listen(onMouseDown);
```

The `onMouseDown` event handler has to know on which cell the click occurred. The mouse event e contains the coordinates of the click in its e.offset.x and e.offset.y properties (lines (3) and (4)). We will obtain the cell's row and column by using a truncating division ~/ operator dividing the x (which gives the column) and y (which gives the row) values by `boxSize`:

```
void onMouseDown(MouseEvent e) {
    int row = e.offset.y ~/ boxSize;                      (3)
    int column = e.offset.x ~/ boxSize;                   (4)
    Cell cell = memory.getCell(row, column);              (5)
    cell.hidden = false;                                  (6)
    cell.twin.hidden = false;                             (7)
}
```

Memory has a collection of cells. To get the cell with a specified row and column value, we will add a getCell method to memory and call it in line (5). When we have the cell, we will set its hidden property and that of its twin cell to false (lines (6) to (7)). The getCell method must return the cell at the given row and column. It loops through all the cells in line (8) and checks each cell, whether it is positioned at that row and column (line (9)). If yes, it will return that cell:

```
Cell getCell(int row, int column) {
    for (Cell cell in cells) {                          (8)
      if (cell.intersects(row, column)) {               (9)
        return cell;
      }
    }
}
```

For this purpose, we will add an intersects method to the Cell class. This checks whether its row and column match the given row and column for the current cell (see line (10)):

```
bool intersects(int row, int column) {
    if (this.row == row && this.column == column) {     (10)
      return true;
    }
    return false;
}
```

Now, we have already added a lot of functionality, but the drawing of the board will need some more thinking:

- How to give a cell (and its twin cell) a random color that is not yet used?

- How to attach a cell randomly to a twin cell that is not yet used?

To end this, we will have to make the constructor of Memory a lot more intelligent:

```
Memory(this.length) {
    if (length.isOdd) {                                 (1)
      throw new Exception(
          'Memory length must be an even integer: $length.');
    }
    cells = new Cells();
    var cell, twinCell;
    for (var x = 0; x < length; x++) {
      for (var y = 0; y < length; y++) {
        cell = getCell(y, x);                           (2)
        if (cell == null) {                             (3)
```

```
            cell = new Cell(this, y, x);
            cell.color = _getFreeRandomColor();          (4)
            cells.add(cell);
            twinCell = _getFreeRandomCell();             (5)
            cell.twin = twinCell;                        (6)
            twinCell.twin = cell;
            twinCell.color = cell.color;
            cells.add(twinCell);
          }
        }
      }
    }
```

The number of pairs given by (*(length * length) / 2*) must be even. This is only true if the length parameter of Memory itself is even, so we checked it in line (1). Again, we coded a nested loop and got the cell at that row and column. However, as the cell at that position has not yet been made (line (3)), we continued to construct it and assign its color and twin. In line (4), we called _getFreeRandomColor to get a color that is not yet used:

```
String _getFreeRandomColor() {
    var color;
    do {
      color = randomColor();
    } while (usedColors.any((c) => c == color));      (7)
    usedColors.add(color);                            (8)
    return color;
}
```

The do...while loop continues as long as the color is already in a list of usedColors (this is elegantly checked with the any functional from *Chapter 3, Structuring Code with Classes and Libraries*). On exiting from the loop, we found an unused color, which is added to usedColors in line (8) and also returned. We then had to set everything for the twin cell. We searched for a free one with the _getFreeRandomCell method in line (5). Here, the do...while loop continues until a (row, column) position is found where cell == null is, meaning that we haven't yet created a cell there (line (9)). We will promptly do this in line (10):

```
Cell _getFreeRandomCell() {
    var row, column;
    Cell cell;
    do {
      row = randomInt(length);
      column = randomInt(length);
```

```
        cell = getCell(row, column);
    } while (cell != null);                                    (9)
    return new Cell(this, row, column);                        (10)
}
```

From line (6) onwards, the properties of the twin cell are set and added to the list. This is all we need to produce the following result:

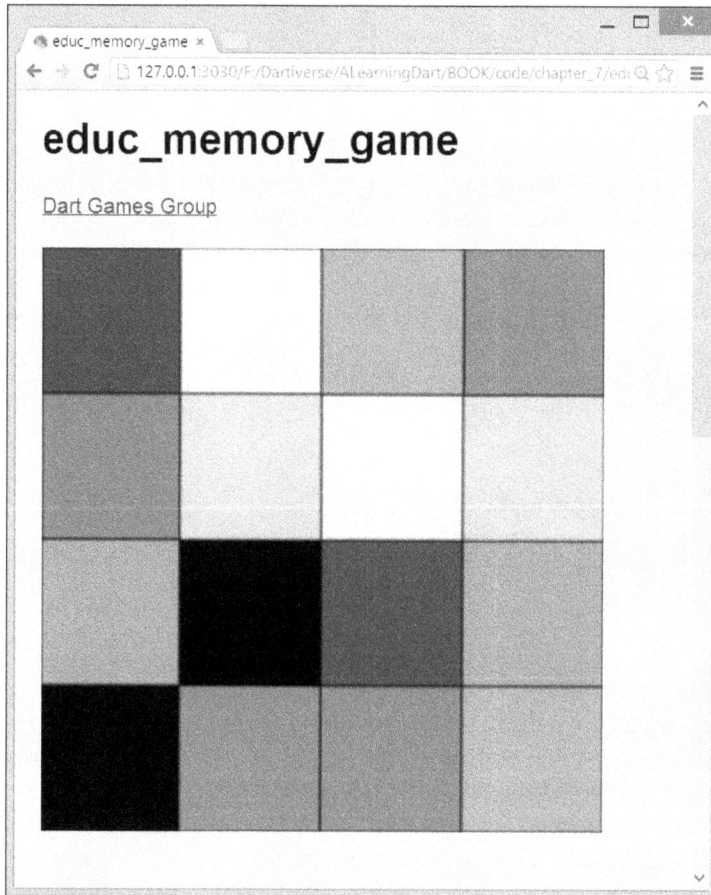

Paired colored cells

Spiral 5 – game logic (bringing in the time element)

Our app isn't playable yet:

- When a cell is clicked, its color must only show for a short period of time (say one second)
- When a cell and its twin cell are clicked within a certain time interval, they must remain visible

[🖊 For the code file for this section, refer to `Chapter 7\code\educ_memory_game\spirals\s05` in the code bundle.]

All of this is coded in the `mouseDown` event handler and we also need a `lastCellClicked` variable of the `Cell` type in the `Board` class. Of course, this is exactly the cell we get in the `mouseDown` event handler. So, we will set it in line (5) in the following code snippet:

```
void onMouseDown(MouseEvent e) {
  // same code as in Spiral 4 -
  if (cell.twin == lastCellClicked && lastCellClicked.shown) {  (1)
    lastCellClicked.hidden = false;                              (2)
      if (memory.recalled)   memory.hide();                      (3)
    } else {
      new Timer(const Duration(milliseconds: 1000), () =>
                      cell.hidden = true);                       (4)
    }
    lastCellClicked = cell;                                      (5)
  }
```

In line (1), we checked whether the last clicked cell was the twin cell and whether this is still shown. Then, we made sure in (2) that it stays visible. The `shown` is a new getter in the `Cell` class to make the code more readable: `bool get shown => !hidden;`. If at that moment all the cells were shown (the memory is recalled), we again hid them in line (3). If the last clicked cell was not the twin cell, we hid the current cell after one second in line (4).The `recalled` is a simple getter (read-only property) in the `Memory` class and it makes use of a Boolean variable in `Memory` that is initialized to `false` (`_recalled = false;`):

```
bool get recalled {
    if (!_recalled) {
      if (cells.every((c) => c.shown)) {            (6)
        _recalled = true;
```

```
        }
    }
    return _recalled;
}
```

In line (6), we tested that if every cell is shown, then this variable is set to true (the game is over).The new method named every, is in the Cells List and a nice functional way to write this is given as follows:

```
bool every(Function f) => list.every(f);
```

The hide method is straightforward: hide every cell and reset the _recalled variable to false:

```
hide() {
    for (final cell in cells) cell.hidden = true;
    _recalled = false;
}
```

This is it, our game works!

Spiral 6 – some finishing touches

A working program always gives its developer a sense of joy, and rightfully so. However, this doesn't that mean you can leave the code as it is. On the contrary, carefully review your code for some time to see whether there is room for improvement or optimization. For example, are the names you used clear enough? The color of a hidden cell is now named simply COLOR_CODE in board.dart, renaming it to HIDDEN_CELL_COLOR_CODE makes its meaning explicit. The List object used in the Cells class can indicate that it is List<Cell>, by applying the fact that Dart lists are generic. The parameter of the every method in the Cell class is more precise—it is a function that accepts a cell and returns bool. Our onMouseDown event handler contains our game logic, so it is very important to tune it if possible. After some thought, we see that the code from the previous spiral can be improved; in the following line, the second condition after && is, in fact, unnecessary:

```
if (cell.twin == lastCellClicked && lastCellClicked.shown) {...}
```

> For the code files of this section, refer to Chapter 7\code\ educ_memory_game\spirals\s06 in the code bundle.

When the player has guessed everything correctly, showing the completed screen for a few seconds will be more satisfactory (line (2)). So, this portion of our event handler code will change to:

```
if (cell.twin == lastCellClicked) {                                (1)
    lastCellClicked.hidden = false;
    if (memory.recalled) { // game over
        new Timer(const Duration(milliseconds: 5000), () =>
                memory.hide());                                    (2)
    }
} else if (cell.twin.hidden) {
        new Timer(const Duration(milliseconds: 800), () =>
                cell.hidden = true);
}
```

Why don't we show a "YOU HAVE WON!" banner. We will do this by drawing the text on the canvas (line (3)), so we must do it in the draw() method (otherwise, it would disappear after INTERVAL milliseconds):

```
void draw() {
  _clear();
  _boxes();
  if (memory.recalled) { // game over
   context.font = "bold 25px sans-serif";
   context.fillStyle = "red";
   context.fillText("YOU HAVE WON !", boxSize, boxSize * 2);   (3)
  }
}
```

Then, the same game with the same configuration can be played again.

We could make it more obvious that a cell is hidden by decorating it with a small circle in the _colorBox method (line (4)):

```
if (cell.hidden) {
   context.fillStyle = HIDDEN_CELL_COLOR_CODE;
   var centerX = cell.column * boxSize + boxSize / 2;
   var centerY = cell.row * boxSize + boxSize / 2;
   var radius = 4;
   context.arc(centerX, centerY, radius, 0, 2 * PI, false);   (4)
}
```

We do want to give our player a chance to start over by supplying a **Play again** button. The easiest way will be to simply refresh the screen (line (5)) by adding this code to the startup script:

```
void main() {
  canvas = querySelector('#canvas');
  ButtonElement play = querySelector('#play');
  play.onClick.listen(playAgain);
  new Board(canvas, new Memory(4));
}

playAgain(Event e) {
  window.location.reload();                                    (5)
}
```

Spiral 7 – using images

One improvement that certainly comes to mind is the use of pictures instead of colors as shown in the *Using images* screenshot. How difficult would that be? It turns out that this is surprisingly easy, because we already have the game logic firmly in place!

> For the code files of this section, refer to chapter 7\educ_
> memory_game in the code bundle. This is the master version
> of the game to be found in the root directory.

In the images folder, we supply a number of game pictures. Instead of the color property, we give the cell a String property (image), which will contain the name of the picture file. We then replace util\color.dart with util\images.dart, which contains an imageList variable with the image filenames. In util\random.dart, we will replace the color methods with the following code:

```
String randomImage() => randomListElement(imageList);
```

The changes to `memory.dart` are also straightforward: replace the `usedColor` list with `List usedImages = [];` and the `_getFreeRandomColor` method with `_getFreeRandomImage`, which will use the new list and method:

```
List usedImages = [];

String _getFreeRandomImage() {
    var image;
    do {
      image = randomImage();
    } while (usedImages.any((i) => i == image));
    usedImages.add(image);
    return image;
}
```

In `board.dart`, we replace `_colorBox(cell)` with `_imageBox(cell)`. The only new thing is how to draw the image on canvas. For this, we need `ImageElement` objects. Here, we have to be careful to create these objects only once and not over and over again in every draw cycle, because this produces a flickering screen. We will store the `ImageElements` object in a `Map`:

```
var imageMap = new Map<String, ImageElement>();
```

Then, we populate this in the `Board` constructor with a for...in loop over `memory.cells`:

```
    for (var cell in memory.cells) {
      ImageElement image = new Element.tag('img');      (1)
      image.src = 'images/${cell.image}';               (2)
      imageMap[cell.image] = image;                     (3)
    }
```

We create a new `ImageElement` object in line (1), giving it the complete file path to the image file as a `src` property in line (2) and store it in `imageMap` in line (3). The image file will then be loaded into memory only once. We don't do any unnecessary network access, but effectively cache the images. In the draw cycle, we will load the image from `imageMap` and draw it in the current cell with the `drawImage` method in line (4):

```
if (cell.hidden) {
    // see previous code
} else {
    ImageElement image = imageMap[cell.image];
    context.drawImage(image, x, y); // resize to cell size (4)
}
```

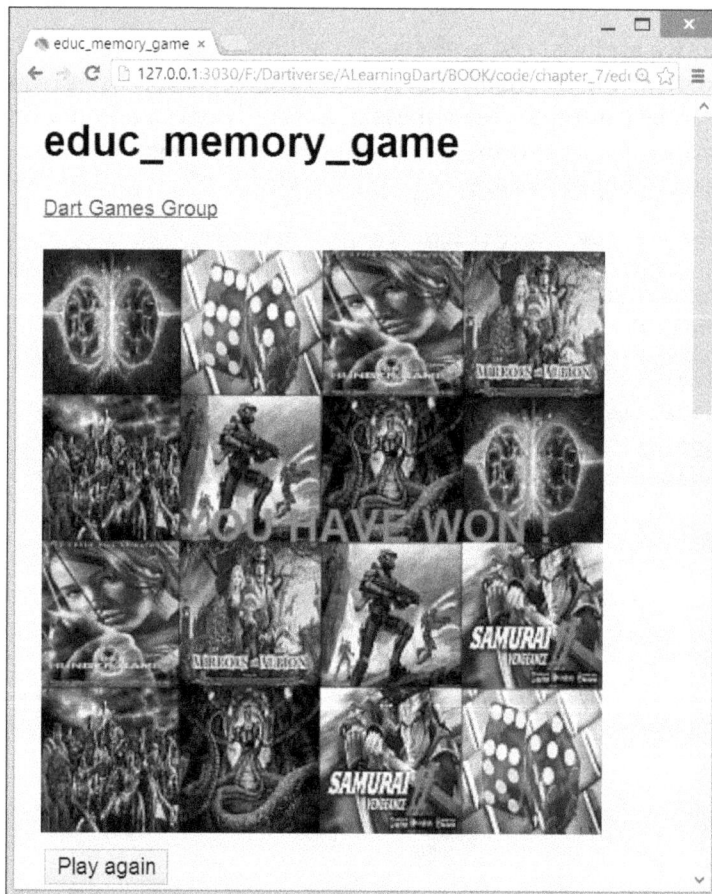

Using images

Perhaps, you can think of other improvements? Why not let the player specify the game difficulty by asking the number of boxes. It is 16 now. Check whether the input is a square of an even number. Do you have enough colors to choose from? Perhaps, dynamically building a list with enough random colors would be a better idea. Calculating and storing the statistics discussed in the model would also make the game more attractive. For ideas, see the *Using an audio library – Collision clones* section. Another enhancement from the model is to support different catalogs of pictures. Go ahead and exercise your Dart skills!

Adding audio to a web page

HTML5 provides us with the `<audio>` element, which specifies a standard way to embed an audio file on a web page. There's no more trouble in installing plugins in your browsers! It needs a *controls* attribute to add audio controls, such as play, pause, and volume (see the following screenshot):

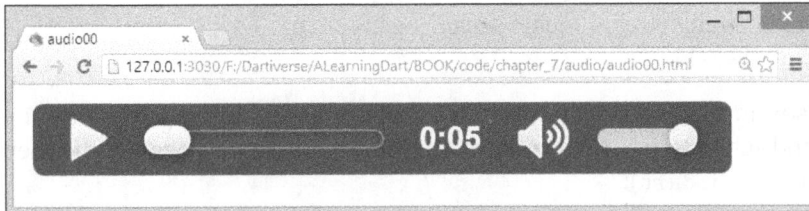

The controls attribute

> For the code file for this section, refer to `chapter 7\audio\` and `chapter 7\audio_dart\` in the code bundle.

Of course, you also need to indicate where the browser can find the source of the sound file through the `<source>` element and its `src` attribute. However, we all know that media files come in different formats, such as MP3, WAV, and OGG. These are the currently supported file formats, and only Chrome supports all three of them. The format is described via the `type` attribute of `<source>`, as in `type="audio/mpeg"` for MP3. Luckily, the `<audio>` element allows multiple `<source>` elements, so we can link to different audio file formats. The browser will use the first recognized format. Try it out with `audio00.html`:

```
<audio controls>
  <source src="dog.mp3" type="audio/mpeg" />
   <source src="dog.ogg" type="video/ogg" />
     The audio tag is not supported in your browser.
     Download the audio <a href="dog.mp3">here</a>.
  </audio>
```

> Best practice is to provide both MP3 and OGG sources in order to take full advantage of HTML5 audio. The browser will take the first recognized format.

Note that Dartium didn't support the `<audio>` format MP3 with local sounds until now. To set up HTML5 audio in the most robust manner, you can also add the `codecs` info to the `type` attribute, as we did in `audio01.html`:

```
<source src="dog.ogg" type="audio/ogg; codecs='vorbis'" />
```

The source can also be a URL reference as in `audio02.html`:

```
src= "http://www.html5rocks.com/en/tutorials/audio/quick/test.mp3"
```

Refer to `http://html5doctor.com/html5-audio-the-state-of-play/` to find out more information. Using sound in Dart is very easy too (see `audio_dart`); just give the `<audio>` element an ID so that you can reference it from code, like this

```
AudioElement thip = querySelector('#thip');
thip.play();
```

Now, the sound file will start to play. We will apply this to enhance our game — we play a sound when two similar images are found, and another when the memory is recalled (in `board.dart`):

```
void onMouseDown(MouseEvent e) {
    // code left out
    if (cell.twin == lastCellClicked) {
        lastCellClicked.hidden = false;
        // play sound found same 2 images:
        AudioElement thip = querySelector('#thip');
        thip.play();
        if (memory.recalled) { // game over
            AudioElement fireballs= querySelector('#fireballs');
            fireballs.play();
        // code left out
    }
}
```

For more serious sound applications, HTML5 introduced the **Web Audio** API. Dart incorporated this in its `dart:web_audio` library. This package makes it possible to process, mix, filter, and synthesize sound in your web applications. A Dart game that uses this is *Pop, Pop, Win!*, a *Minesweeper* variant by Kevin Moore. You can play it at `https://www.dartlang.org/samples/` and find the source at `https://github.com/dart-lang/pop-pop-win`. You can find detailed information on Web Audio at `http://www.html5rocks.com/en/tutorials/webaudio/intro/`.

If you need less sophistication, you can use the `simple_audio` library written by John McCutchan, which you can find at `https://github.com/johnmccutchan/simple_audio`.

The `AudioManager` class is the main entry point in this library. You can create `AudioClips` and `AudioSources` and play clips from the sources with the manager. This library is used in the game **Collision Clones**, which will come next.

The Collision Clones game

This game shows a field of moving cars of different sizes and colors. The player controls the red car (initially at the top-left corner) through the mouse cursor. The objective is to move the red car within the time limit with as few collisions as possible. The lower the speed limit, the slower the cars. The game runs until the time limit is over (in minutes). You will lose if the number of collisions during that time is greater than the time elapsed in seconds. You win if you survive the time limit. If the red car is hit, it will shrink to a small black car. In order to revive it, move the cursor to one of the borders of the board. After a certain number of collisions, clone cars will appear. Here is a typical game screen:

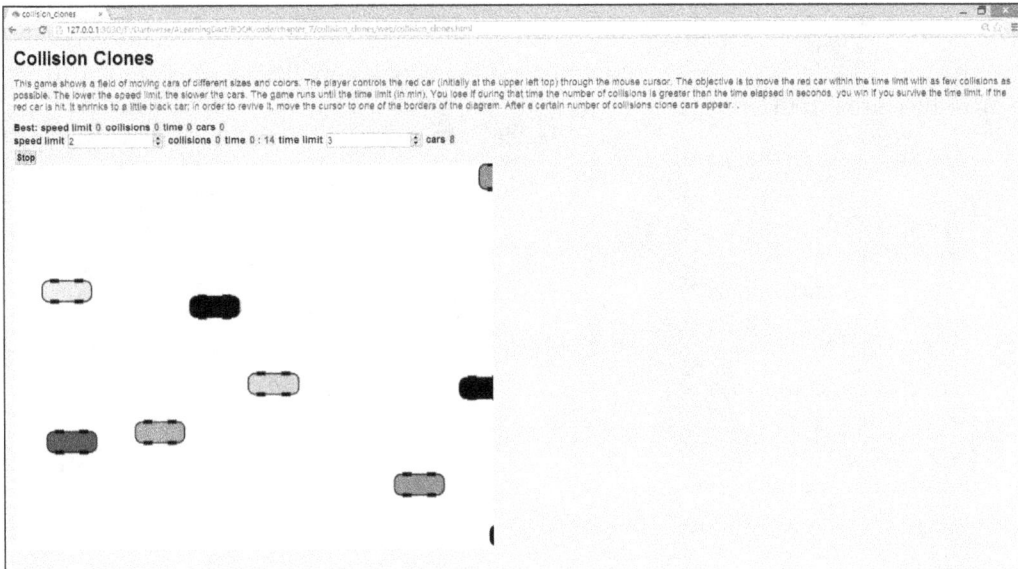

Collision Clones game screen

> For the code file of this section, refer to chapter 7\collision_
> clones and chapter 7\car_collisions in the code bundle. You
> can also get them from GitHub using the following commands:
> **git clone git://github.com/dzenanr/collision_clones.git**
> **git clone git://github.com/dzenanr/car_collisions.git**

This is our first example of a web app, where all the code is assembled in a
collision_clones library that resides in its own lib folder. Because it is also stored
in the packages folder, it can be imported (line (1)) in the start up web\collision_
clones.dart script, where a new object of the Board class is created:

```
import 'package:collision_clones/collision_clones.dart';        (1)
```

```
main() {
  new Board();
}
```

Now, look at pubspec.yaml:

```
dependencies:
  browser: any
```

In the lib\collision_clones.dart library file, all the constituent packages and
source files are imported:

```
library collision_clones;

import 'dart:html';
import 'dart:async';
import "dart:convert";
import 'dart:math';

part 'game_board.dart';
part 'cars.dart';
part 'score.dart';
part 'util/color.dart';
part 'util/git_commands.dart';
part 'util/random.dart';
```

Again, the `view` class is called `Board` (in `game_board.dart`) and its instantiation starts and animates the game. The viewable objects in this game are the cars and, specifically, the red car. They have corresponding classes in `lib\cars.dart` and the `Board` class contains `List<Car>` and a `redCar` variable. Because they share many properties, we let them both inherit from a `Vehicle` abstract class:

```
abstract class Vehicle
class Car extends Vehicle
class RedCar extends Vehicle
```

The `abstract` class contains all that is needed to draw a car in its constructor and the `draw` method: getting the canvas context, calculating a random position (*x*, *y*) and the color code, and the methods on the canvas context we saw in *Chapter 5, Handling DOM in a New Way*, are put to use. The `draw` method is given as follows:

```
draw() {
    context
        ..beginPath()
        ..fillStyle = colorCode
        ..strokeStyle = 'black'
        ..lineWidth = 2;
    roundedCorners(context, x, y, x + width, y + height, 10);
    context
        ..fill()
        ..stroke()
        ..closePath();
    // wheels
    context
        ..beginPath()
        ..fillStyle = '#000000'
        ..rect(x + 12, y - 3, 14, 6)
        ..rect(x + width - 26, y - 3, 14, 6)
        ..rect(x + 12, y + height - 3, 14, 6)
        ..rect(x + width - 26, y + height - 3, 14, 6)
        ..fill()
        ..closePath();
}
```

Every `Car` object has a different speed specified in its constructor: a random number that is lesser than the speed limit:

```
Car(canvas, speedLimit) : super(canvas) {
    var speedNumber = int.parse(speedLimit);
    dx = randomNum(speedNumber);
    dy = randomNum(speedNumber);
}
```

The Car class contains a move method, which is called from displayCars() in Board, that changes the position (line (1)), taking into account that cars must bounce from the borders (line (4)). In line (2), we will test whether the car referred to by it has had a collision with the red car and, in line (3), we will test whether this car has had a collision with the red car:

```
move(RedCar redCar, List<Car> cars) {
    x += dx;                                                    (1)
    y += dy;
    if (redCar.big) {
       redCar.collision(this);                                 (2)
    }
    for (Car car in cars) {                                     (3)
      if (car != this) {
        car.collision(this);
      }
    }
    if (x > canvas.width || x < 0) dx = -dx;                    (4)
    if (y > canvas.height || y < 0) dy = -dy;
}
```

The red car contains some Booleans to determine whether it is in its big or small state and when it is movable. The onMouseDown and onMouseMove events are defined on document property of canvas, and are also there in the red car constructor:

```
RedCar(canvas) : super(canvas) {
    colorCode = bigColorCode;
    width = bigWidth;
    height = bigHeight;
    canvas.document.onMouseDown.listen((MouseEvent e) {   (1)
      movable = !movable;
      if (small) {
        bigger();
      }
    });
    canvas.document.onMouseMove.listen((MouseEvent e) {   (2)
      if (movable) {
        x = e.offset.x - 35;
        y = e.offset.y - 35;
        if (x > canvas.width) {
          bigger();
          x = canvas.width - 20;
        }
// some code left out for brevity
```

The first event handler (line (1)) makes the red car movable after a click on the **Play** button at the beginning of the game or after a click on the **Stop** button. The second handler (line (2)) makes sure the red car is contained within the board's dimensions and that it is revived at the limits of the board after a collision. When the red car collides with another car, the `collision` method in RedCar invokes `smaller()`:

```
smaller() {
    if (big) {
        small = true;
        colorCode = smallColorCode;
        width = smallWidth;
        height = smallHeight;
        collisionCount++;
    }
}
```

The Board class constructs a Score object, a Red Car object, and the other cars. In the code following line (1), the score will be updated, displayed, and stored in the local storage every 1,000 milliseconds (see `save()` and `load()` in the Score class):

```
Board() {
    var bestScore = new Score();
    // code left out
    redCar = new RedCar(canvas);
    cars = new List();
    for (var i = 0; i < carCount; i++) {
        var car = new Car(canvas, score.currentSpeedLimit);
        cars.add(car);
    }
    // code left out
    // active play time:
    new Timer.periodic(const Duration(milliseconds: 1000), (t) {
        if (!stopped && redCar.big) {                              (1)
        // code left out
}
```

Here is a portion of the `displayCars()` code:

```
displayCars() {
    // code left out
    clear();              // nested function !
    for (var i = 0; i <cars.length; i++) {
        cars[i].move(redCar, cars);
        cars[i].draw();
    }
    redCar.draw();
    // code left out
```

The Score class also contains a supporting code to keep track of the counters. This is it, you can find some suggestions for change or improvement in doc\todo.txt.

An important improvement can still be made. The Car class contains both the state information (position, color, and so on) as well as the way to draw itself. The model should not concern itself with the user interface. This separation is achieved in the car_collisions variant, where everything related to drawing is moved to the view class Board. Compare both the versions and see how the separation makes the project much easier to understand and maintain.

Adding video to a web page

Adding video to a web page is as easy to do as adding audio: just add a <video> tag to the HTML with an embedded <source> tag specifying src and type, and Dartium will render this nicely (see video01.html):

```
<video poster="wildlife.jpg" controls>
  <source src="wildlife.ogv" type='video/ogg; codecs="theora,
    vorbis"' />
  <source src="wildlife.webm" type='video/webm; codecs="vp8,
    vorbis"' />
    The video tag is not supported in your browser. Download the
      video <a href="wildlife.webm">here</a>.
</video>
```

> For the code file of this section, refer to chapter 7\video\ in the code bundle.

The `poster` attribute from `<video>` serves to provide the initial image, as shown in the following screenshot:

The poster image with the `<video>` tag

The three important formats you should care about are WEBM, MP4, and OGV. For MP4, use the following type:

```
type='video/mp4; codecs="avc1.42E01E, mp4a.40.2"'
```

Both `<audio>` and `<video>` support other attributes, such as `autoplay` and `loop`.

> For more information, consult `http://www.html5rocks.com/en/tutorials/video/basics/`.

Calling a video from Dart is nothing more than creating a `VideoElement` class that references the `<video>` tag, as in `video2.dart`. The `loop` property will show the video continuously:

```
VideoElement video = querySelector('#video');
video.loop = true;
```

Summary

By thoroughly investigating two games applying all of Dart we have already covered, your Dart star begins to shine. For other Dart games, visit `http://www.builtwithdart.com/projects/games/`.

You can find more information at `http://www.dartgamedevs.org/` on building games. In the next chapter, we will embark on the quest for the holy grail of modern web development: web components.

8
Developing Business Applications with Polymer Web Components

Web components are the hottest new thing, where everybody is looking into and working in the web universe. We will show you how they fit together with HTML5, why they are needed in the web applications of the future, and how Dart brings this to you through Polymer. The following topics will be covered in this chapter:

- How web components change web development
- Web components with `Polymer.dart`
- Two-way data binding in `Polymer.dart`
- The polymer links project
- The category links project
- The project tasks application

How web components change web development

Developers in object oriented languages such as Java (for example, in Swing) and C# / VB.NET (for example, in Windows Forms, ASP.NET, WPF, and Silverlight) are keen to apply inheritance and reuse the components of their app user interfaces (in short, UI). Controls are adapted to specific needs by extending basic UI classes, and controls are assembled into reusable parts of screens (commonly called user or custom controls). Web developers want to be able to do the same; for example, extend a `<button>` tag, encapsulate a piece of markup for reuse, or have a simple way to bind data to an HTML element. However, until now, this wasn't possible in web development. This is exactly the promise of web components: extending HTML, they bring to web development what OO developers expect in their toolkit. Web components enable you to specialize HTML elements with style and code, and W3C is actively engaged in the standardization of this technology. They can be thought of as extending (often, they extend `<div>`, `<span>`, or `<section>` tags) or even as new HTML elements; they create encapsulated, reusable views to be embedded in several places of your application or even across several applications. So, web components give you what you need in order to write data-driven, scalable web applications, namely:

- **Encapsulation**: This is a concept in which structure, style, and behavior are defined separate from the pages in which the component is used

- **Reusability**: This is used by importing components into web pages; a direct consequence from encapsulation

- **Data-binding**: This is to view (one-way) and change (two-way) model data

The code that we need to write is considerably simplified: while using web components, Dart doesn't manipulate the DOM directly anymore, as was done in *Chapter 5*, *Handling DOM in a New Way*, and *Chapter 6*, *Combining HTML5 Forms with Dart*. On the other hand, when it is useful, both the techniques can be combined. For instance, while drawing an icon on the canvas, this can very well be done inside the web component by manipulating the DOM.

The first package, which the Dart team developed for this was called **Web UI**, and some projects were built using it (see *Chapter 10, Local Data and Client-Server Communication*). However, in mid July 2013, the Dart team announced `Polymer.dart`, a Dart port of the Polymer framework (`http://www.polymer-project.org`), in close collaboration with the Google Polymer developers. The Polymer project is a new library on top of Web (or Custom) Components, Model-Driven Views, Shadow DOM (also called Shady Dom, which is new in Polymer 1.0), and many more emerging standards for the web platform to simplify and improve the development process. Although the work is still in progress, Polymer promises to provide a broad set of reusable custom components for developers.

Web components with Polymer.dart

The `Polymer.dart` framework provides a set of Polymer (UI and other) components, but it will only work in the most recent versions of browsers: IE9, IE10, Safari 6, Firefox, and the latest Chrome version (also for Android). It is important to know that, in Polymer, you can only have a single Dart script tag on an HTML document. So, get started with creating a new Polymer application, `polymer1`, by selecting the **Polymer Web application** project template (using the `polymer` library) in Dart Editor.

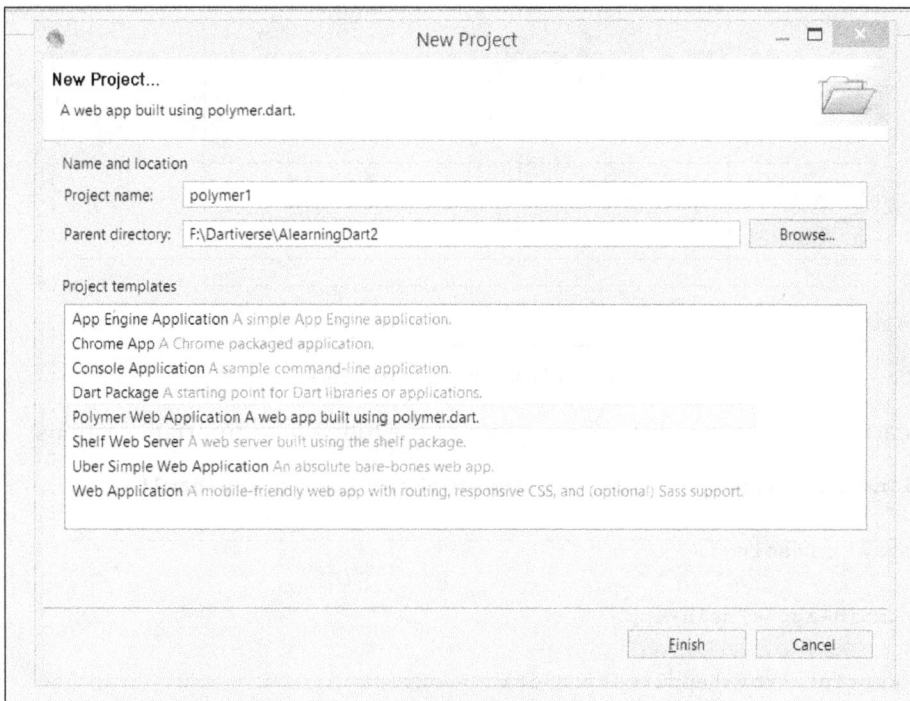

A new Polymer application

Inspecting `pubspec.yaml` will reveal the `polymer` dependency as well as a transformer:

```
dependencies:
  browser: '>=0.10.0 <0.11.0'
  paper_elements: '>=0.7.0 <0.8.0'
  polymer: '>=0.16.0 <0.17.0'
transformers:
- polymer:
    entry_points: web/index.html
```

Pub is invoked automatically and it installs `polymer` and a whole group of packages needed by `polymer` (such as `observe`, `polymer_expressions`, `web_components`, and so on). We'll now examine in detail how a web component is defined in Polymer.

Declaring and instantiating a web component

This is what we will see when the `web\index.html` file is run: a web component from the `paper_elements` package, which expects input and a <p> tag to show the reversed text:

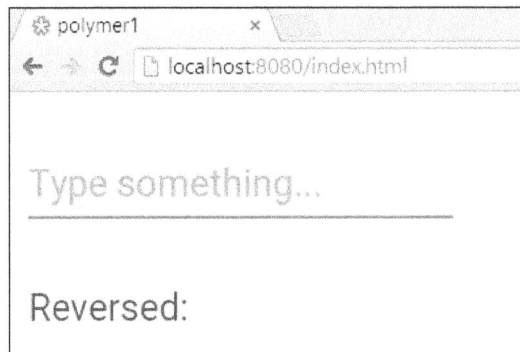

The clickable counter in polymer1

This start up `index.html` HTML file contains the following important sections:

```
<link rel="import" href="packages/polymer1/main_app.html">   (1)

<body unresolved>

  <main-app></main-app>                                       (2)

  <script type="application/dart"> export
    'package:polymer/init.dart';</script>                     (3)
</body>
```

We need `polymer/init.dart` in line (3) to automatically initialize the `polymer` elements. **`<main-app></main-app>`**, in line (2), is the placeholder where our web component will appear. Its definition is imported through the **`<link>`** import in line (1).

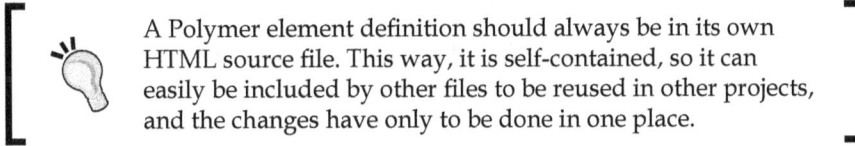

> A Polymer element definition should always be in its own HTML source file. This way, it is self-contained, so it can easily be included by other files to be reused in other projects, and the changes have only to be done in one place.

The name of a component must contain a dash (-); in general, the first half of the name should make it unique (for example, by including a project or a business name) so as to avoid conflicts with the other components. Now, let's turn our attention to the definition of the web component. The structure and style of the `<main-app>` web component is defined in the `lib\main_app.html` file inside `<template>` in a `<polymer-element>` tag, whose name attribute in line (4) is the name of the web component:

```
<polymer-element name="main-app">                    (4)
    <template>
        <style>
            :host {
                display: block;
            }
        </style>

        <paper-input label="Type something..." on-
            keyup="{{reverseText}}"></paper-input>        (5)

        <p>
            Reversed: {{ reversed }}                      (6)
        </p>
    </template>
<script type="application/dart"
    src="main_app.dart"></script>                        (7)
</polymer-element>
```

In general, the `<template>` section contains markup outlining the UI appearance of the web component. We observe that an HTML file containing a Polymer element definition does not need `<html>`, `<head>`, or `<body>` tags. Line (5) shows that `<main-app>` is a paper-input element that reacts on the `keyup` event by calling a `reverseText` method. Line (6) tells us that a `reversed` variable is shown with the polymer expression `{{reversed}}`. This is the typical `{{ expression }}` syntax used for data binding to an expression but, as shown in line (5), an event handler is also called in the same way.

The behavior of the component is defined in the `main_app.dart` Dart script referenced in the `<script>` tag in line (7). This does a lot of things:

```
import 'dart:html';
import 'package:paper_elements/paper_input.dart';
import 'package:polymer/polymer.dart';                         (8)
@CustomTag('main-app')                                         (9)
class MainApp extends PolymerElement {                        (10)
  @observable String reversed = '';                           (11)
  /// Constructor used to create instance of MainApp.
  MainApp.created() : super.created();                        (12)

void reverseText(Event event, Object object, PaperInput target) {
    reversed = target.value.split('').reversed.join('');       (13)
  }
}
```

In line (8), the `polymer` package is imported. `@CustomTag`, in line (9), registers `main-app` as an element in the Polymer framework. Our model is represented by the `MainApp` class in line (10), which has to inherit from the `PolymerElement` class and override its `created()` constructor in line (12). This is because the `polymer` elements are legitimate HTML elements. Note that the name of the Dart class is obtained after converting the first letter of each word separated by - into an uppercase letter, and removing -.

The Polymer framework provides for synchronization of the model with screen data. In this case, it is the `reversed` variable that is annotated with `@observable` in line (11) to indicate simple, one-way (model to screen) data binding. Finally, it contains the `reverseText` method in line (13), which is called at the key up event; this will set `reversed` to the reversed input text. This change will automatically be shown on the web page. In general, the Dart script implements the behavior of the component and can change the model's data. Each time a custom element is instantiated, as in line (2) in the `index.html` file, an instance of the Dart class is created and associated with the custom element. Data bindings in the template are bound to fields in that instance.

> As a best practice, a web component has two files to separate the HTML markup from the Dart code. In some simple examples, you will see the code embedded in the `<script>` tag in the HTML file, but this is not recommended. When both the files have the same name, it is easier to recognize them as parts of the same component.

Developing web applications with web components is a new approach that will let us divide a page in sections and use a web component for each section. If web components become reusable in different contexts, we may have a catalog of web components that would allow us to select and reuse them in a few lines of code. A page can also contain multiple instances of the same component, each behaving independently from each other. A `polymer` element is like a supercharged custom element, with functionality provided by the Polymer framework. It automatically allows for simple component registration and uses the Shadow DOM. This means that its markup is hidden in the web page in which it is embedded, thus providing encapsulation by itself. Polymer uses the composability of elements as much as possible, to the extent that the framework advocates proclaim that everything is a component in Polymer. Let's now examine data binding a bit closer.

Two-way data binding in Polymer.dart

Model Driven View (**MDV**) is a set of techniques to help you bind data to your views in a more direct way than we did in *Chapter 6, Combining HTML5 Forms with Dart*. The idea here is simple:

- We have one or more classes (with properties) in a model
- Our app contains one or more views (implemented as web components) to present the model's data (the data binding)

> For the code files of this section, refer to `code\chapter_8\bank_terminal` in the code bundle.

Data binding can be one-way (model to view) with or without observing the changes in the model: this means that the data from our model (a variable or a method that returns a value) is shown (read-only) on the page, and we do this by writing `{{var}}` on the web page and marking the `var` variable in code as `@observable var`. When its value changes, the altered value will be shown on the web page. In general, you can show any Dart expression with the `{{ expression }}` notation, but be careful that the expression doesn't cause any unwanted side effects by changing the variables. Use `@published var`, when `var` is also an attribute in a tag. Data binding can also be two-way (model to view and view to model), meaning that the data can be shown, but the input from the web page also changes the Dart variables. In other words, the data and the web page are then synchronized.

Data binding combined with event listeners allows us to create simple and sophisticated views for our model in a declarative way, thereby reducing the need to manually create controller objects that do these bindings. They can be exploited fully only as a part of the web components, that is to say, the `polymer` elements. This is what we will do in the following projects in this chapter. Let's apply this first to our Bank Terminal project; we now build a form that also takes an input amount that is deposited in our account, changing the balance on the screen, as shown in the following screenshot:

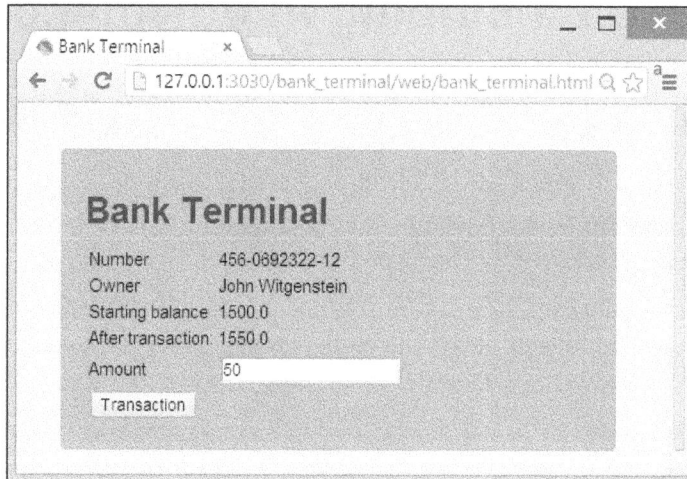

Two-way data binding

The start up `bank_terminal.html` page will show a `<bank-app>` web component through:

```
<h1>Bank Terminal</h1>
<bank-app></bank-app>
```

This web component is linked in with `<link rel="import" href="bank_app.html">`. Our component uses the following markup in the `bank_app.html` file to show the data:

```
<link rel="import" href="bank_account.html">
<link rel="import" href="../../packages/polymer/polymer.html">
<polymer-element name="bank-app">
<template>
  <bank-accountp bac="{{bac}}"></bank-accountp>          (1)
 </template>
 <script type="application/dart" src="bank_app.dart">
  </script>                                              (2)
</polymer-element>
```

In the template in line (1), a second polymer element named `<bank-accountp>` is instantiated. The `bank_app.dart` script publishes and initializes the `BankAccount` object `bac` in lines (3) and (4), respectively:

```
import 'package:polymer/polymer.dart';
import 'package:bank_terminal/bank_terminal.dart';

@CustomTag('bank-app')
class BankApp extends PolymerElement {
  @published BankAccount bac;                           (3)
  BankApp.created() : super.created()  {  }
  attached() {
    super.attached();
    var jw = new Person("John Witgenstein");
    bac = new BankAccount(jw, "456-0692322-12", 1500.0);  (4)
  }
}
```

We also have to override the `attached` method of the `PolymerElement` class, which is called when the element is inserted into the document. The `bac` object is passed to the `<bank-account>` web component in line (1) in the preceding code. The markup of this component is then found in the `bank_account.html` file:

```
<polymer-element name="bank-accountp">
<style> // left out
<template>
<table class="auto-style1" on-keypress="{{enter}}">
    <tr>
     <td class="auto-style2">Number</td>
     <td> {{ bac.number }} </td>                        (1)
    </tr>
```

```
        <tr>
         <td class="auto-style2">Owner</td>
         <td> {{ bac.owner.name}} </td>                  (2)
         <td></td>
        </tr>
        <tr>
         <td class="auto-style2">Starting balance</td>
         <td> {{bac.balance}}</td>
        </tr>
        <tr>
         <td class="auto-style2"> After transaction:</td>
         <td> {{balance}}</td>                            (3)
        </tr>
        <tr>
          <td class="auto-style2">Amount transaction</td>
          <td><input id="amount" type="text"/></td>      (4)
          <td></td>
        </tr>
        <tr>
         <td><button class="btns" on-click="{{transact}}">  (5)
             Transaction</button></td>
        </tr></table></template>
   <script type="application/dart"
     src="bank_account.dart"></script>
```

As the `bac` object is bound to the component, its properties can be shown like `bac.number` in line (1) or even nested properties like in line (2). In line (4), we take in a money amount, which is bound to a variable with the same name in line (13) as in the accompanying `bank_account.dart` script (see the next code). A click on the button in line (5) starts the `transact` event handler in line (11), which changes the `balance` in line (12). To show `balance` in line (3), we need to mark it as `@published` in line (9). In lines (6) to (8), we see the required code to define a Polymer web component. Line (10) shows the `BankAccount.created` constructor, which our web component has to override from the `PolymerElement` class:

```
import 'dart:html';
import 'package:polymer/polymer.dart';                   (6)
@CustomTag('bank-accountp')                               (7)

class BankAccountp extends PolymerElement {               (8)
  @published var bac;
  @published double balance;                              (9)
```

```
  double amount = 0.0;
  BankAccount.created() : super.created() {  }              (10)
  attached() {
    super.attached();
    var jw = new Person("John Witgenstein");
    bac = new BankAccount(jw, "456-0692322-12", 1500.0);
    balance = bac.balance;
  }
  transact(Event e, var detail, Node target) {             (11)
    InputElement amountInput =
    shadowRoot.querySelector("#amount");
    if (!checkAmount(amountInput.value)) return;
    bac.transact(amount);
    balance = bac.balance;                                 (12)
  }
  enter(KeyboardEvent  e, var detail, Node target) {
    if (e.keyCode == KeyCode.ENTER) {
      transact(e, detail, target);
    }
  }
  checkAmount(String in_amount) {
    try {
      amount = double.parse(in_amount);                    (13)
    } on FormatException catch(ex) {
      return false;
    }
    return true;
  }
}
```

Creating the web_links project

Get the code with `git clone git://github.com/dzenanr/web_links.git` command. We start our discussion with the first spiral in the `web_links\web_links_s01` project.

Spiral s01

In this spiral, we just show a web component that contains a list of links of the String type, as shown in the following screenshot:

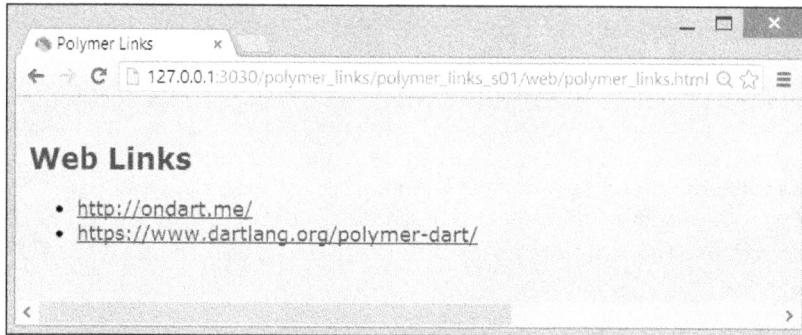

Spiral s01 of web_links

The web\index.html start up HTML page imports the web component with:

```
<link rel="import" href="packages/web_links/links_app.html">
```

The component with the links-app name is instantiated in the <body> tag of the page:

```
<links-app></links-app>
```

The lib\links_app.html file contains the UI definition of the component:

```
<link rel="import" href="../../packages/web_links/link_list.html">
<polymer-element name="links-app">
  <template>
    <link-list></link-list>
  </template>
  <script type="application/dart" src="links_app.dart"></script>
</polymer-element>
```

This in its turn imports a <link-list> web component defined in link_list.html:

```
<polymer-element name="link-list">
  <template>                                          (1)
    <ul>
      <template repeat="{{link in links}}">           (2)
```

```
      <li>
        <a href="{{link}}">                           (3)
          {{link}}
        </a>
      </li>
    </template>
  </ul>
</template>
<script type="application/dart" src="link_list.dart"></script> (4)
</polymer-element>
```

The outer template in line (1) is required. The template in line (2) uses a `repeat` statement to iterate over the `links`: `repeat="{{link in links}}` list. The `link` variable takes on the value of each list item in succession, and is shown through `{{link }}` in the next line. The list is constructed in the `link_list.dart` script referenced in line (4):

```
import 'package:polymer/polymer.dart';
@CustomTag('link-list')
class LinkList extends PolymerElement {
  List links =
    ['http://ondart.me/',
      'https://www.dartlang.org/polymer-dart/'];
  LinkList.created() : super.created();
}
```

Spiral s02

Now, we will base the web component on a model with one simple concept: a web link. This has two attributes: a `name` and a `url`. The `Link` class is defined in `lib\model\links.dart`:

```
class Link {
  String name;
  Uri url;
  Link(this.name, String link) {
    url = Uri.parse(link);
  }
}
```

It is a best practice to put our model in its own links library in a separate lib folder. The Polymer framework is based on the statement: everything is a component. We use a <links-app></links-app> web component in index.html that encapsulates the user interface and is also imported through a <link> tag <link rel="import" href="packages/web_links/links_app.html">. We show all our links as a <link-list> component in links_app.html, so the <link-list> component is embedded in <links-app>:

```
<link rel="import" href="../../packages/web_links/view/link_list.
html">
<polymer-element name="links-app">
  <template>
    <link-list links="{{links}}"></link-list>                    (1)
  </template>
  <script type="application/dart" src="links_app.dart"></script>
</polymer-element>
```

This component in its turn is defined in view\link_list.html and view\link_list.dart.

> Name the definition files of the web component like the component, replacing - with _ . This keeps a more complex project with different components structured.

In the links_app.dart file, we find the code for the <links-app> component that constructs a links collection called links:

```
import 'package:web_links/web_links.dart';
import 'package:polymer/polymer.dart';
@CustomTag('links-app')
class LinksApp extends PolymerElement {
  var links = toObservable(new List<Link>());
  LinksApp.created() : super.created() {
    var link1 = new Link('On Dart', 'http://ondart.me/');
    var link2 = new Link('Polymer.dart'
'https://www.dartlang.org/polymer-dart/');
    var link3 = new Link('Books To Read',
    'http://www.goodreads.com/');
    links..add(link1)..add(link2)..add(link3);          (2)
  }
}
```

Our <links-app> component is now instantiated through the template in line (1) in the preceding code; it needs a links variable, which is made in the LinksApp constructor in line (2).

The web component in `link_list.html` also uses the repeating template introduced in spiral s01, but now shows the names of the links:

```
<template repeat="{{link in links}}">
   <li>
      <a href="{{link.url.toString()}}">
        {{link.name}}
      </a>
   </li>
</template>
```

The `link_list.dart` file now also imports our model from the `links` library and annotates the `links` variable with `@published` in line (3) to show its contents:

```
import 'package:web_links/web_links.dart';
import 'package:polymer/polymer.dart';
@CustomTag('link-list')
class LinkList extends PolymerElement {
  @published List<Link> links;                           (3)
  LinkList.created() : super.created();
}
```

When you run the preceding code, it will look like the following screenshot:

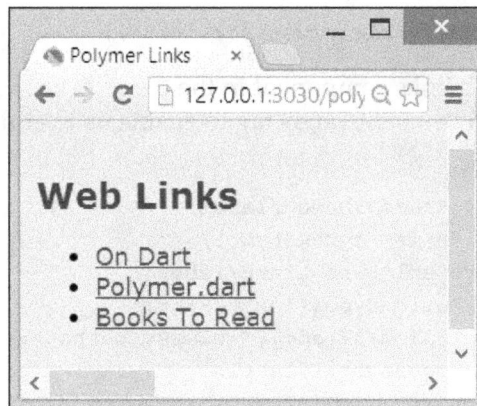

Spiral s02 of web_links

Apart from some added style in spiral s03, the `<links-app>` component is identical to the one in spiral s02.

Spiral s04

In this spiral, we will also provide the possibility to add a web link by the user:

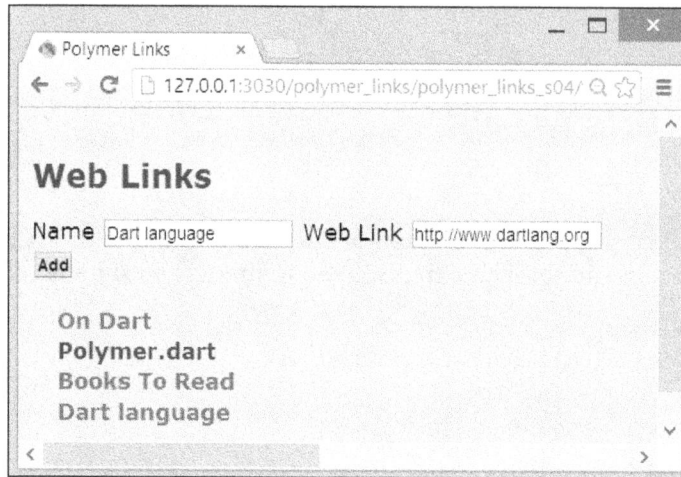

Adding a web link

A new link has to be shown; in order to accomplish this, we have to mark the list with `toObservable` in the `links_app.dart` file:

```
var links = toObservable(new List<Link>());
```

The definition of the web links component in the `link_list.html` file now contains additional UI markup in its `<template>` tag to enable us to add links:

```
<div>
    <label for="name">Name</label>
    <input id="name" type="text"/>
    <label for="url">web Link</label>
    <input id="url" type="text"/><br/>
    <button on-click="{{add}}" class="button">Add</button>    (1)
    <label id="message"></label>
</div>
<ul> <!-- repeating template --> </ul></template>
<script type="application/dart" src="link_list.dart"></script>
```

The add method from line (1) is found in the `link_list.dart` script:

```
add(Event e, var detail, Node target) {                         (2)
    InputElement name = shadowRoot.querySelector("#name");      (3)
    InputElement url = shadowRoot.querySelector ("#url");
    LabelElement message = shadowRoot.querySelector ("#message");
```

```
        var error = false;
        message.text = '';
        if (name.value.trim() == '') {
          message.text = 'name is mandatory; ${message.text}';
          error = true;
        }
        if (url.value.trim() == '') {
          message.text = 'web link is mandatory; ${message.text}';
          error = true;
        }
        if (!error) {
          var weblink = new Link(name.value, url.value);
          weblinks.add(weblink);                              (4)
        }
      }
```

Notice how in line (1) the add event handler is called in { { } }. In line (2), we can see that it has three arguments: the third one is a direct reference to the target element on which the event happened. In line (3) and the ones that follow, we see how to get a reference to the inner markup of a web component. The familiar querySelector method call is now preceded by shadowRoot:

```
shadowRoot.querySelector("#name");
```

Spiral s05

In spiral s05, we add the functionality to store our web links in the local storage by adding the code needed to load and save data to the model. The save functionality is implemented in the link_list.dart script of the <link-list> component. In the preceding code, after line (4), we will now add:

```
if (!error) {
  // previous code
    save();
}
```

We will then add this save method:

```
save() {
  window.localStorage['web_links'] =
  JSON.encode(toJson());
}
```

We want to save our data in the JSON format. To do this, our `Link` model class needs to know how to transform itself in a Map (with a `toJson` method) or to construct itself from a Map (using the `Link.fromJson` constructor):

```
Map<String, Object> toJson() {
    var linkMap = new Map<String, Object>();
    linkMap['name'] = name;
    linkMap['url'] = url.toString();
    return linkMap;
}


Link.fromJson(Map<String, Object> linkMap) {
    name = linkMap['name'];
    url = Uri.parse(linkMap['url']);
}
```

Spiral s06

The constructor `LinksApp()` method in `links_app.dart` first creates a list in line (4), and then calls the `load()` method in line (5) to read the data from the local storage:

```
    var links = toObservable(new List<Link>());           (4)
LinksApp.created() : super.created() {
  load();                                                 (5)
}


load() {
  String json = window.localStorage['web_links'];
  if (json == null) {
    init();                                               (6)
  } else {
    fromJson(JSON.decode(json));                          (7)
  }
}
```

If nothing was stored yet, the `Model` object is initialized via the `init()` method in line (6), otherwise, it is parsed from local storage in line (7). In line (4), the `List` object of links is created. As there is only one `model` object, we can safely refer to the unique links object of `model` to feed links within the web component's Dart code.

In spiral s06, the possibility is added to remove links, as shown in the following screenshot:

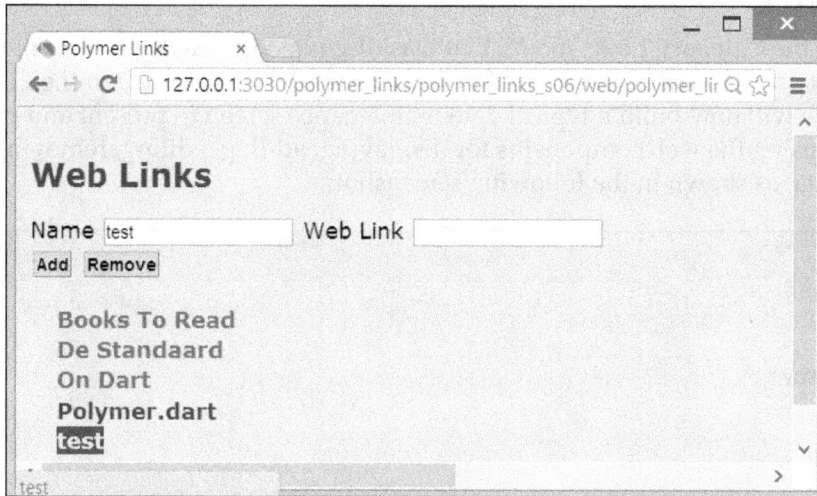

Removing a web link

To allow this, a second button is placed inside the `<template>` tag of the `<link-list>` component:

```
<button on-click="{{delete}}" class="button">Remove</button>
```

The `delete` method is implemented in the script of the `link_list.dart` component:

```
delete(Event e, var detail, Node target) {
  InputElement name = shadowRoot.querySelector("#name");
  InputElement url = shadowRoot.querySelector ("#url");
  LabelElement message = shadowRoot.querySelector("#message");
  message.text = '';
  Link link = links.find(name.value);
  if (link == null) {
    message.text = 'web link with this name does not exist';
  } else {
    url.value = link.url.toString();
    if (links.remove(link)) save();
  }
}
```

Using Polymer for the category links project

On top of the Category Links model that was discussed in *Chapter 4, Modeling Web Applications with Model Concepts and Dartlero* (the model is contained in the `lib` folder), we will now build a typical data maintenance screen to present and change link data using the web components for displaying, adding, editing, removing, and saving data, as shown in the following screenshot:

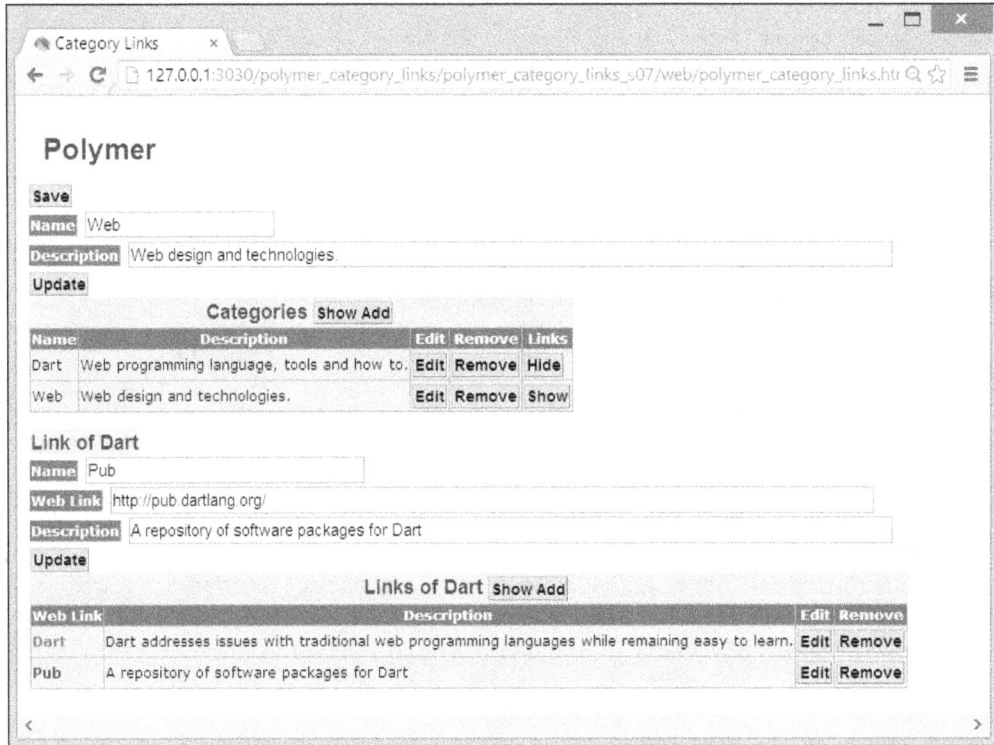

The category_links application

You can get the code with the following command:

```
git clone
git://github.com/dzenanr/polymer_category_links.git
```

In the final spiral, there are three web components per concept of the model: table (for a list), add (to add an element to the list), edit (to edit an element of the list); they can be found in the web\component folder. In the Spiral s01 section, only the Category entity is defined as ConceptEntity together with its categories collection. The test\categories_entities_test.dart script applies unittest on this model. In spiral s01, we build a component for the Category entity: this is the first step toward the upper part of the preceding screenshot. In this spiral, we only show a table with the category data, using a <category-table> web component, as shown in the following screenshot:

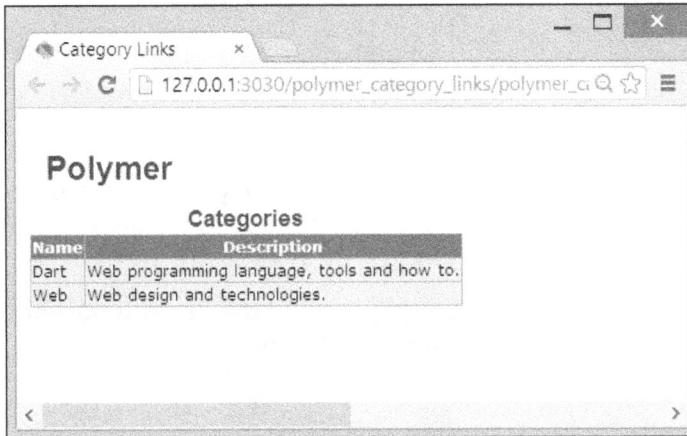

Category_links spiral s01

The polymer_category_links.html page exposes a <polymer-app> web component defined in the polymer_app.html file:

```
    <link rel="import"
    href="view/component/category/category_table.html">        (1)
<polymer-element name="polymer-app">
    <template>
    <category-table categories="{{categories}}">
</category-table>                                               (2)
    </template>
    <script type="application/dart"
    src="polymer_app.dart"></script>
</polymer-element>
```

This contains the `<category-table>` component in line (2) that shows the data
from the `categories` collection, which is made and filled with data in line (4) in
`polymer_app.dart`:

```dart
import 'package:polymer_category_links/category_links.dart';   (3)
import 'package:polymer/polymer.dart';
@CustomTag('polymer-app')
class PolymerApp extends PolymerElement {
  @observable Categories categories;
  PolymerApp.created() : super.created() {
    var categoryLinksModel = new CategoryLinksModel();
    categoryLinksModel.init();                                 (4)
    categories = categoryLinksModel.categories;
  }
}
```

Line (3) imports the model. The `categories` variable in the `<category-table>`
component gets its value from the `{{ categories }}` polymer expression, where
the `categories` object in the expression is the property of the `<polymer-app>`.

In this way, data from the application is passed to the web component. The
`<category-table>` component is imported through line (1) and is defined
in the `category_table.html` file:

```html
<polymer-element name="category-table">
  <template>
    // <style> markup omitted
    <table>
      <caption class="marker">
        Categories
      </caption>
      <tr>
        <th>Name</th>
        <th>Description</th>
      </tr>
      <tbody template repeat="{{category in
      categories.toList()}}">                                  (5)
        <tr>
          <td>{{category.code}}</td>
          <td>{{category.description}}</td>
        </tr>
      </tbody>
    </table>
  </template>
  <script type="application/dart" src="category_table.dart"></script>
</polymer-element>
```

The `repeat-template` in the `<tbody>` tag in line (5) iterates through `List` to show the categories declared in the `category_table.dart` file:

```dart
import 'package:polymer_category_links/category_links.dart';
import 'package:polymer/polymer.dart';
@CustomTag('category-table')
class CategoryTable extends PolymerElement {
  @published Categories categories;
  CategoryTable.created() : super.created();
}
```

In spiral s02, the application is enriched with the add functionality, as shown in the following screenshot. Now, we can add new categories.

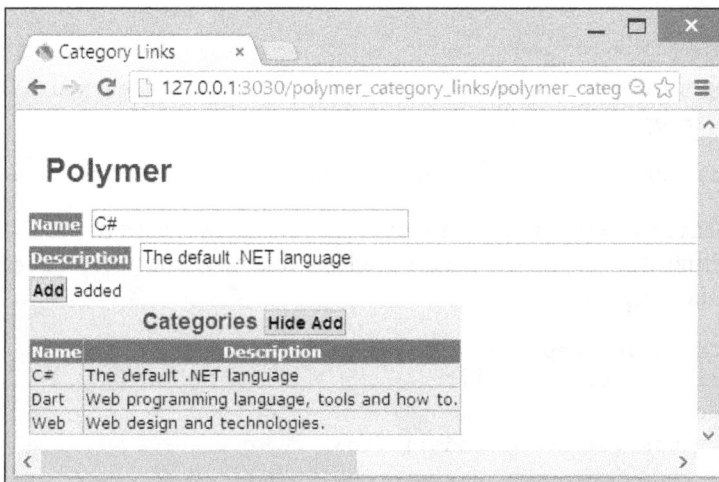

Category_links spiral s02

This is achieved through a `<category-add>` component that is embedded in the `<category-table>` component. It is only shown when `showAdd` is `true`:

```html
<template if="{{showAdd}}">
    <category-add
      categories="{{categories}}">
    </category-add>
</template>
```

In the **Categories** caption (in the table header), a button is added to toggle the appearance of the `add` component:

```html
<button id="show-add" on-click="{{show}}">Show Add</button>
```

The button is monitored by the `showAdd` Boolean variable marked as `observable` in the script:

```
@observable bool showAdd = false;
show(Event e, var detail, Node target) {
  ButtonElement addCategory = shadowRoot.querySelector("#show-
  add");
  if (addCategory.text == 'Show Add') {
    showAdd = true;
    addCategory.text = 'Hide Add';
  } else {
    showAdd = false;
    addCategory.text = 'Show Add';
  }
}
```

Now, the categories data can change, so we must mark it as `observable`. This is done in `polymer_app.dart` through:

```
categories.internalList = toObservable(categories.internalList);
```

This `internalList` is a property of the `ConceptEntities` class in the Dartlero model and is inherited by the `Categories` class. It is now shown in `category-table` through the following code:

```
<tbody template repeat="{{category in
categories.internalList}}">
    <tr>
      <td>{{category.code}}</td>
      <td>{{category.description}}</td>
    </tr>
</tbody>
```

Our `add` component defined in the `\category_add.html` component contains two input text fields and an **Add** button with an `add` event handler that checks whether a name is given and the category is not yet in use. The code property is inherited from `ConceptEntity` in Dartlero and used as a category name; the inherited `add` method checks that the code is unique. Here is the code from `category_add.dart`:

```
add(Event e, var detail, Node target) {
    InputElement code = shadowRoot.querySelector("#code");
    InputElement description = shadowRoot.querySelector
        ("#description");
    Element message = shadowRoot.querySelector("#message");
    var error = false;
    message.text = '';
```

```
    if (code.value.trim() == '') {
      message.text = 'category name is mandatory;
                    ${message.text}';
      error = true;
    }
    if (!error) {
      var category = new Category();
      category.code = code.value;
      category.description = description.value;
      if (categories.add(category)) {
        message.text = 'added';
        categories.order();
      } else {
        message.text = 'category name already in use';
      }
    }
  }
}
```

Spiral s03 adds an **Edit** functionality analogous to **Add**. This is achieved by a second embedded <category-edit> web component, again shown through a conditional template:

```
<template if="{{showEdit}}">
  <category-edit categories="{{categories}}"
    category="{{category}}">
  </category-edit>
</template>
```

Here, the categories and category properties of the category table component are passed to the <category edit> component by using the {{categories}} and {{category }} expressions. We will also add a new button in the table row:

```
<td><button on-click="{{edit}}" category-
code={{category.code}}>Edit</button></td>
```

This button has the following event handler:

```
edit(Event e, var detail, Element target) {
  String code = target.attributes['category-code'];    (1)
  category = categories.find(code);
  showEdit = true;
  }
```

Notice how we get the category code as the value of an attribute in line (1). The edit component is defined in component\category_edit.html. It is nearly identical to the add component, but the **Name** field is read-only. The following is a snippet of the HTML code:

```
<input readonly="true" value="{{category.code}}"/>
<br/>
<input id="{{category.code}}-description"
   type="text" size="96" value="{{description}}"/>        (2)
```

To be able to change the description, we will have to use a description variable in line (2) that is marked as @published and set to the category description in the attached method in category_edit.dart in line (3):

```
@published String description;
   CategoryEdit.created() : super.created();
   attached() {
     super.attached();
     description = category.description;              (3)
   }
```

The **Update** button calls the corresponding method in the same script:

```
update(Event e, var detail, Node target) {
   category.description = description;
   categories.order();                               (4)
   var polymerApp = querySelector('#polymer-app');
   var categoryTable =
polymerApp.shadowRoot.querySelector('#category-
   table');                                          (5)
   categoryTable.showEdit = false;                   (6)
}
```

The sorting of categories in line (4) is also needed to show the new description. A previously instantiated web component can also be retrieved by querySelector. Line (5) uses this to toggle the appearance of the edit component in line (6).

Adding local storage

Spiral s04 adds persistency to the browser local storage; our model `Category` class implements the necessary `toJson` and `fromJson` methods. In the body of the `<polymer-app>` component, a **Save** button is added, which is coupled to a `save()` method in `polymer_app.dart`:

```
save(Event e, var detail, Node target) {
    window.localStorage['polymer_category_links'] =
        JSON.encode(categories.toJson());
  }
```

The data is then read from the local storage in the constructor of the `<polymer-app>` component in line (1) of the following code (see `polymer_app.dart`):

```
PolymerApp.created() : super.created() {
  var categoryLinksModel = new CategoryLinksModel();
  categories = categoryLinksModel.categories;
  String json = window.localStorage['polymer_category_links']; (1)
  if (json == null) {
    categoryLinksModel.init();
  } else {
    categories.fromJson(JSON.decode(json));
  } .
  categories.internalList = toObservable(categories.internalList);
}
```

If the data is not in the local storage, the `init()` method is called and the model is populated. Spiral s04 also adds a **Remove** functionality through a new button in every table row, which will invoke the following method in `category_table.dart`:

```
delete(Event e, var detail, Element target) {
    String code = target.attributes['category-code'];
    category = categories.find(code);
    categories.remove(category);
  }
```

Now, how about viewing the links for each category? This is taken care of in spiral s05, first by adding the Link and Links classes to our model in lib\model\link_ entities.dart. Being good Dartlero citizens, they know to construct themselves the fromJson method and deconstruct the toJson method, so they are ready for (local storage) persistence. Test programs are also provided in test\model. When the app is run, a **Show** button is added to every category row. If this is clicked on, a new <link-table> web component will appear with the links of the selected category shown; this was added to <category-table>. This can be seen in the *Category_links spiral s01* screenshot, where the **Web Link** column contains real hyperlinks:

```
<template if="{{showCategoryLinks}}">
    <link-table category="{{category}}"></link-table>      (2)
</template>
```

Here is the code for the **Show** button:

```
<button on-click="{{showLinks}}" category-
code={{category.code}}>Show</button>
```

When clicked on, the showLinks method from category_table.dart will be executed:

```
showLinks(Event e, var detail, Element target) {
  String code = target.attributes['category-code'];
  ButtonElement categoryLinks = target;
  if (!showCategoryLinks && categoryLinks.text == 'Show') {
    showCategoryLinks = true;
    category = categories.find(code);
    categoryLinks.text = 'Hide';
  } else if (showCategoryLinks && categoryLinks.text == 'Hide')
  {
    showCategoryLinks = false;
    categoryLinks.text = 'Show';
  }
}
```

This code toggles the appearance of the <link-table> component in line (2) in the preceding code, which also passes the category variable; the <link-table> component gets this value in its attached() method in link_table.dart:

```
class LinkTable extends PolymerElement {
  @published Category category;
  @published Links links;
  @observable bool showAdd = false;
  attached() {
```

```
super. attached();
links = category.links;
links.internalList = toObservable(links.internalList);
}
```

The links are shown in a repeating template in the `link_table.html` file:

```
<tbody template repeat="{{link in links.internalList}}">
    <tr>
      <td>
        <a href="{{link.url.toString()}}">
          {{link.code}}
        </a>
      </td>
      <td>{{link.description}}</td>
    </tr>
</tbody>
```

This `<link-table>` web component also has a **Show Add** button to activate a `<link-add>` component in a conditional template. This is shown when `@observable bool showAdd` becomes true and toggled in the code of the `show` method of the `LinkTable` class.

The `link-add` web component is very similar to `category-add`. So, with what we discussed here, you should be able to analyze the code for yourself.

Spiral s06 introduces the edit functionality for links through a new `<link-edit>` component and finally, in spiral s07, you can remove links from a category. Now, you have all the knowledge to completely understand the code in these last spirals. Moreover, you are able to apply the model and build a web components app for every (*1-n*) relation between data, such as `Departments` and `Employees`, or `Orders` and `Order Details`. We now look at using web components in a (*n-m*) or many-to-many relationship.

Applying web components to the project tasks app

> Get the code with the following command:
> ```
> git clone
> git://github.com/dzenanr/polymer_project_tasks.git
> ```

The model that forms the basis for this app is a typical many-to-many relationship between the two entry concepts: project and employee. A project has many employees, and an employee works on many projects. The many-to-many relationship between project and employee is normalized into two one-to-many relationships by introducing the intermediary task concept; a project consists of many tasks and an employee has many tasks: project (*1-n*) task and employee (*1-n*) task.

A project has a name (its ID), a description, and a tasks collection. An employee has an `email` (its ID), a `lastName`, and a `firstName` (both required) attributes, and a tasks collection. A task has a project, an employee, and a description: its ID is composed of the IDs of the project and employee, so an employee can only have, at the most, one task in a project. The code for this model is based on the Dartlero framework and can be found in the `lib\model` folder. Let's say that we want to look up a project first, and then display its tasks. In this case, the relationship between project (*1-n*) and task is internal. This means that you will have two hierarchical structures: projects with their tasks and employees only (employees without tasks). In each task, you will have a reference to its employee. The data could be saved as two JSON documents in two different files or in the local storage under two different keys. You will be able to see the difference in code by looking at the `toJson` methods for project in the `projects.dart` file:

```
Map<String, Object> toJson() {
    Map<String, Object> entityMap = new Map<String, Object>();
    entityMap['code'] = code;
    entityMap['name'] = name;
    entityMap['description'] = description;
    entityMap['tasks'] = tasks.toJson(); // saving tasks
    return entityMap;
}
```

Compare this with the same method for employee in the `employee.dart` file (the same is true for the `fromJson` methods):

```
Map<String, Object> toJson() {
    Map<String, Object> entityMap = new Map<String, Object>();
    entityMap['code'] = code;
    entityMap['lastName'] = lastName;
    entityMap['firstName'] = firstName;
    entityMap['email'] = email;
    return entityMap;
}
```

When you load the data, you will need to recreate the relationship between employee (*1-n*) and task in both directions by using the employee's `email` in each task. After the load, all the relationships become internal and there are no reference IDs in the model (no `employee email` in every task, only the `employee` and `project` properties), which means that the model in the main memory is an object model. On the startup, our app instantiates the `<polymer-app>` component in the `polymer_project_tasks.html` file, which fires the `PolymerApp.created()` constructor. Here, the model objects are created and the data is either loaded from the local storage or, if the data was not saved yet, it is initialized by calling the `tasksModel.init()` method:

```
static const String EMPLOYEE_TASKS = 'polymer-employee-tasks';
static const String PROJECT_TASKS = 'polymer-project-tasks';
PolymerApp.created() : super.created() {
  tasksModel = TasksModel.one();
  employees = tasksModel.employees;
  projects = tasksModel.projects;
  // tasksModel.init()  // comment load to reinit
  load();
  employees.internalList= toObservable(employees.internalList);(1)
  projects.internalList = toObservable(projects.internalList);  (2)
}

load() {
  loadEmployees();
  loadProjects();
}

loadEmployees() {
  String json = window.localStorage[EMPLOYEE_TASKS];
  if (json == null) {
    tasksModel.init();
  } else {
```

```
        employees.fromJson(JSON.decode(json));
    }
    employees.order();
}


loadProjects() {
    String json = window.localStorage[PROJECT_TASKS];
    if (json != null) {
        projects.fromJson(JSON.decode(json));
    }
    projects.order();
}
```

Lines (1) and (2) are there so that the web components show employee or project updates when a new employee or project is added or removed: this is done by annotating the List with toObservable. The web component defined in the polymer_app.html file shows a **Save** button:

```
<button on-click="{{save}}">Save</button>
```

The save() method is also contained in the polymer_app.dart file and saves the data in the local storage:

```
save(Event e, var detail, Node target) {
    saveEmployees();
    saveProjects();
}
saveEmployees() {
    window.localStorage[EMPLOYEE_TASKS] =
        JSON.encode(employees.toJson());
}
saveProjects() {
    window.localStorage[PROJECT_TASKS] =
        JSON.encode(projects.toJson());
}
```

The initial screen shows all **Projects** and all **Employees**, as shown in the following screenshot:

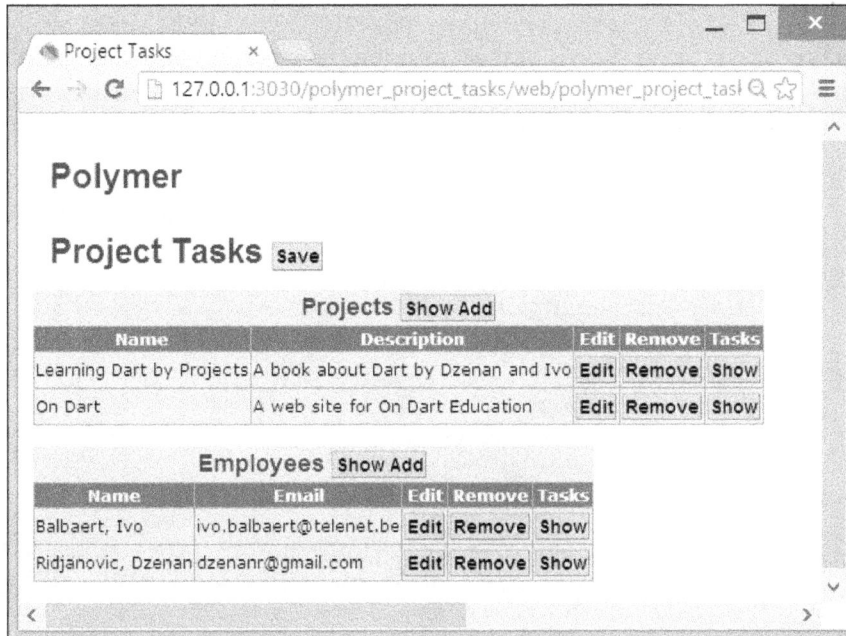

Startup of app Project Tasks

Here, we use two `<project-table>` and `<employee-table>` web components:

```
<project-table id="project-table"
    projects="{{ projects }}">
</project-table>
<employee-table id="employee-table"
    employees="{{ employees }}">
</employee-table>
```

They are imported through:

```
<link rel="import" href="component/employee/employee_table.html">
<link rel="import" href="component/project/project_table.html">
```

As usual, the code of the components resides in `lib\view\component`. We see that both the entities have an **Add** functionality together with **Edit**, **Remove**, and **Show** tasks. The `<employee-table>` component defined in the `employee_table.html` file is indeed composed of three other components: `<employee-add>`, `<employee-edit>`, and `<task-table>`, again shown in the conditional templates controlled by the `showAdd`, `showEdit`, and `showTasks` Boolean variables; these are all marked as `@observable` in the `EmployeeTable` class:

```
<template if="{{showAdd}}">
  <employee-add employees="{{employees}}"></employee-add>
</template>
<template if="{{showEdit}}">
  <employee-edit employees="{{employees}}"
    employee="{{employee}}"></employee-edit>
</template>
<template if="{{showTasks}}">
  <task-table id="task-table" employee="{{employee}}">
  </task-table>
</template>
```

The employees are shown through a repeating template in an HTML table:

```
<tbody template repeat="employee in employees.internalList">
  <tr>
    <td>{{ employee.name }}</td>
    <td>{{ employee.email }}</td>
    <td><button on-click="{{edit}}" code="{{employee.code}}>(2)
        Edit</button></td>
    <td><button on-click="{{delete}}" code="{{employee.code}}>
      Remove</button></td>
    <td><button on-click="{{showEmployeeTasks}}"
    code="{{employee.code}}>Show</button></td>
  </tr>
</tbody>
```

The behavior of the **`<employee-table>`** component is defined in the **`employee_table.dart`** file:

```
@CustomTag('employee-table')
class EmployeeTable extends PolymerElement {
  @published Employees employees;
  Employee employee;
  @observable bool showAdd = false;
  @observable bool showEdit = false;
  @observable bool showTasks = false;
```

```
show(Event e, var detail, Node target) {
  ButtonElement showAddButton = $['show-add'];          (3)
  if (showAddButton.text == 'Show Add') {
    showAdd = true;
    showAddButton.text = 'Hide Add';
  } else {
    showAdd = false;
    showAddButton.text = 'Show Add';
  }
}
edit(Event e, var detail, Element target) {
  String code = target.attributes['code'];              (4)
  employee = employees.find(code);
  showEdit = true;
}
delete(Event e, var detail, Element target) {
  String code = target.attributes['code'];
  employee = employees.find(code);
  for (var task in employee.tasks) {
    task.project.tasks.remove(task);
  }
  employees.remove(employee);
  showTasks = false;
}
showEmployeeTasks(Event e, var detail, Element target) {
  String code = target.attributes['code'];
  ButtonElement tasksButton = target;
  if (!showTasks && tasksButton.text == 'Show') {
    showTasks = true;
    employee = employees.find(code);
    employee.tasks.internalList =
  toObservable(employee.tasks.internalList);
    employee.tasks.order();
    tasksButton.text = 'Hide';
  } else if (showTasks && tasksButton.text == 'Hide') {
    showTasks = false;
    tasksButton.text = 'Show';
  }
}
}
```

In line (3), we have used $['show-add'] as an alternative way of writing `querySelector('#show-add')`. It will probably remind you of jQuery and is included in Polymer. Note how the edit event handler (as well as delete and showEmployeeTasks) gets passed the employee code through line (4), because it is an attribute of the button (see line (2)). If we expand the three subcomponents of the `<employee-table>` component, we will get the following screen:

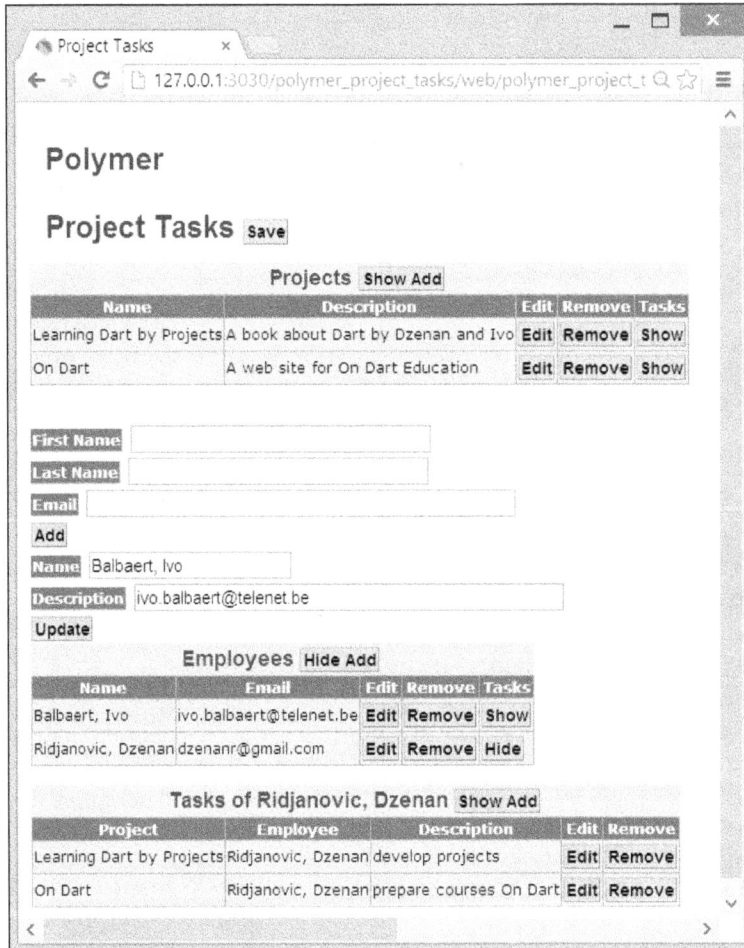

All components of employee activated

The `<employee-add>` component is defined in the `employee_add.html` file:

```
<polymer-element name="employee-add">
  <template>
    <style> // left out </style>
    <br/>
    <label for="first-name">First Name</label>
    <input id="first-name" type="text" size="32"/>
    <br/>
    <label for="last-name">Last Name</label>
    <input id="last-name" type="text" size="32"/>
    <br/>
    <label for="email">Email</label>
    <input id="email" type="text" size="48"/>
    <br/>
    <button on-click="{{add}}">Add</button>
    <span id="message"></span>
  </template>
  <script type="application/dart"
  src="employee_add.dart"></script>
  </polymer-element>
```

The `add` method in the `employee_add.dart` file verifies that all the fields are filled in. If so, a new `Employee` object is made and added (only when the employee was new) to the `employees` collection:

```
class EmployeeAdd extends PolymerElement {
  @published Employees employees;
  add(Event e, var detail, Node target) {
    InputElement firstName = $['first-name'];
    InputElement lastName = $['last-name'];
    InputElement email = $['email'];
    Element message = $['message'];
    var error = false;
    message.text = '';
    if (firstName.value.trim() == '') {
      message.text = 'employee first name is required;
       ${message.text}';
      error = true;
    }
    if (lastName.value.trim() == '') {
```

```
        message.text = 'employee last name is required;
        ${message.text}';
        error = true;
      }
      if (email.value.trim() == '') {
        message.text = 'employee email is required;
        ${message.text}';
        error = true;
      }
      if (!error) {
        var employee = new Employee();
        employee.firstName = firstName.value;
        employee.lastName = lastName.value;
        employee.email = email.value;
        if (employees.add(employee)) {
          message.text = 'added';
          employees.order();                              (1)
        } else {
          message.text = 'employee email already in use';
        }
      }
    }
  }
```

The `<employee-table>` component shows the newly added employee because of line (1). The UI of the `<employee-edit>` component is defined in the employee_edit.html file; the update is called in the employee_edit.dart file:

```
class EmployeeEdit extends PolymerElement {
  @published Employees employees;
  @published Employee employee;
  EmployeeEdit.created() : super.created();



  update(Event e, var detail, Node target) {
      var polymerApp = querySelector('#polymer-app');
      EmployeeTable employeeTable =
          polymerApp.shadowRoot.querySelector('#employee-table');
      employeeTable.showEdit = false;
      polymerApp.saveData();
      window.location.reload();
  }}
```

Deleting an employee is covered in the `delete` method of the `employee_table.dart` file. The **Show Tasks** button activates the `<task-table>` component. Its `<template>` definition in the `task_table.html` file repeats over all the tasks:

```
<tbody template repeat="{{task in tasks.internalList}}">
  <tr>
    <td>{{task.project.name}}</td>
    <td>{{task.employee.name}}</td>
    <td>{{task.description}}</td>
    <td><button on-click="{{edit}}"
  code="{{task.code}}">Edit</button></td>
    <td><button on-click="{{delete}}"
      code="{{task.code}}">Remove</button></td>
  </tr>
</tbody>
```

The browser now shows the name of the employee or project. This component also envelops two other components: tasks can be added through the `<task-add>` component, edited through the `<task-edit>` component, and also be removed.

The Add and Remove task propagations

A new task must be related to one project and one employee. This means that a new task, as one and only one object, must be added to two different collections of tasks: one for the project and the other for the employee. In this application, the internal project-task relationship is used to add a task to its project. The external task-employee relationship is used to lookup an employee for the new task of the project. In this application, a task cannot be added to an employee.

When a task is removed from the project's tasks, it must also be removed from the employee's tasks and vice versa. When a project is removed, its tasks cannot be accessed anymore. These tasks must be removed from the collections of tasks related to the employees found in the project's tasks. Similarly, when an employee is removed, its tasks cannot be accessed anymore. These tasks must be removed from the collections of tasks related to the projects found in the employee's tasks.

The **Add** and **Remove** propagations of the tasks in the model must be reflected in the display of the web components. When a task is updated (description only in this application), there is no need to update the propagations in the model because there is only one task with the same project and the same employee. However, the same task (with the same project and the same employee) may be displayed in two different web components. When this task is updated, the new description must show up in the display of both the web components.

As it is built in exactly the same way, you should now be able to understand the other web components: `<project-table>`, and its `<project-add>` and `<project-edit>` subcomponents, together with `<task-table>`. Used in the project context, the task table also shows a `<task-add>` component and a remove functionality. Now, here is the lookup of an employee while adding a task in the `task_add.html` file:

```
<select id="employee-lookup">
      <option template repeat="{{employee in
  employees.internalList}}"> {{employee.code}} </option>
</select>
```

In the `add` event handler, its value is retrieved with the following code:

```
SelectElement employeeLookup = $['employee-lookup'];
String code = employeeLookup.value;
```

Summary

This chapter showed you that it is easy to build web apps that work with data using data binding and web components in `Polymer.dart`. We did this by exploring three projects: links, category links, and project-tasks-employee; the last two by building up the model starting from the Dartlero framework. Web components through Polymer will revolutionize the way future web apps are built.

In the next chapter, we will focus on how to build web apps following the MVC pattern and using the dartling modeling framework.

9
Modeling More Complex Applications with dartling

In *Chapter 4*, *Modeling Web Applications with Model Concepts and Dartlero*, we discussed the importance of modeling the data in your domain before starting your app. We used model concepts to visually represent the model, and showed a simple modeling framework called **Dartlero**. In this chapter, we will discuss the full blown domain modeling framework dartling, which can take the JSON export of model concepts as an input to generate code for the model as well as to generate default app code. We do this by developing the Travel Impressions model and app.

Next, we look at the **Model View Controller** (**MVC**) design pattern and why it is a good fit for web applications. This is put into practice by developing a `todomvc` application in spirals. Again, model concepts and dartling are used to generate the basic application code. So, the following are the topics of this chapter:

- The dartling domain modeling framework
- Design of the Travel Impressions model in spirals
- Code generation of Travel Impressions from the model
- Initializing the Travel Impressions model with data
- Testing the Travel Impressions model
- What is the MVC pattern and why is it used in software development?
- The TodoMVC app

The dartling domain modeling framework

The dartling (`https://github.com/dzenanr/dartling`) is a domain model framework for the development of complex models with many concepts and relationships. It takes care of a lot of functionality, greatly reducing the amount of code you would need to write. A dartling model is first designed in the graphical tool model concepts, as shown in *Chapter 4*, *Modeling Web Applications with Model Concepts and Dartlero*. A dartling model consists of **concepts**, concept **attributes**, and concept **neighbors**. Two neighbors make a **relationship** between two concepts. A relationship has two directions; each direction going from one concept to another neighbor concept. Standard **one-to-many**, **many-to-many**, and **is-a** relationships are supported. When both concepts are the same, the relationship is reflexive. When there are two relationships between the same but different concepts, the relationships are twins.

The code for a dartling model is generated from the JSON representation of a graphical model. The model is initialized with some basic data and tested (models' tests are the best way to start learning dartling). We can also generate a default web application; whose purpose is to validate the model by a user in order to discover missing concepts, attributes, and relationships; and improve the existing ones.

A dartling model has access to actions, action pre and post validations (these are validations of the data done before and after actions), error handling, select data views, view update propagations, reaction events, transactions (a transaction is an action that contains other actions), and sessions with the history of actions and transactions so that *undos* and *redos* on the model may be done.

In dartling, there may be multiple domains and multiple models within the domains, which can be used together. A model has **entry points** that are entities. From an entity in one of the entry entities, child entities may be obtained. Data navigation is done by following the parent or child neighbors. You can add, remove, update, find, select, and order (sort) the data. Actions or transactions may be used to support unrestricted undos and redos in a domain session. The domain allows any object to react to actions (action events) in its models.

To understand what else you can do with dartling, clone it from Git and examine its API defined in the abstract classes with its API at the end of their names. The two most important ones are `EntitiesApi` and `EntityApi`; they provide the public methods available in dartling to handle the entities. Dart generics are used to enforce a specific type for a dartling entity, as shown in the following code snippet:

```
abstract class EntitiesApi<E extends EntityApi<E>> implements
Iterable<E> {
  Concept get concept;
  ValidationErrorsApi get errors;
```

```
    EntitiesApi<E> get source;

    E firstWhereAttribute(String code, Object attribute);
    E random();
    E singleWhereOid(Oid oid);
    EntityApi singleDownWhereOid(Oid oid);
    E singleWhereCode(String code);
    E singleWhereId(IdApi id);
    E singleWhereAttributeId(String code, Object attribute);

    EntitiesApi<E> copy();
    // sort, but not in place
    EntitiesApi<E> order([int compare(E a, E b)]);
    EntitiesApi<E> selectWhere(bool f(E entity));
    EntitiesApi<E> selectWhereAttribute(String code, Object
      attribute);
    EntitiesApi<E> selectWhereParent(String code, EntityApi parent);
    EntitiesApi<E> skipFirst(int n);
    EntitiesApi<E> skipFirstWhile(bool f(E entity));
    EntitiesApi<E> takeFirst(int n);
    EntitiesApi<E> takeFirstWhile(bool f(E entity));
    List<Map<String, Object>> toJson();
    void clear();
    void sort([int compare(E a, E b)]); // in place sort
    bool preAdd(E entity);
    bool add(E entity);
    bool postAdd(E entity);
    bool preRemove(E entity);
    bool remove(E entity);
    bool postRemove(E entity);
}

abstract class EntityApi<E extends EntityApi<E>> implements Comparable
{
    Concept get concept;
    ValidationErrorsApi get errors;
    Oid get oid;
    IdApi get id;
    String code;

    Object getAttribute(String name);
    bool setAttribute(String name, Object value);
    String getStringFromAttribute(String name);
```

```
    bool setStringToAttribute(String name, String string);
    EntityApi getParent(String name);
    bool setParent(String name, EntityApi entity);
    EntitiesApi getChild(String name);
    bool setChild(String name, EntitiesApi entities);

    E copy();
    Map<String, Object> toJson();
}
```

Note that `EntityApi` implements `Comparable`, and `EntitiesApi` implements `Iterable`. Thus, all the public members of `Iterable` are available in the dartling entities. There are several dartling examples at GitHub; you can look at (all the URLs have the same structure, `https://github.com/dzenanr/`, followed by the name of the project, for example, `https://github.com/dzenanr/art_pen`):

- `art_pen`: This is a drawing tool based on the Logo programming language for children

- `game_parking`: This is a game based on *Rush Hour*

- `dartling_examples`: This contains different types of relationships

- `concept_attribute`: This deals with different categories of test data that can be used in the generation of tests

- `travel_impressions`: This is the model we will discuss to illustrate dartling in this chapter

- `dartling_todos`: This is a web application based on `TodoMVC` with dartling, action undos, and web components

Schematically, the following sections show how to:

1. Design a graphical model step by step:
    ○ **Tool to use**: Model Concepts (`https://github.com/dzenanr/model_concepts`)
    ○ **End result**: Visual model and export to the JSON format, `model.json`

2. Generate code for the dartling model from `model.json`:
    ○ **Tool to use**: dartling_gen (which uses dartling) (`https://github.com/dzenanr/dartling_gen`)
    ○ The generated app presents the data of the model in a web page inherited from the `dartling_default_app` tool (which uses dartling, `https://github.com/dzenanr/dartling_default_app`)

3. Initialize the dartling model with some basic data.

4. Test the model.

> If you want to follow new developments in dartling, consult On Dart Blog (http://dzenanr.github.io/) and On Dart Education (http://ondart.me/).

Design of the Travel Impressions model in spirals

We will start the project by designing a domain model in spirals (see the model directory in the project); this is step one in our schema. This new project will allow readers to follow our approach in order to make their development of a first web application with dartling easier. The project will evolve, but in a way that reflects the usual project progression with dartling.

> The project can be found at https://github.com/dzenanr/travel_impressions.

The domain of the new project is Travel. The principal model of the Travel domain is called Impressions. The objective is to create a web application that will allow young travelers to inform their families and friends about their impressions of the visited places without losing too much time. With the help from someone in the family or from a friend, their impressions of the visited places may be enriched by web links. Even a traveler may send only an e-mail message about the impressions of visiting certain places to a friend, and the friend may use the web application to present impressions about the visited places expressed in the message to other interested people in a more informative and pleasing way. Of course, the traveler can do all of this without help from other people. The first spiral (refer to the Travel Impressions model figure) starts with the most important concepts from the chosen domain. In our Travel domain, the key concepts are Traveler, Place, and Impression.

In general, a traveler visits many different places and may have an impression (or more than one) for each place. A place is something of interest for a traveler. It may be as general as a city, or as specific as a monument in a city. It may also be a village or a nature spot. The important thing is that a traveler has impressions about visited places to share with family and friends.

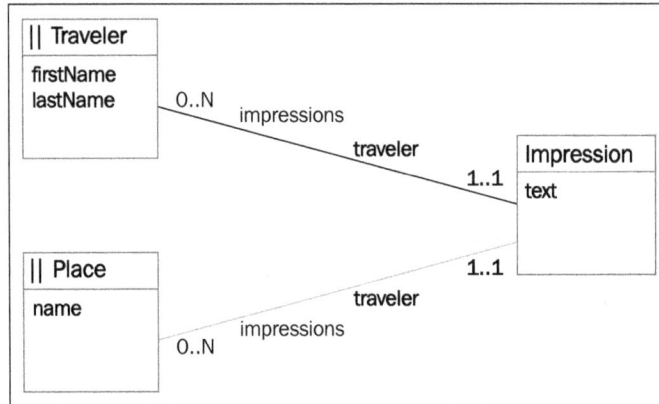

Spiral 1 of the Travel Impressions model

The first cut domain model is created in model concepts. There are three concepts and two relationships in the model. Each relationship has two directions. The direction from the `Traveler` concept to the `Impression` concept is also a neighbor of the `Traveler` concept. Thus, the `Traveler` concept has two attributes and one neighbor (attributes and neighbors are properties). The attributes are `firstName` and `lastName`, and the neighbor is `impressions`. As in Dart, the names of the concepts and properties are standardized. Since the concept corresponds to a class, its name starts with a capital letter. An attribute name starts with a small letter and, if a name is composed of several subnames, each subname starts with a capital letter. Spaces, hyphens, or underscores are not used in names. Since a neighbor is a relationship property, its name also starts with a small letter. The meaning of the impression's neighbor for the `Traveler` concept is expressed in the following way: a traveler may have 0 to N impressions. In the opposite direction, an impression has at least one and at the most one traveler, so it turns to be exactly one traveler. Similarly, a place may be mentioned in many impressions and an impression is about exactly one place. The `Impression` concept is an intersection concept between the `Traveler` and `Place` concepts. This means that a relationship between the `Traveler` and `Place` concepts is many-to-many. A traveler may refer to many places in his or her impressions, and a place may be noted by many travelers. There are two entry concepts that allow a user to navigate through the model's data, starting with travelers or places. The two concepts have the | | entry sign in the left section of their title areas.

The relationship between the `Traveler` and `Impression` concepts is **internal**. The relationship between the `Place` and `Impression` concepts is **external**, which is indicated by a lighter line. A concept with more than one parent must have only one internal relationship. This means that impressions may be saved within their `traveler` and not within the same place. By introducing internal and external relationships, the choice of which is rather subjective, a model may be decomposed into hierarchical submodels by starting with entry concepts and following internal relationships.

What happens if a traveler sends a rather long e-mail message to his family and if he describes more than one place in the same message? This common situation is introduced in a new spiral of the model with some improvements with respect to the previous spiral. In the spiral approach, each design or development iteration brings more clarifications and more details. If the reasoning behind the spirals is recorded in the documentation of the model, it would be easy for newcomers to get familiar with the model in a step-bystep fashion.

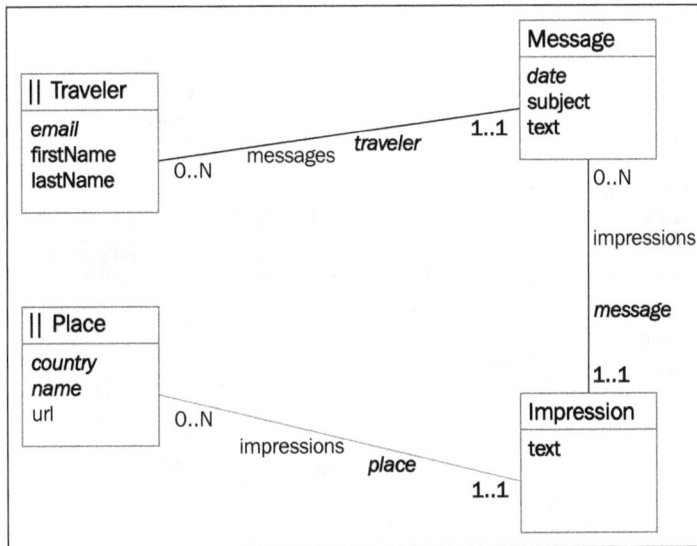

Spiral 2 of the Travel Impressions model

There is a new concept representing a message with the impressions of the visited places. `Traveler` may send many messages on his or her trip. A `Message` may contain `impressions` about several visited places. A traveler would send an e-mail and someone from a circle of family and friends would enter specific impressions about the visited places by extracting portions of the message text. A `Traveler` must have an e-mail attribute (as is the case with names, indicated by bold). A message must have a date when it is sent, a subject of the message, and a full text of the message. An impression's text, the country, and the name of a place are mandatory. The identifier (ID) of the `Traveler` concept is its e-mail (indicated by italics). The identifier of the `Place` concept consists of the `country` and `name` attributes. This means that each place name must be unique within its country. An impression is identified by its source message and the place about which the impression is formed (IDs of neighbors). Thus, the identifier of the `Impression` concept is composed of two neighbors. A message is identified by the traveler that sent the message and by the date when the message was sent. Further analysis leads to the model in the following figure:

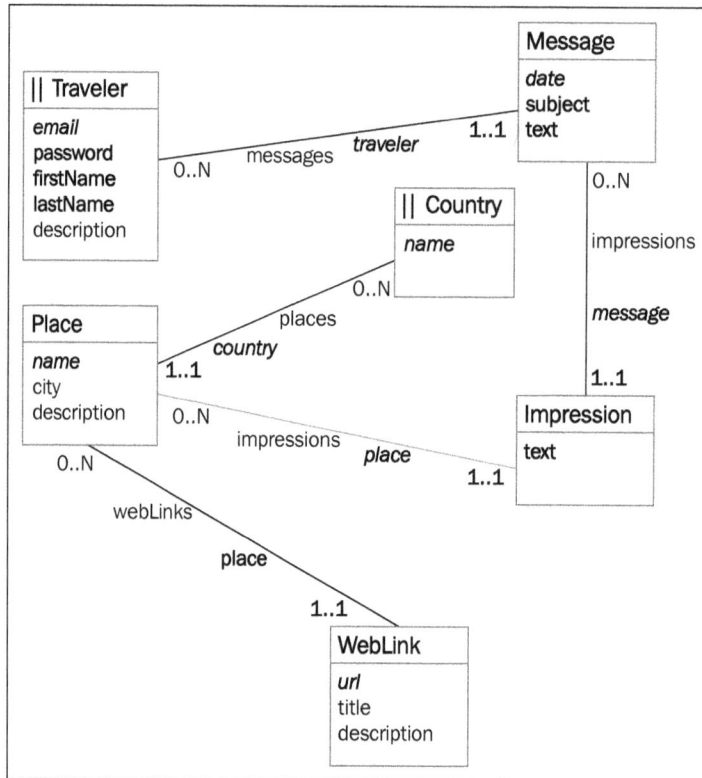

Spiral 3 of the Travel Impressions model

A place must be located in a specific country. Often, a visited place will be in a city. However, there are many interesting places that are not located in cities. A short description may be entered about a new place. Web links that are relevant to the visited place may be added. If we want to allow a traveler's friend to help the traveler by entering some data about her trip, the following concept should be added to the model (refer to the following figure):

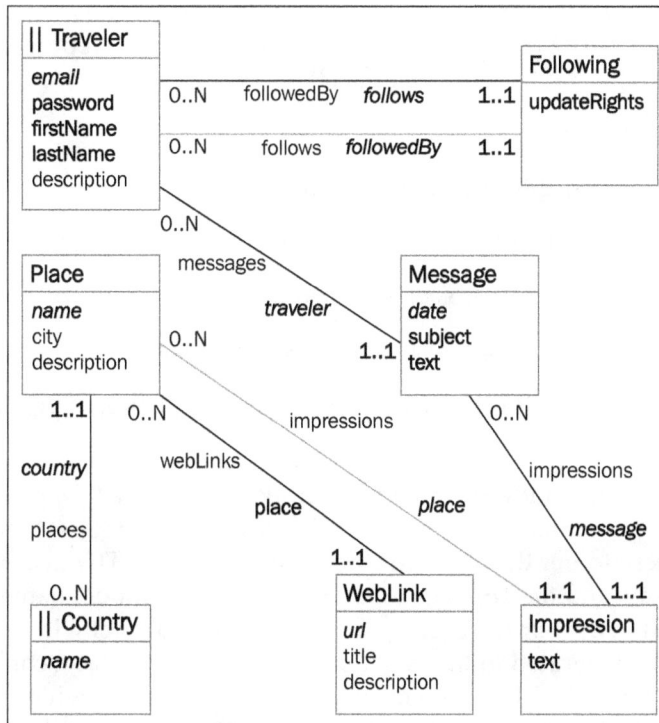

Spiral 4 of the Travel Impressions model

This concept represents a many-to-many relationship between travelers (real and virtual). In addition, there is a small change in the Message concept. The text attribute is now optional, allowing a traveler with update rights to use text only in the Impression concept. The model could be further extended with more concepts, attributes, and relationships. It is a good practice to spend more time on the model by introducing additional spirals. The new spirals may clarify some issues and provide new ideas. However, it is also a good practice to start programming with a less ambitious model, but with the knowledge of a richer model.

Generating the Travel Impressions code from the model

The JSON representation of the last model spiral is generated in the Model Concepts tool and then copied to the `model.json` file that is placed in the empty `travel_impressions` folder of the new app. The project's model code is generated by `dartling_gen`; this is step two in our schema. In **Run** | **Manage Launches** of Dart Editor, create a `dartling_gen.dart` command-line launch pointing to the following script in the `dartling_gen` project:

bin/dartling_gen.dart

In the Script arguments, enter the following argument:

--genall projectpath domain model

For the `travel_impressions` project, the arguments are as follows:

--genall c:/dart/travel_impressions travel impressions

The arguments are similar for the project path in Linux: `/home/dart/travel_impressions`.

The `--genall` argument indicates that the complete project will be generated. The `c:/dart/travel_impressions` argument replaces the `projectpath` parameter — a path to the project's folder that contains the `model.json` file. The `travel` argument is the domain name and the `impressions` argument is the model name. By running the `main` function in the `bin/dartling_gen.dart` file, a project with its domain and model will be generated in the `project` directory. This project contains the `doc`, `lib`, `test`, and `web` folders, as well as a `pubspec.yaml` file, which specifies that our project is dependent on dartling and `dartling_default_app`. In the generated project, the `lib` folder has the `gen` and `travel` (domain) folders. The `gen` folder also has the `travel` (domain) folder. The `travel` folder, both in `lib` and `gen`, has the `impressions` (model) folder. The `gen` folder keeps the generic code (not to be edited!) that is to be regenerated when the model changes. However, the `travel` subfolder in `lib` contains the specific code that is open for changes. The generic code extends the code in dartling, while the specific code extends the generic code.

```
▼ 📂 travel_impressions
  ► 📦 packages [package:]
    📄 pubspec.lock
    📄 pubspec.yaml
  ► 📂 doc
  ▼ 📂 lib
    ▼ 📂 gen
      ▼ 📂 travel
        ▼ 📂 impressions
          📄 countries.dart
          📄 entries.dart
          📄 followings.dart
          📄 impressions.dart
          📄 messages.dart
          📄 places.dart
          📄 travelers.dart
          📄 web_links.dart
        📄 models.dart
        📄 repository.dart
    ▼ 📂 travel
      ▼ 📂 impressions
        ► 📂 json
        📄 countries.dart
        📄 followings.dart
        📄 impressions.dart
        📄 init.dart
        📄 messages.dart
        📄 places.dart
        📄 travelers.dart
        📄 web_links.dart
      📄 travel_impressions.dart
      📄 travel_impressions_app.dart
  ▼ 📂 test
```

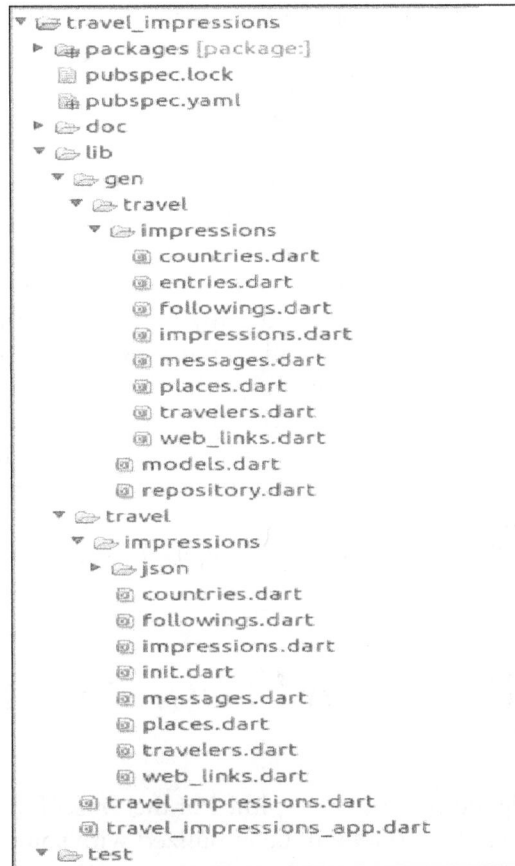

Structure of the generated project

However, what if the model changes? Then, update the JSON representation of the model in the `model.json` file. Regenerate only the `lib/gen` directory by giving these arguments:

```
--gengen projectpath domain model
```

> The generated code in `lib/gen` must not be edited by a programmer. The specific code, which is outside of the `lib/gen` folder, will be changed in the evolution of the application.

If you regenerate only the generic code in the lib/gen folder, you may need to adjust some specific code. When the complete project is generated, the content of the model.json file is reproduced in the lib/travel/impressions/json/ model.dart file as the content of its travelImpressionsModelJson variable. This variable, and not the model.json file, is used in the running of the application. In this way, you may experiment with some minor changes in the model (for example, changing essential attributes) without losing the content of the model.json file. However, if you want to keep these changes, you should update the JSON file before the next code generation. After the code is generated, the README.md and travel_impressions_web.html files are usually updated in a minor way to reflect the project in question. To run the application, the travel_impressions_web.html web page (in the web/travel/impressions folder) is selected. If you run the app, it will show two buttons with the **Show Travelers** and **Show Countries** text. When these buttons are pushed, they show a grid with dummy data. The two travel_ impressions_web files (.dart and .html) are the only web files, in addition to CSS files, in the project. However, they rely on dartling_default_app. The objective of this application is to validate the model by using its data. The next step is to create this data.

Initializing the Travel Impressions model with data

After the model is designed (refer to the spiral 4 of the *Travel Impression Model* figure) and its code is generated, the model will be initialized with some basic data starting with its entries. This is done in the lib/travel/impressions/init.dart file:

```
initTravelImpressions(var entries) {
  _initCountries(entries);
  _initTravelers(entries);
}
```

We will start by creating a country and some of its places, together with the web links, from the entries parameter:

```
_initCountries(var entries) {
  var countries = entries.countries;
  var country = new Country(countries.concept);
  country.code = 'BA';
  country.name = 'Bosnia and Herzegovina';
  countries.add(country);
```

In the Country concept of the graphical model, there is no code attribute of the String type. The code attribute is inherited from dartling. In a concept, you do not need to use the inherited code attribute. However, if you use it, its values must be unique. Note that a new country is added to the countries' entities. Once the first country is created, its first place may be created:

```
var place = new Place(country.places.concept);
place.name = 'Bascarsija';
place.city = 'Sarajevo';
place.description = 'old town';
place.country = country;
country.places.add(place);
```

After a new place is created, its country is established and added to the country's places. Then, the web links for the Bascarsija place are created:

```
var webLink = new WebLink(place.webLinks.concept);
webLink.url =
Uri.parse('http://en.wikipedia.org/wiki/Bašаršija');
webLink.title = 'Wikipedia';
webLink.description =
    "Sarajevo's old bazaar and the historical and cultural
       center.";
webLink.place = place;
place.webLinks.add(webLink);

webLink = new WebLink(place.webLinks.concept);
webLink.url =
  Uri.parse('http://en.wikipedia.org/wiki/File: Bašаršija
  _2006.jpg');
webLink.title = 'image';
webLink.place = place;
place.webLinks.add(webLink);
```

Other countries, places, and web links may be created in a similar way. Travelers, with their messages and impressions, are created with their entry into the model:

```
_initTravelers(var entries) {
  var countries = entries.countries;
  var travelers = entries.travelers;

  var traveler = new Traveler(travelers.concept);
  traveler.email = 'dzenan@gmail.com';
  traveler.password = 'dzenan';
  traveler.firstName = 'Dzenan';
```

```
traveler.lastName = 'Ridjanovic';
traveler.description = 'working hard on Dart projects';
travelers.add(traveler);

var message = new Message(traveler.messages.concept);
message.subject = 'first day in Sarajevo';
message.traveler = traveler;
traveler.messages.add(message);

var country = countries.singleWhereCode('BA');
var place = country.places.firstWhereAttribute('name',
  'Bascarsija');
var impression =
    new Impression.withId(message.impressions.concept, place,
      message);
impression.text = 'as usual, my first meal is "cevapcici"';
message.impressions.add(impression);
place.impressions.add(impression);

place = country.places.firstWhereAttribute('name',
  'Bjelasnica');
impression =
    new Impression.withId(message.impressions.concept, place,
      message);
impression.text = 'after "cevapcici", hiking at Bjelasnica is
  calling';
message.impressions.add(impression);
place.impressions.add(impression);

place = country.places.firstWhereAttribute('name', 'Dariva');
impression =
  new Impression.withId(message.impressions.concept, place,
    message);
impression.text = 'however, short walk will do';
message.impressions.add(impression);
place.impressions.add(impression);
```

The `Impression` concept has two parents: `Message` and `Place`. A place is found within a country. A country's code is unique and the `singleWhereCode` method is used on the country's entry to find the country. A place's name is a part of the identifier (the place within the country) and the `firstWhereAttribute` method is used on `country.places` to find the place. Once some basic data is created, a default web application (`web/travel/impressions/travel_impressions.html`) may be run to validate the model by navigating from the model's entries and discovering the missing concepts, attributes, and relationships. This default application is an example of generic programming based on the meta model of dartling. Its code is in the `dartling_default_app` project that is imported based on the pub declaration in the generated `pubspec.yaml` file:

```
name: travel_impressions
author: Your Name
homepage: http://ondart.me/
version: 0.0.1
description: travel_impressions application that uses dartling for its
model.
dependencies:
  browser: any
  dartling:
    git: git://github.com/dzenanr/dartling.git
  dartling_default_app:
    git: git://github.com/dzenanr/dartling_default_app.git
```

This generates the following code in the `web/travel/impressions/travel_impressions_web.dart` file:

```
import "dart:html";
import "package:dartling/dartling.dart";
import "package:dartling_default_app/dartling_default_app.dart";
import "package:travel_impressions/travel_impressions.dart";

initTravelData(TravelRepo travelRepo) {
    var travelModels =
        travelRepo.getDomainModels(TravelRepo.travelDomainCode);
    var travelImpressionsEntries =
        travelModels.getModelEntries(TravelRepo.travelImpressionsModel
        Code);
    initTravelImpressions(travelImpressionsEntries);
    travelImpressionsEntries.display();
    travelImpressionsEntries.displayJson();
}

showTravelData(TravelRepo travelRepo) {
```

```
    var mainView = new View(document, "main");
    mainView.repo = travelRepo;
    new RepoMainSection(mainView);
  }

  void main() {
    var travelRepo = new TravelRepo();
    initTravelData(travelRepo);
    showTravelData(travelRepo);
  }
```

In dartling, a repository may have many domains and a domain may have many models. However, in a default web application, only one domain and one model is used. After the travel repository is created with the Travel domain and the Impressions model, the model is initialized with some data and it is shown in a web page of the default application. Data is also displayed in the Dart Editor's console. Note that this is the only code written manually for the time being. The next step is to test the model, and more specific code will be added to the project.

Testing the Travel Impressions model

After the model is designed, generated, and initialized with some data, the model should be tested to validate it further. In addition, writing tests by applying the techniques we learned in *Chapter 3, Structuring Code with Classes and Libraries*, is the best way to start learning dartling. Testing is done in the test/travel/ impressions/travel_impressions_test.dart file. The main function creates a repository based on the JSON definition of the model and passes it to the testTravelData function:

```
  testTravelData(TravelRepo travelRepo) {
    testTravelImpressions(travelRepo, TravelRepo.travelDomainCode,
        TravelRepo.travelImpressionsModelCode);
  }

  void main() {
    var travelRepo = new TravelRepo();
    testTravelData(travelRepo);
  }
```

The `testTravelImpressions` function accepts the repository and the names of the domain and the model. In a group of tests, before each test, a setup is done to first obtain the three variables: `models`, `session`, and `entries`. The models (here, only one) are obtained from the repository based on the domain's name. A session, with a history of actions and transactions of dartling, is created by the `newSession` method of the `models` object. The `entries` variable for the only model is obtained from the model's object by using the model's name:

```
testTravelImpressions(Repo repo, String domainCode, String modelCode)
{
  var models;
  var session;
  var entries;

  Countries countries;
  Country bosnia;
  Oid darivaOid, oid;
    Travelers travelers;
  group("Testing ${domainCode}.${modelCode}", () {
    setUp(() {
      models = repo.getDomainModels(domainCode);
      session = models.newSession();
      entries = models.getModelEntries(modelCode);
      expect(entries, isNotNull);

      countries = entries.countries;
      travelers = entries.travelers;
      initTravelImpressions(entries);

      var code = 'BA';
      bosnia = countries.singleWhereCode(code);
      darivaOid = bosnia.places.firstWhereAttribute('name',
        'Dariva').oid;
    });
    tearDown(() {
      entries.clear();
    });
    test("Not empty entries test", () {
      expect(!entries.isEmpty, isTrue);
    });
    // code left out
```

The countries and travelers are the entry entities. The `initTravelImpressions` function is called to initiate the model with some basic data. After the initialization, the country Bosnia is found in the `countries` object based on its unique code. A single place, with the `Dariva` name, is retrieved from the `bosnia` object and its `oid` is kept in the `darivaOid` variable. The `oid` attribute is inherited from dartling. It is a unique timestamp used as a system identifier in a collection of entities. Each test has an access to all these variables. After a test is run, the entries object is cleared so that the `setUp` function may start from the empty model. The first test is run to show that the entries object is not empty after the setup. A single country is found by the `singleWhereCode` method based on the inherited code attribute. In the `Country` concept, the `code` attribute is used. In the `countries` object, each country must have a unique code:

```
test('Find country by code', () {
  var code = 'BA';
  Country country = countries.singleWhereCode(code);
  expect(country, isNotNull);
  expect(country.name, equals('Bosnia and Herzegovina'));
});
```

A single entity may be found by its user identifier. In the `Country` concept, the user identifier is the `name` attribute:

```
test('Find country by id', () {
  Id id = new Id(countries.concept);
  id.setAttribute('name', 'Bosnia and Herzegovina');
  Country country = countries.singleWhereId(id);
  expect(country, isNotNull);
  expect(country.code, equals('BA'));
});
```

If a concept has one attribute identifier (simple identifier), a creation of an ID object may be avoided by using a shortcut method called `singleWhereAttributeId`:

```
test('Find country by name attribute id', () {
  var name = 'Bosnia and Herzegovina';
  Country country = countries.singleWhereAttributeId('name',
    name);
  expect(country, isNotNull);
  expect(country.code, equals('BA'));
});
```

The first entity with an attribute value equal to a value given to the
`firstWhereAttribute` method will then be obtained. If this attribute is
an identifier, methods that use identifiers will perform faster:

```
test('Find country by name attribute', () {
  var name = 'Bosnia and Herzegovina';
  Country country = countries.firstWhereAttribute('name',
    name);
  expect(country, isNotNull);
  expect(country.code, equals('BA'));
});
```

If an entity is not a member of a collection of entities, a `search` method will
return `null`:

```
test('Find country by name attribute id', () {
  var name = 'Poland';
  Country country = countries.singleWhereAttributeId('name',
    name);
  expect(country, isNull);
});
```

The `Place` concept has a composite identifier, composed of the country neighbor and
the `name` attribute. If only the name attribute is used, `singleWhereAttributeId` will
return `null`:

```
test('Find country and (not) place by name id', () {
  var countryName = 'Bosnia and Herzegovina';
  Country country = countries.singleWhereAttributeId('name',
    countryName);
  var placeName = 'Dariva';
  Places places = country.places;
  Place place = places.singleWhereAttributeId('name',
    placeName);
  expect(place, isNull);
});
```

The `name` attribute may be used to find both a country and its place:

```
test('Find country and place by name attribute', () {
  var countryName = 'Bosnia and Herzegovina';
  bosnia = countries.firstWhereAttribute('name', countryName);
  expect(bosnia, isNotNull);
  var placeName = 'Dariva';
  Places places = bosnia.places;
  Place place = places.firstWhereAttribute('name', placeName);
  expect(place, isNotNull);
  expect(place.city, equals('Sarajevo'));
});
```

However, the use of identifiers is recommended for performance reasons:

```
test('Find country and place by id', () {
    var countryName = 'Bosnia and Herzegovina';
    bosnia = countries.singleWhereAttributeId('name', countryName);
    var placeName = 'Dariva';
    Places places = bosnia.places;
    Id id = new Id(bosnia.concept);
    id.setParent('country', bosnia);
    id.setAttribute('name', placeName);
    Place place = places.singleWhereId(id);
    expect(place, isNotNull);
    expect(place.city, equals('Sarajevo'));
});
```

The same results may be obtained by using more elegant method cascades. Note that the bosnia variable is used in order to avoid searching for the country. Besides, in the last line, the place's oid attribute is assigned to the oid variable that will be used in the next test:

```
test('Find country and place by id (method cascades)', () {
    var placeName = 'Dariva';
    Places places = bosnia.places;
    Id id = new Id(bosnia.concept)
        ..setParent('country', bosnia)
        ..setAttribute('name', placeName);
    Place place = places.singleWhereId(id);
    expect(place, isNotNull);
    expect(place.city, equals('Sarajevo'));
    oid = place.oid;
});
```

In the model, the Country concept is an entry. The relationship between the Country and Place concepts is internal. A place may be searched by its oid attribute starting with the countries' entry, followed by the internal neighbors from the Country concept:

```
test('Find place by oid by searching from countries down',
    {
    Place place = countries.singleDownWhereOid(darivaOid);
    expect(place, isNotNull);
    expect(place.name, equals('Dariva'));
});
```

A specific method that does a job of finding an entity based on an identifier value may be used:

```
test('Find place by a specific method', () {
  var placeName = 'Dariva';
  Place place = bosnia.places.findById(placeName, bosnia);
  expect(place, isNotNull);
  expect(place.city, equals('Sarajevo'));
});
```

The `findById` method is added to the `Places` class in the `lib/travel/impressions/places.dart` file:

```
Place findById(String name, Country country) {
  return singleWhereId(new Id(concept)..setAttribute('name',
    name)..
    setParent('country', country));
}
```

The `city` attribute of the `Place` concept is not required (not in bold in the Travel Impression model figure). Thus, it is not an identifier or a part of an identifier (not in italics). All the places in the city of Sarajevo may be selected by the `selectWhereAttribute` method. The `select` methods return a new collection of entities:

```
test('Select places in Sarajevo', () {
  Places places = bosnia.places.selectWhereAttribute('city',
    'Sarajevo');
  expect(places.length, greaterThan(0));
    for (var place in places) {
      expect(place.city, equals('Sarajevo'));
      }
});
```

A specific read-only property (with only the `get` method) may be used in an anonymous function of the `selectWhere` method to select a subset of entities:

```
test('Select places by function', () {
  Places places = bosnia.places.selectWhere((place) =>
    place.old);
  expect(places.length, greaterThan(0));
  for (var place in places) {
    expect(place.description, contains('old')));
    }
});
```

The old property with the `get` method is added to the `Places` class in the `lib/travel/impressions/places.dart` file:

```
bool get old => description.contains('old') ? true : false;
```

The places of the `bosnia` object are sorted by the `city` attribute:

```
test('Sort places by city in Bosnia and Herzegovina', () {
  bosnia.places.sort(
      (place1, place2) => place1.city.compareTo(place2.city));
});
```

A new place is not added because the required values for the `name` attribute and the country neighbor are missing. The corresponding error messages are added to the `errors` property of the `places` object:

```
test('Add place required error', () {
  Places places = bosnia.places;
  var placesCount = places.length;
  var place = new Place(places.concept);
  expect(place, isNotNull);

  var added = places.add(place);
  expect(added, isFalse);
  expect(places.length, equals(placesCount));
  places.errors.display(title:'Add place required error');

  expect(places.errors.length, equals(2));
  expect(places.errors.toList()[0].category,
     equals('required'));
  expect(places.errors.toList()[0].message,
       equals('Place.name attribute is null.'));
  expect(places.errors.toList()[1].category,
     equals('required'));
  expect(places.errors.toList()[1].message,
       equals('Place.country parent is null.'));
});
```

The error messages also appear in the console of the Dart Editor.

If we want to add a place that already exists according to its identifier, the `add` method will not be successful:

```
test('Add place unique error', () {
  Places places = bosnia.places;
  var placesCount = places.length;
  var place = new Place(places.concept);
  expect(place, isNotNull);

  place.name = 'Dariva';
  place.country = bosnia;
  var added = places.add(place);
  expect(added, isFalse);
  expect(places.length, equals(placesCount));

  places.errors.display(title:'Add place unique error');
  expect(places.errors.length, equals(1));
  expect(places.errors.toList()[0].category,
    equals('unique'));
});
```

In dartling, there are pre and posthooks for the `add` and `remove` methods. A pre-add hook may be used to validate a specific constraint that is not defined in the model:

```
test('Add place pre validation error', () {
  Places places = bosnia.places;
  var placesCount = places.length;
  var place = new Place(places.concept);
  expect(place, isNotNull);
  place.name =
  'A new place with a name longer than 32 cannot be accepted';
  place.country = bosnia;
  var added = places.add(place);
  expect(added, isFalse);
  expect(places.length, equals(placesCount));
  places.errors.display(title:'Add place pre validation
    error');
  expect(places.errors.length, equals(1));
  expect(places.errors.toList()[0].category, equals('pre'));
});
```

The specific `preAdd` method is defined in the `Places` class. The method is called by the `add` method of dartling:

```
bool preAdd(Place place) {
  bool validation = super.preAdd(place);
  if (validation) {
    validation = place.name.length <= 32;
    if (!validation) {
      var error = new ValidationError('pre');
      error.message =
          '${concept.codePlural}.preAdd rejects the
            "${place.name}" '
          'name that is longer than 32.';
      errors.add(error);
    }
  }
  return validation;
}
```

Finally, a new place is added:

```
test('Add place', () {
  Places places = bosnia.places;
  var placesCount = places.length;
  var place = new Place(places.concept);
  expect(place, isNotNull);

  place.name = 'Ilidza';
  place.city = 'Sarajevo';
  place.country = bosnia;
  var added = places.add(place);
  expect(added, isTrue);
  expect(places.length, equals(++placesCount));
});
```

The Travel Impressions app is further worked out to show all the data that was input: the countries and their places, the impressions, and the web links associated with each place, or the travelers and their impressions. These screens are not application-specific, but use the views, menu bars, and so on in the included `dartling_default_app` library, showing the advantage of starting with a modeling framework.

Defining and using the MVC pattern

Conceptually, there are several basic modules in almost any software. The **model** is a data container and the **user interface** (**UI**) is a way to communicate with the model. A relationship between the model and the UI is bidirectional. Data from the model is displayed to a user and a user may change the model's data. The model may keep some or all of the data in the main memory and store the data in an external storage, such as files or **databases** (**db**). A relationship between the model and the data storage is also bidirectional. The UI has one or many **views** of data, which present data in a format useful to users, and one or many **controllers**, which channel changes in the data to the model. For example, a web application, after a user request, retrieves data from a database and displays it in a presentable way. After the user changes the data, the application updates the database. There is a flow of data between the UI and the db. For a simple data model and a simple application, the view is often combined with the model. However, a coupling of these parts produces maintenance problems. One problem is that the UI tends to change more often than the model of the db. Another problem is that an application may have business rules that are more than simple data transmissions. It is important to organize a software application to allow for easy modifications of its parts. There are many design patterns that may help in detailing this software architecture. The most popular one, with a long history of different variations, is the **Model View Controller** (**MVC**) pattern.

MVC (http://en.wikipedia.org/wiki/Model-view-controller) is a design pattern that isolates an application's data from the UI. In the MVC, the model represents the data of the application and the business rules used to manipulate the data, the view corresponds to the elements of the UI such as the text fields, and the controller manages the details involving the communication between the model and the views and handles business logic. There may be many views and only one controller or many views and many controllers. A view and its controller may be separate or combined together. A view might have its own model in addition to the model for all the views. All these and the other variations exist in the different versions of MVC that even have some new names such as MVP (http://en.wikipedia.org/wiki/Model-view-presenter), MVVM (http://en.wikipedia.org/wiki/Model_View_ViewModel), MOVE (http://cirw.in/blog/time-to-move-on), and MDV (http://www.polymer-project.org/docs/polymer/databinding.html). There are also many articles about MVC and its variations (www.mvccentral.net, www.infoq.com/ASP-NET-MVC/articles/).

Thus, for a learner, it is not easy to grasp the essence of MVC. The following sentence provides this in a nutshell (refer to the MVC pattern figure): a user action triggers a UI event that changes the model's data by invoking data actions in a controller. A view registers with the model to be informed about the data changes. When a view is informed about the changes, it reacts by refreshing its display. Implementing this pattern makes our app obey the *Separation of Concerns* design principle (the code of views, controllers, and models are loosely coupled). Thus, the different layers in the MVC can be developed independently from each other so that the code is better maintainable. This is especially important for web applications, where the views are presented in the client's browser and the data source (which interacts with the model) sits on a server. The model and controller code can be executed on the server (as in the traditional web applications) or on the client (as in the RIA apps), or be distributed.

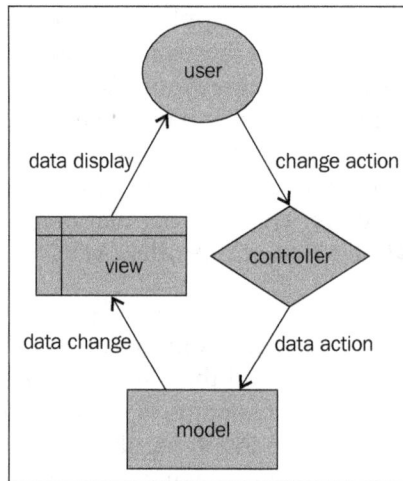

The MVC pattern

It is important to note that the model does not depend on the controller and views. In other words, there are no references to the controller and the views in the model (this is the reason why a view registers with the model to be informed about the changes in the data). However, the controller and views depend on the model. In this way, the model may be developed and tested without the views and controllers. In addition, new views of the model may be added easily. Even different applications may use the same model.

The TodoMVC app

We will now show how the MVC functions in a Dart version of the famous TodoMVC application (http://todomvc.com/), which is used as a standard to compare different web frameworks. This application is developed in spirals in the dartling_todo_mvc project and is built by using the dartling framework for the model. Download the code from https://github.com/dzenanr/dartling_todo_mvc_spirals. In the following screenshot, you will see a glimpse of the end result (spiral 6):

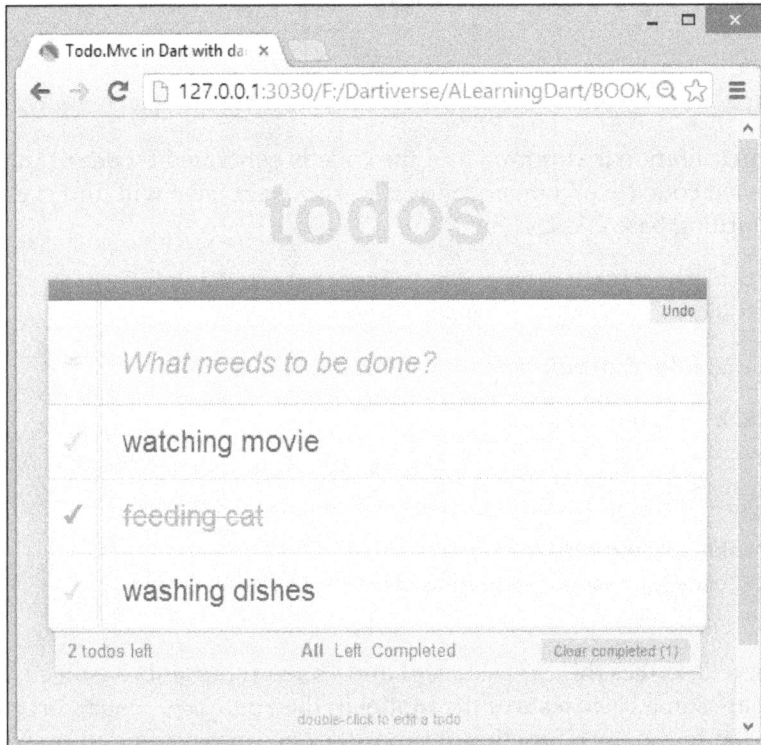

The TodoMVC app

The todo items can be added, edited, marked as complete, and deleted. Overviews of all the tasks, or only the completed or remaining ones can be shown. The user has undo/redo possibilities after making a mistake. Moreover, it is really useful because the data is stored in the local storage (using the JSON format).

Spiral 0 – generating a class model

Spiral 0 does not have any UI; it contains only a simple model with one `Task` concept and two properties: `title` and `completed`. This is designed in Model Concepts with a `Todo` domain name and `Mvc` model name, as shown in the following figure:

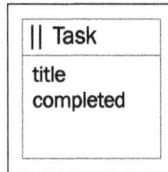

The TodoMVC model

Its JSON representation is exported and the code is generated by `dartling_gen`. In the generated code (`lib/gen/todo/mvc/tasks.dart`), we will find classes that extend the dartling base classes:

```
abstract class TaskGen extends ConceptEntity<Task>
abstract class TasksGen extends Entities<Task>
```

In the `lib/todo` folder, developers may specialize the model:

```
class Task extends TaskGen {
  Task(Concept concept) : super(concept);
}

class Tasks extends TasksGen {
  Tasks(Concept concept) : super(concept);
}
```

The `Task` class describes the `Task` concept and `Tasks` represents a collection of tasks. There are some basic tests of the model in the `todo_mvc_test.dart` file of the `test` folder. In the `main` function, a repository is constructed and passed to the `testTodoMvc` function, together with the domain name and the model name:

```
testTodoData(TodoRepo todoRepo) {
  testTodoMvc(todoRepo, TodoRepo.todoDomainCode,
      TodoRepo.todoMvcModelCode);
}

void main() {
  var todoRepo = new TodoRepo();
  testTodoData(todoRepo);
}
```

The model entries of the MvcEntries type are obtained from the models object of the repository:

```
var models = repo.getDomainModels(domainCode);
entries = models.getModelEntries(modelCode);
```

The tasks variable of the Tasks type is the only entry into the model:

```
tasks = entries.tasks;
```

All the tests are done on the tasks object. The web folder contains a default web application of the model.

Spiral 1 – adding todo tasks

In the todo_mvc_s01 spiral, there is a new lib/app folder. In the todo_app.dart file, the TodoApp class has three properties: tasks, todoWidgets, and todoListElement. The Tasks class is generated by dartling in the lib/todo/mvc folder:

```
class TodoApp {
  Tasks tasks;
  var todoWidgets = new List<TodoWidget>();
  Element todoListElement = query('#todo-list');
    }
```

The TodoWidget class is defined in the lib/app/todo_widget.dart file. The id to-do list is used in the web/todo_mvc.html file to get access to the corresponding DOM element:

```
<section id="todoapp">
    <header id="header">
      <h1>todos</h1>
      <input id="new-todo" placeholder="What needs to be done?"
autofocus>
    </header>
    <section id="main">
      <ul id="todo-list"></ul>
    </section>
  </section>
```

At the beginning of the constructor of the `TodoApp` class, the dartling repository is used to get the `todo` domain. There is only one model in the domain and only one entry into the model, which is an empty collection of tasks:

```
TodoApp(repo) {
    var todo = repo.getDomainModels(TodoRepo.todoDomainCode);
    var mvc = todo.getModelEntries(TodoRepo.todoMvcModelCode);
    tasks = mvc.getEntry('Task');

    InputElement newTodoElement = query('#new-todo');
    newTodoElement.on.keyPress.add((KeyboardEvent e) {
      if (e.keyCode == KeyCode.ENTER) {
        var title = newTodoElement.value.trim();
        if (title != '') {
          var task = new Task(tasks.concept);
          task.title = title;
          addTodo(task);
          newTodoElement.value = '';
        }
      }
    });
}
```

The application is created in the main function of the `web/todo_mvc.dart` file:

```
main() {
        new TodoApp(new TodoRepo());
}
```

A new `todo` task is entered by a user into the input element. The entered value becomes the title of a newly created task, which is then added to tasks by the `addTodo` method:

```
addTodo(Task task) {
        tasks.add(task);
        var todoWidget = new TodoWidget(task);
        todoWidgets.add(todoWidget);
        todoListElement.nodes.add(todoWidget.createElement());
}
```

A `todo` widget is constructed based on the task and added to the list of `todo` widgets. A new DOM node is created by the `createElement` method and added to the `todo` list element. The `todo` widget may be toggled to the completed state:

```
class TodoWidget {
  Task task;
  Element element;
  Element toggleElement;

  TodoWidget(this.task);

  Element createElement() {
    element = new Element.html('''
<li ${task.completed ? 'class="completed"' : ''}>
  <div class='view'>
        <input class='toggle' type='checkbox'
          ${task.completed ? 'checked' : ''}>
    <label class='todo-content'>${task.title}</label>
  </div>
</li>
    ''');

    toggleElement = element.query('.toggle');
    toggleElement.on.click.add((MouseEvent e) {
      toggle();
    });

    return element;
  }

  void toggle() {
    task.completed = !task.completed;
    toggleElement.checked = task.completed;
    if (task.completed) {
      element.classes.add('completed');
    } else {
      element.classes.remove('completed');
    }
  }
}
```

I have taken the `web/css/base.css` file as it is. The completed CSS class is shown here:

```
#todo-list li.completed label {
  color: #a9a9a9;
  text-decoration: line-through;
}
```

Spiral 2 – showing how many todo tasks are left

In the `todo_mvc_s02` spiral, there is a footer with a count of items (tasks) left to do:

```
<footer id="footer">
      <span id="todo-count"><strong>0</strong> item left</span>
</footer>
```

There is a change in the `lib/todo/mvc/tasks.dart` file. There are two new properties (methods) in the `Tasks` class. A subset of entities (here tasks) may be obtained in dartling by using an anonymous Boolean function as the argument of the select method:

```
int get completed => select((task) => task.completed).count;
int get left => count - completed;
```

There are two new elements in the `TodoApp` class located in the `lib/app/todo_app.dart` file. One element is identified by the `footer` ID and the other by the `todo-count` ID:

```
class TodoApp {
  Tasks tasks;
  var todoWidgets = new List<TodoWidget>();
  Element todoListElement = querySelector('#todo-list');
  Element footerElement = querySelector ('#footer');
  Element countElement = querySelector ('#todo-count');
}
```

When a new task is added, the `updateFooterDisplay` method is called to prepare the style display value and to update the count of the tasks left to be done:

```
void updateFooterDisplay() {
    var display = todoWidgets.length == 0 ? 'none' : 'block';
    footerElement.style.display = display;
    updateCount();
}

void updateCount() {
    countElement.innerHTML =
        '<b>${tasks.left}</b> item${tasks.left != 1 ? 's' : ''} left';
}
```

When a task is completed, the number of tasks to do will change. In the `TodoWidget` class in the `lib/app/todo_widget.dart` file, a reaction to the click event on the toggle element now includes a call to the `updateCount` method of the `TodoApp` class:

```
toggleElement.on.click.add((MouseEvent e) {
        toggle();
        todoApp.updateCount();
    });
```

To be able to call the `updateCount` method, the application object will be passed to the constructor of the `TodoWidget` class:

```
class TodoWidget {
    Task task;
    TodoApp todoApp;
    Element element;
    Element toggleElement;

    TodoWidget(this.task, this.todoApp);
}
```

Spiral 3 – removing a single task and completed tasks

In the `todo_mvc_s03` spiral, there is a button that clears the completed tasks.

```
<button id="clear-completed">Clear completed</button>
```

In addition, a single task completed or left to do may be removed by clicking on the x icon at the far right end of a task. There is a new element in the `TodoApp` class located in the `lib/app/todo_app.dart` file:

```
class TodoApp {
  Tasks tasks;
  var todoWidgets = new List<TodoWidget>();
  Element todoListElement = query('#todo-list');
  Element footerElement = query('#footer');
  Element countElement = query('#todo-count');
  Element clearCompletedElement = query('#clear-completed');
}
```

A click on the `clear completed` button triggers a traversal of `todo` widgets. If a `todo` widget is completed, it will be removed:

```
clearCompletedElement.on.click.add((MouseEvent e) {
    var newList = new List<TodoWidget>();
    for (TodoWidget todoWidget in todoWidgets) {
      if (todoWidget.task.completed) {
        todoWidget.element.remove();
      } else {
        newList.add(todoWidget);
      }
    }
    todoWidgets = newList;
    updateFooterDisplay();
  });
```

A single task completed or not may be removed by clicking on the x icon at the far right end of a task. A button with the `destroy` CSS class is added to the `createElement` method of the `TodoWidget` class:

```
Element createElement() {
    element = new Element.html('''
      <li ${task.completed ? 'class="completed"' : ''}>
        <div class='view'>

          <button class='destroy'></button>
```

```
            </div>
          </li>
        ''');
    }
```

The button with the `destroy` CSS class is queried in the `createElement` method. The click event removes the element and calls the two methods of the `todo` application:

```
removeTodo() {
    element.remove();
    todoApp.removeTodo(this);
    todoApp.updateFooterDisplay();
}

element.query('.destroy').on.click.add((MouseEvent e) {
    removeTodo();
});
}
```

Based on the given `todo` widget, in the `removeTodo` method of the `TodoApp` class, the corresponding task is removed from the model and the list of widgets is updated:

```
removeTodo(TodoWidget todoWidget) {
    var task = todoWidget.task;
    tasks.remove(task);
    todoWidgets.removeAt(todoWidgets.indexOf(todoWidget));
}
```

Spiral 4 – saving in the local storage

In the `todo_mvc_s04` spiral, tasks are loaded from a local storage and saved in the local storage as a JSON document. The list represents tasks, and each map { } is a task with four attributes. The `oid` attribute is generated by dartling and it represents an object identifier, which is a unique time stamp. The `code` attribute also comes from dartling, but it is not used in this application.

Here is a typical JSON document for tasks:

```
[
    {
        "completed":"false",
        "oid":"1355408619267",
        "title":"explain dartling todos",
        "code":null
    },
    {
        "completed":"true",
        "oid":"1355412503471",
        "title":"explain spiral 03",
        "code":null
    },
    {
        "completed":"false",
        "oid":"1355412519900",
        "title":"explain spiral 04",
        "code":null
    }
]
```

There are two new methods in the TodoApp class: load() and save():

```
load() {
    var json = window.localStorage['todos'];
    if (json != null) {
        try {
            var todoList = JSON.parse(json);
            for (Map todo in todoList) {
                var task = new Task(tasks.concept);
                task.fromJson(todo);
                add(task);
            }
        } catch (e) {
            window.console.log(
                'Could not load todos from the local storage. ${e}');
        }
    }
}

save() {
    window.localStorage['todos'] = JSON.stringify(tasks.toJson());
}
```

The `load` method retrieves the text value of the `todos` key from the local storage. This value, if it exists, is parsed to produce a list of maps. Each map in the list is a task, which is then converted into a dartling object by the `fromJson` method inherited from the `ConceptEntity` class of dartling. The `save` method converts a list of tasks into a string. The list is obtained by the `toJson` method inherited from the `Entities` class of dartling. The two abstract classes located in the `lib/gen/todo/mvc/tasks.dart` file are generated by dartling. They should not be updated by a programmer to allow code regeneration if the model changes:

```
abstract class TaskGen extends ConceptEntity<Task> {

  TaskGen(Concept concept) : super.of(concept);

  String get title => getAttribute("title");
  set title(String a) => setAttribute("title", a);

  bool get completed => getAttribute("completed");
  set completed(bool a) => setAttribute("completed", a);

  Task newEntity() => new Task(concept);

}


abstract class TasksGen extends Entities<Task> {

  TasksGen(Concept concept) : super.of(concept);

  Tasks newEntities() => new Tasks(concept);

}
```

The two specific classes located in the `lib/todo/mvc/tasks.dart` file are also generated by dartling. However, they may be changed by a programmer to add some specific methods that do not exist in dartling. In this example, the completed and left properties have been added to simplify programming in the application classes:

```
class Task extends TaskGen {

  Task(Concept concept) : super(concept);

}

class Tasks extends TasksGen {
```

```
    Tasks(Concept concept) : super(concept);

    int get completed => select((task) => task.completed).count;
    int get left => count - completed;


}
```

The constructor of the `TodoApp` class now receives the tasks as its parameter. The `load` method is called at the very beginning of the constructor:

```
TodoApp(this.tasks) {
    load();
}
```

The `main` function in the `todo_mvc.dart` file obtains the `tasks` object from the model entries. There is only one entry in the model and only one model in the `todo` domain, which is contained in the dartling repository:

```
main() {
  var repo = new TodoRepo();
  var todo = repo.getDomainModels(TodoRepo.todoDomainCode);
  var mvc = todo.getModelEntries(TodoRepo.todoMvcModelCode);
  Tasks tasks = mvc.getEntry('Task');
  new TodoApp(tasks);
}
```

The `TodoWidget` class is renamed as `Todo`. The `task` or `tasks` refer to the model and `todo` and `todos` refer to the application. The element property becomes `todo` and `elementToggle` is simply `toggle`:

```
class Todo {
  Task task;
  TodoApp todoApp;
  Element todo;
  Element toggle;

  Todo(this.task, this.todoApp);

  Element createElement() {
    todo = new Element.html('''
      <li ${task.completed ? 'class="completed"' : ''}>

      </li>
    ''');
  }
}
```

In the `TodoApp` class, `todoWidgets` there are now `todos`:

```
class TodoApp {
  Tasks tasks;
  var todos = new List<Todo>();
}
```

Spiral 5 – displaying completed todos

In the `todo_mvc_s05` spiral in the upper-left corner of `todos`, there is a checkbox to complete all the `todos` by clicking on its unusual display. See `#toggle-all-completed` in the `web/css/base.css` file for a display different from a regular checkbox. The `web/todo_mvc.html` file is renamed to `web/todos.html` and `web/todo_mvc.dart` to `web/todos.dart`:

```
<section id="main">
    <input id="toggle-all-completed" type="checkbox">
    <ul id="todo-list"></ul>
</section>
```

The `lib/app/todo_app.dart` file becomes `lib/app/todos.dart`. There is now a new input element in the `TodoApp` class:

```
class TodoApp {
  Tasks tasks;
  var todos = new List<Todo>();

  Element main = query('#main');
  InputElement allCompleted = query('#toggle-all-completed');
}
```

In the constructor of the `TodoApp` class, a click event is defined, where all the incomplete `todos` become complete or all the completed `Todo` instances are changed to incomplete:

```
allCompleted.on.click.add((Event e) {
    InputElement target = e.currentTarget;
    for (Todo todo in todos) {
      if (todo.task.completed != target.checked) {
        todo.toggleCompleted();
      }
    }
    updateCounts();
});
```

The updateCounts method of the TodoApp class, renamed from updateTodoCount, reflects well the number of tasks left to be done and the number of tasks completed (to be cleared by a click on the button):

```
updateCounts() {
    allCompleted.checked = (tasks.completed == tasks.count);
    todoCount.innerHTML =
        '<b>${tasks.left}</b> todo${tasks.left != 1 ? 's' : ''} left';
    if (tasks.completed == 0) {
        clearCompleted.style.display = 'none';
    } else {
        clearCompleted.style.display = 'block';
        clearCompleted.text = 'Clear completed (${tasks.completed})';
    }
    save();
}
```

The createElement method in the Todo class is renamed as create. Also, the CSS class of the input checkbox element for a single todo is renamed from toggle to toggle-completed:

```
Element create() {
    todo = new Element.html('''
        <li ${task.completed ? 'class="completed"' : ''}>
          <div class='view'>
            <input class='toggle-completed' type='checkbox'
              ${task.completed ? 'checked' : ''}>
            <label class='todo-content'>${task.title}</label>
            <button class='remove'></button>
          </div>
        </li>
        ''');
}
```

Finally, the toggleTodo method in the Todo class is renamed to toggleCompleted:

```
toggleCompleted() {
    task.completed = !task.completed;
    toggle.checked = task.completed;
    if (task.completed) {
        todo.classes.add('completed');
    } else {
        todo.classes.remove('completed');
    }
}
```

Spiral 6 – editing a task and testing the model

In the `todo_mvc_s06` spiral, a todo file may be edited. The `TodoApp` class is renamed to `Todos`:

```
class Todos {
  Tasks tasks;
  var todos = new List<Todo>();

  Element main = query('#main');
  Element allCompleted = query('#toggle-all-completed');
  Element todoList = query('#todo-list');
  Element footer = query('#footer');
  Element leftCount = query('#left-count');
  Element clearCompleted = query('#clear-completed');
}
```

The `create` method in the `Todo` class has two elements that represent two different states of the `todo` element. The `todoContent` element is double-clicked to edit the task title in the `edit` element. The double-click event adds the editing CSS class to the `todo` element, then selects and focuses on the `edit` element. The key press event on the `edit` element calls the `editingDone` function when the *ENTER* key is used. The `editingDone` function updates the corresponding task title and the displayed value of the `todoContent` element. After the editing CSS class is removed from the `todo` element, `todos` are saved in the local storage:

```
Element create() {
    todo = new Element.html('''
      <li ${task.completed ? 'class="completed"' : ''}>
        <div class='view'>
          <input class='toggle-completed' type='checkbox'
            ${task.completed ? 'checked' : ''}>
          <label class='todo-content'>${task.title}</label>
          <button class='remove'></button>
        </div>
        <input class='edit' value='${task.title}'>
      </li>
    ''');

    Element todoContent = todo.query('.todo-content');
    Element edit = todo.query('.edit');

    todoContent.on.doubleClick.add((MouseEvent e) {
      todo.classes.add('editing');
      edit.select();
```

```
        edit.focus();
      });

      editingDone(event) {
        task.title = edit.value.trim();
        if (task.title != '') {
          todoContent.text = task.title;
          todo.classes.remove('editing');
          todos.save();
        }
      }

      edit.on.keyPress.add((KeyboardEvent e) {
        if (e.keyCode == KeyCode.ENTER) {
          editingDone(e);
        }
      });
```

In the `test/todo/mvc/todo_mvc_test.dart` file, there are 27 tests of the dartling model. When the file is run in Dart Editor, all the tests pass:

PASS: Testing Todo.Mvc Empty Entries Test

PASS: Testing Todo.Mvc From Tasks to JSON

PASS: Testing Todo.Mvc From Task Model to JSON

PASS: Testing Todo.Mvc From JSON to Task Model

PASS: Testing Todo.Mvc Add Task Required Title Error

PASS: Testing Todo.Mvc Add Task Pre Validation

PASS: Testing Todo.Mvc Find Task by New Oid

PASS: Testing Todo.Mvc Find Task by Attribute

PASS: Testing Todo.Mvc Random Task

PASS: Testing Todo.Mvc Select Tasks by Function

PASS: Testing Todo.Mvc Select Tasks by Function then Add

PASS: Testing Todo.Mvc Select Tasks by Function then Remove

PASS: Testing Todo.Mvc Order Tasks by Title

PASS: Testing Todo.Mvc Copy Tasks

PASS: Testing Todo.Mvc Copy Equality

PASS: Testing Todo.Mvc True for Every Task

PASS: Testing Todo.Mvc Find Task then Set Oid with Failure

PASS: Testing Todo.Mvc Find Task then Set Oid with Success

PASS: Testing Todo.Mvc Update New Task Title with Failure

```
PASS: Testing Todo.Mvc Update New Task Oid with Success
PASS: Testing Todo.Mvc Find Task by Attribute then Examine Code and Id
PASS: Testing Todo.Mvc Add Task Undo and Redo
PASS: Testing Todo.Mvc Remove Task Undo and Redo
PASS: Testing Todo.Mvc Add Task Undo and Redo with Session
PASS: Testing Todo.Mvc Undo and Redo Update Task Title
PASS: Testing Todo.Mvc Undo and Redo Transaction
PASS: Testing Todo.Mvc Reactions to Task Actions
```

```
All 27 tests passed.
unittest-suite-success
```

There are three packages imported in the test file: the `test` package to use the testing facility, the `dartling` package to inherit the methods on the entities of the model, and the `todo_mvc` package to use the specific code added to the model:

```
import "package:test/test.dart";
import "package:dartling/dartling.dart";
import "package:todo_mvc/todo_mvc.dart";
```

The `todo` repository is created in the `main` function of the testing file and passed as an argument to the `testTodoData` function:

```
testTodoData(TodoRepo todoRepo) {
  testTodoMvc(todoRepo, TodoRepo.todoDomainCode,
      TodoRepo.todoMvcModelCode);
}

void main() {
  var todoRepo = new TodoRepo();
  testTodoData(todoRepo);
}
```

The `testTodoData` function finds the domain and model names and calls the `testTodoMvc` function. In the `setUp` function (the setup for each test), based on the domain name (code in dartling), a collection of models (in this example, only one) of the domain are retrieved. A new session is defined. Based on the model name (code), entries (in this example, only one—`tasks`) of the model are obtained.

This code tests the MVC model in the `todo` domain:

```
testTodoMvc(Repo repo, String domainCode, String modelCode) {
  TodoModels models;
  DomainSession session;
  MvcEntries entries;
  Tasks tasks;
  int count = 0;
  Concept concept;
  group("Testing ${domainCode}.${modelCode}", () {
    setUp(() {
      models = repo.getDomainModels(domainCode);
      session = models.newSession();
      entries = models.getModelEntries(modelCode);
      expect(entries, isNotNull);
      tasks = entries.tasks;
      expect(tasks.count, equals(count));
      concept = tasks.concept;
      expect(concept, isNotNull);
      expect(concept.attributes.list, isNot(isEmpty));
    }
  }
```

Three tasks are created in the setup for each test. Each test starts with three tasks:

```
var design = new Task(concept);
      expect(design, isNotNull);
      design.title = 'design a model';
      tasks.add(design);
      expect(tasks.count, equals(++count));

      var json = new Task(concept);
      json.title = 'generate json from the model';
      tasks.add(json);
      expect(tasks.count, equals(++count));

      var generate = new Task(concept);
      generate.title = 'generate code from the json document';
      tasks.add(generate);
      expect(tasks.count, equals(++count));
```

The `tearDown` function is called after each test to clear all the tasks. The `setUp` function is called before every test to create several tasks.

After every test, tasks are cleared:

```
tearDown(() {
    tasks.clear();
    expect(tasks.empty, isTrue);
    count = 0;
});
```

The first test clears all the entries. Since there is only one entry to the model, which is tasks, the tasks are cleared and the entries become empty. This means that the model does not have any data:

```
test('Empty Entries Test', () {
    entries.clear();
    expect(entries.empty, isTrue);
});
```

The three tasks created in the setUp function are transformed by dartling into a list of maps, a map for each task, and then printed:

```
test('From Tasks to JSON', () {
    var json = tasks.toJson();
    expect(json, isNotNull);
    print(json);
});
```

Here is the printed list of maps displayed in the console of Dart Editor:

```
[
    {
        completed:false,
        oid:1357225270729,
        title:design a model,
        code:null
    },
    {
        completed:false,
        oid:1357225270731,
        title:generate json from the model,
        code:null
    },
    {
        completed:false,
        oid:1357225270732,
        title:generate code from the json document,
        code:null
    }
]
```

Summary

In this chapter, we used the domain modeling framework, dartling, to build an app, from designing the model to generating and testing the application's code. Then, we discussed the universally applied MVC pattern and used it together with dartling to build a complete and usable `todo` app. In this process, the advantages of using a domain modeling framework became apparent. Once a model is designed, its code is generated, which is a big deal for large models. Although the code for the model is generated, a programmer may add some specific code that will not be lost if the model is regenerated. The API of dartling, for example, for entities, is rich and it allows the handling of identifiers and relationships, which is not done in Dartlero. The code in the `TodoMVC` application clearly shows that, after the code is generated, there is not much model programming left to do, allowing a developer to focus on the UI.

In the next chapter, we'll get an overview of the MVC and UI frameworks built by the Dart community.

10

Local Data and Client-Server Communication

Data goes around in applications, but, eventually, new and modified data has to be stored; this can be done on the client or server. In the previous chapters, we used local storage (also called web storage) in the browser. Here, we will investigate a better client-side storage mechanism called **IndexedDB** and a layer called **Lawndart** that automatically chooses the best local storage mechanism available on the client. Most of the time, the data needs to be available to many people, so it needs to be stored centrally on a server. We will see how to communicate data between the client and server with JSON and, in the next chapter, how to store this data in a database on the server-side. Then, we'll see that Dart can be used for both sides of a client-server app. To do this, we need to learn how Dart works with asynchronous calls using the `Future` objects and how it can run as a web server. The following are the topics for this chapter:

- What are the options for browser storage?
- Asynchronous calls and `Future` objects
- How to use IndexedDB with Dart
- Using Lawndart
- A Dart web server
- Using JSON web services

The options for browser storage

Using client-side data storage reduces bandwidth traffic, decreases network response times (latency), increases UI performance, and, best of all, allows your application to run offline. The local storage mechanism that we've used until now is a very simple key/value store and does have good cross-browser coverage. However, it can only store strings and is a blocking (synchronous) API; this means that it can temporarily stop your web page from responding while it is doing its job. This can be bad for performance when your app wants to store or read large amounts of data, such as images. Moreover, it has a space limit of 5 Mb (this varies with the browsers); you can't detect when you are nearing this limit and you can't ask for more space! These properties make it only as useful as a temporary data storage tool—better than cookies, but not suited for a reliable database kind of storage.

On the other hand, IndexedDB is the future of offline, local object storage for your web app. It has all the advantages of a local storage, but no size limit. It is a database which comprises a lot of functionality; however, being an indexed object store, it belongs to the family of NoSQL databases (similar to MongoDB and CouchDB on the server). It is on the track to becoming an official standard and it does have Chrome, Firefox, and Internet Explorer (a version greater than or similar to 10) implementations. Using indexes, it provides a far better search performance than web storage, but programming it is more complex (the equivalent of relational database storage in the browser also exists and is called Web SQL DB. However, its specification is no longer maintained and Firefox and Internet Explorer do not support it. This is why we won't discuss it here). IndexedDB works in a non-blocking way for our app and, before we dive into how to use it, we will explore Dart's mechanism to program non-blocking codes called the `Future` objects.

Asynchronous calls and Future objects

How should our app handle a situation where it needs a service that can take some time to return its result, for example, when we have to fetch or store data, read a large file, or need a response from a web service. Obviously, the app can't wait for this to end and the result to arrive (the so-called **synchronous** way), because this would freeze the screen (and the app) and frustrate users. A responsive web app must be able to call this service and immediately continue with what it was doing. Only when the result returns should it react and call some function on the response data. This is called working in an **asynchronous**, non-blocking way. Most of the methods in `dart:io` for server-side Dart apps work in this way.

Developers with a Java or C# background would perhaps think of starting another thread to do additional work, but Dart can't do it. Dart has to compile to JavaScript, so similar to JavaScript, it also works in a single-threaded model that is tightly-controlled by the browser's event loop. On the Web (client as well as server), the code has to execute as asynchronously as possible in order to not block the browser from serving its user or a server process from serving its many thousands of client requests. The JavaScript world has long solved this issue using **callbacks**; this is a function that is "called" when the result of the first function called returns ("backs"). In the following code snippet, the first function that will return the result is `doStuff` and `handle` is registered as a callback that will work on the result; when an error occurs (`onError`), `handleError` is invoked:

```
doStuff((result) {
    handle(result);
}, onError: (e) {
    handleError(e);
});
```

The same mechanism can be used in Dart; but, here, we have a more elegant way to handle this with objects appropriately called the `Future` objects. Now, we will define `doStuff` to return a `Future` object; this is a value (which could be an error) that is not yet available when `doStuff` returns. However, it will be available sometime in the future after `doStuff` has been executed (indicated using the `then` keyword). The same code snippet written using the `Future` objects will then be much more readable:

```
doStuff()
    .then( (result) => handle(result) )
    .catchError( (e) => handleError(e) );
```

The `doStuff` method returns a `Future` object, so it could have been written as:

```
Future fut1 = doStuff();
fut1.then( (result) => handle(result) )
    .catchError( (e) => handleError(e) );
```

However, the first or even the following shorter way is idiomatically used:

```
doStuff()
    .then(handle)
    .catchError(handleError);
```

Then, it registers the `handle` callback and `catchError` calls `handleError` when an error occurs, which stops the error from propagating. It could be considered as the asynchronous version of a try/catch construct (there is also a `.whenComplete` handler that is always executed and it corresponds with finally). The syntax advantage becomes even clearer when callbacks are nested to enforce the execution order, because this results in ugly and difficult-to-read code (sometimes referred to as callback hell). Suppose a `doStuff2` computation has to occur between `doStuff` and `handle`, the first snippet will become much less readable:

```
doStuff((result){
doStuff2((result){
handle((result) {
      });
   }, onError: (e) {
  handleError(e);
  });
}, onError: (e) {
  handleError(e);
  });
```

However, the version using the `Future` objects remains very simple:

```
doStuff()
  .then(doStuff2)
  .then(handle)
  .catchError(handleError);
```

Through this chaining syntax, it looks like synchronous code, but it is purely an asynchronous code executing; `catchError` catches any errors that occur in the chain of the `Future` objects. As a simple, but working, example, suppose a `future1` app needs to show or process a large `bigfile.txt` file and we don't want to wait until this I/O is completely done:

```
import 'dart:io';                                           (1)
import 'dart:async';

var file;                                                   (2)

main() {
  file = new File('bigfile.txt');                           (3)
  // using Future:
  readFileFuture();
  // using async / await
  readFileAsync();
    .then( (text) => print(text) )
    .catchError( (e) => print(e) );
```

```
    // do other things while file is read in
    ...                                                        (7)
}
readFileFuture() {
    file.readAsString()                                        (4)
                .then((text) => print(text))                   (5)
                .catchError((e) => print(e));                  (6)
// shorter version:
//   file.readAsString()
//     .then(print)
//     .catchError(print);
}

readFileAsync() async {
  try {
      var text = await file.readAsString();
      await print(text);
  }
  catch (e) {
    print(e);
  }
}
```

To work with files and directories, dart:io is needed in line (1); the Future
functionality comes from dart:async (line (2)). In line (3), a File object is created.
In line (4), the action to read the file is started asynchronously. However, the
program immediately continues executing lines (7) and beyond. When the file is
completely read through, line (5) prints its contents; should an e error (for example,
a nonexisting file) have occurred, it is printed in line (6). You can even leave out the
intermediary variables and write:

```
file.readAsString()
  .then(print)
  .catchError(print);
```

In the readFileAsync method, we do the same, but now with the newer async
/ await syntax (see *Chapter 3, Structuring Code with Classes and Libraries*). Error
handling can be applied here with normal try/catch. Asynchronous functions
return the Future objects, so it will boil down to the same mechanism, but the
syntax will be more readable.

You can find more information at https://www.dartlang.org/articles/
futures-and-error-handling/.

Using IndexedDB with Dart

IndexedDB is a transactional database system like a SQL-based RDBMS. However, while the latter uses tables with fixed columns, IndexedDB is a JavaScript-based object-oriented database. IndexedDB lets you store and retrieve objects that are indexed with a key. You need to specify the database schema, open a connection to your database, and retrieve and update the data within a series of transactions. Operations in IndexedDB are done asynchronously, so as to not block the rest of the application's running.

We will learn how to work with IndexedDB and JSON web services through the `indexed_db_spirals` project (`https://github.com/dzenanr/indexed_db_spirals`), which is a `todo` app like the ones we've built in the previous chapters. However, this stores its data in IndexedDB. Get a copy of the code with a `git` clone:

`https://github.com/dzenanr/indexed_db_spirals.git`.

Spiral s00

In this spiral, the `todo` tasks can be entered. They are stored in IndexedDB. The following is a screenshot:

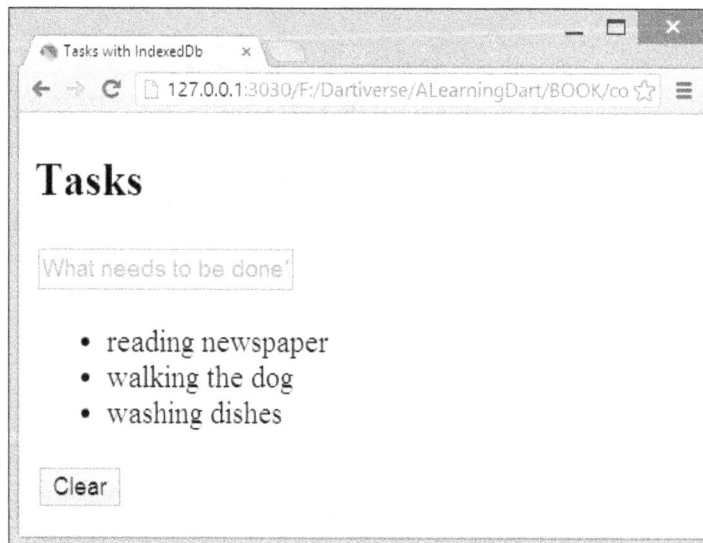

The Tasks screen of Spiral s00

Our model class is called `Task` and it lives in `model.dart`; with `toDb` and `FromDb`, it can transform an object to or make an object from a map:

```
class Task {
  String title;
  bool completed = false;
  DateTime updated = new DateTime.now();
  var key;

  Task(this.title);

  Task.fromDb(this.key, Map value):
    title = value['title'],
    updated = DateTime.parse(value['updated']),
    completed = value['completed'] == 'true' {
  }


  Map toDb() {
    return {
      'title': title,
      'completed': completed.toString(),
      'updated': updated.toString()
    };
  }
}
```

Besides `Task`, the model also contains the `TasksStore` class, which contains `List<Task>` and interacts with IndexedDB. To do this, we need to import the `dart:indexed_db` library to `model.dart`, which will provide the Dart API to use IndexedDB:

```
import 'dart:indexed_db';
```

The web page is `view.html` and references `view.dart`; this contains all the UI code setup from the `main()` entry point:

```
import 'dart:html';
import 'model.dart';

Element taskElements;
TasksStore tasksStore;

main() {
```

```
  taskElements = querySelector('#task-list');
  tasksStore = new TasksStore();
  tasksStore.open().then((_) {                               (1)
    loadElements(tasksStore.tasks);
  });

  InputElement newTask = querySelector('#new-task');
  newTask.onKeyPress.listen((KeyboardEvent e) {
    if (e.keyCode == KeyCode.ENTER) {
      var title = newTask.value.trim();
      if (title != '') {
        tasksStore.add(title).then((task) {                  (2)
          addElement(task);
        });
        newTask.value = '';
      }
    }
  });

  ButtonElement clear = querySelector('#clear-tasks');
  clear.onClick.listen((MouseEvent e) {
    tasksStore.clear().then((_) {                            (3)
      clearElements();
    });
  });
}
Element newElement(Task task) {
  return new Element.html('''
    <li>
      ${task.title}
    </li>
  ''');
}

addElement(Task task) {
  var taskElement = newElement(task);
  taskElements.nodes.add(taskElement);
}

loadElements(List tasks) {
  for (Task task in tasks) {
```

```
      addElement(task);
    }
  }

  clearElements() {
    taskElements.nodes.clear();
  }
}
```

All the interactions with IndexedDB are asynchronous and return the `Future` objects; this is why we use `then` in lines `(1)` to `(3)`, respectively, while opening a database and adding a task or removing all the tasks. The `loadElements`, `addElement`, and `clearElements` callback functions update the screen after the database has been changed (the code is straightforward; see `view.dart`). In line `(1)`, we see that for the parameter of the `then` callback function, `(_)` is written; this means there is one parameter, but we don't need it, so we won't name it. What happens now, in line `(1)` in the preceding code, with the `open()` call on `TaskStore`? You can imagine that we need to open the database or create it the first time the page is requested. This is done with a call to `window.indexedDB.open` in line `(4)` in `model.dart`:

```
class TasksStore {
  static const String TASKS_STORE = 'tasksStore';
  final List<Task> tasks = new List();
  Database _db;

  Future open() {
    return window.indexedDB.open('tasksDb00',                (4)
        version: 1,
        onUpgradeNeeded: _initDb)                            (5)
      .then(_loadDb);                                        (6)
  }
// code left out
```

The open() method takes three parameters: the first two are listed in an alphabetical order by the name of the database and the third by the version number. When the app is first started on a client, a database with its name and version 1 is created; every subsequent time, it is simply opened. On creating it, the third onUpgradeNeeded parameter kicks in to fire an upgrade event, which calls _initDb in line (5). You can upgrade a database to a higher version by opening it with a new version number. Then, an upgrade event will take place and the previous version of the database will not exist anymore. Our tasksDb00 database needs one or more object stores; these can only be created during an upgrade event. Here, in _initDb, we get a reference to the database object in line (7), and, in line (8), we create an object store (that can contain data records) named TasksStore. The value of the constant is TASKS_STORE:

```
void _initDb(VersionChangeEvent e) {
    var db = (e.target as Request).result;              (7)
    var objectStore = db.createObjectStore(TASKS_STORE  (8)
        autoIncrement: true);
}
```

The autoIncrement property, when true, lets the database generate unique primary keys for you. In a later spiral, we will also create an index to enhance query speed. A database can contain multiple object stores if needed and our app can have access to multiple databases at once. After initialization, the then callback in line (6) kicks in, calling _loadDb:

```
Future _loadDb(Database db) {
    _db = db;
    var trans = db.transaction(TASKS_STORE, 'readonly');    (9)
    var store = trans.objectStore(TASKS_STORE);
    var cursors = store.openCursor(autoAdvance:             (10)
        true).asBroadcastStream();
    cursors.listen((cursor) {                               (11)
        var task = new Task.fromDb(cursor.key, cursor.value);
        tasks.add(task);
    });

    return cursors.length.then((_) {                       (12)
        return tasks.length;
    });
}
```

To make sure it is reliable, every operation on the database happens within a transaction. So, this transaction is created in line (9) and attached to the object store (this is also required for reads; the second argument can be `readonly`, `readwrite`, or `versionchange`). Database transactions take time, so the results are always provided via the `Future` objects. Getting records from a database is mostly done using a `Cursor` object, which is created here in line (10) with the `openCursor` method on the object store. The `cursors` object indicates the current position in the object store, and returns the records one by one through a `Stream` object automatically because of the `autoAdvance` parameter (otherwise, use the `next()` method). For each record that returns, a `listen` event fires the code defined in line (11). Here, the `cursor.key` and `cursor.value` database values are passed to the task constructor named `fromDb`, so a new task is created and added to the list. A `BroadcastStream` method also returns the length of the cursor as the final event in line (12), which is also the length of the tasks collection. When a task is added, the `add` method on the store will be called in line (2):

```
Future<Task> add(String title) {
    var task = new Task(title);
    var taskMap = task.toDb();                                  (13)

    var transaction = _db.transaction(TASKS_STORE, 'readwrite');
    var objectStore = transaction.objectStore(TASKS_STORE);

    objectStore.add(taskMap).then((addedKey) {                  (14)
      task.key = addedKey;
    });

    return transaction.completed.then((_) {                     (15)
      tasks.add(task);
      return task;
    });
}
```

The `Task` class has a `toDb` method called in line (13) to transform the `Task` object into a map. A read/write transaction is created and the `add` method is called on the store in line (14) with the task data. This also returns a the `Future` object, resulting in the key generated by the database (`addedKey`), which is also stored in the task object. When the transaction completes in line (15), the task is added to the collection and returned as the `Future` object's result, which is then used in `view.dart` to update the view. Removing all the objects from the store is easy; calling `clear` on the store in line (3) executes:

```
Future clear() {
    var transaction = _db.transaction(TASKS_STORE, 'readwrite');
    transaction.objectStore(TASKS_STORE).clear();
```

```
    return transaction.completed.then((_) {
      tasks.clear();
    });
}
```

This results in the clearing of the tasks collection and then the updating of the view. To see the data in your IndexedDB database at any moment, navigate to **Chrome View** | **Developer** | **Developer Tools**, and then choose **Resources** from the tabs along the top of the window:

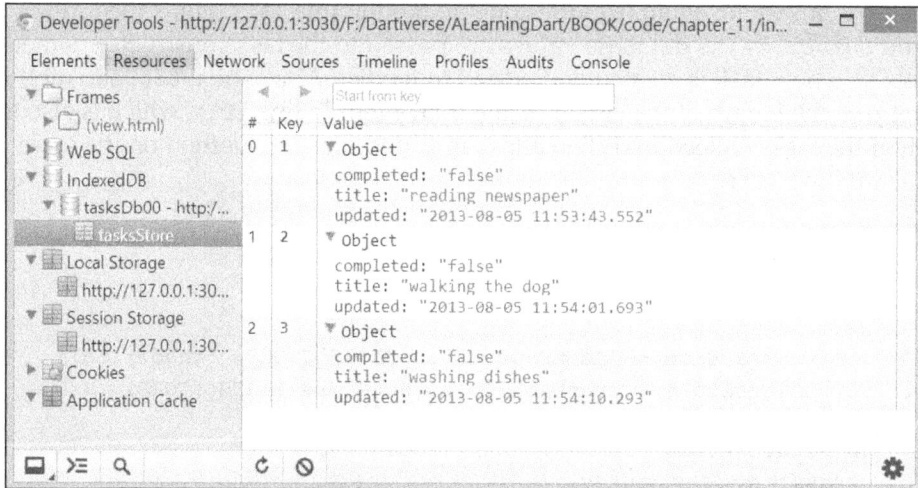

Viewing IndexedDb with developer tools

Spiral s01

No new functionality is added here, but the start up web page is renamed to app. html and the layout is improved through CSS. Furthermore, the methods are made private where possible and the app architecture is refactored to MVC by introducing a library in line (1); all of the UI code is moved from view.dart to the TasksView class in lib/view/view.dart, and the model code to lib/model/model.dart. Both are now contained in the lib/indexed_db.dart library file:

```
library indexed_db;                                              (1)

import 'dart:async';
import 'dart:html';
import 'dart:indexed_db';

part 'model/model.dart';
part 'view/view.dart';
```

The main `app.dart` Dart file imports our new library in line (2) and uses a `TasksView` object:

```
import 'package:indexed_db/indexed_db.dart';                    (2)

main() {
  var tasksStore = new TasksStore();
  var tasksView = new TasksView(tasksStore);
  tasksStore.open().then((_) {
    tasksView.loadElements(tasksStore.tasks);
  });
}
```

Spiral s02

Now, we can remove a task or mark it as completed using the x button, as shown in the following screenshot:

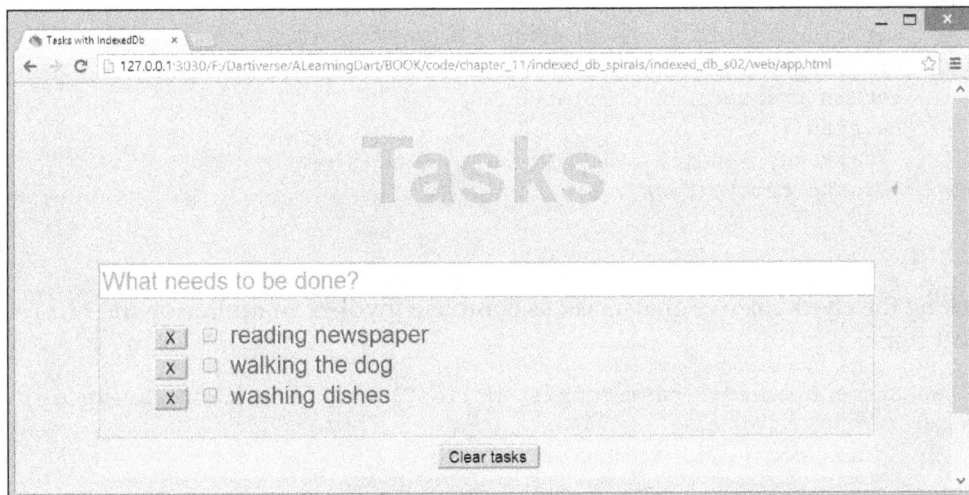

The screen of Spiral s02

To accomplish this, the `newElement` method is expanded a bit to draw the checkbox and remove button:

```
Element _newElement(Task task) {
    return new Element.html('''
        <li>
            <button class='task-button remove-task'>X</button>
            <input class='task-completed' type='checkbox'
              ${task.completed ? 'checked' : ''}>
```

```
            <label class='task-title'>${task.title}</label>
        </li>
    ''');
    }
```

The `Element.html` file performs default validations and removes all the scriptable elements and attributes so that no code injection takes place.

In `_addElement`, a click event handler on the x button is added, which removes the task from the object store:

```
tasksStore.remove(task).then((_) {
    _taskElements.nodes.remove(taskElement);
    _updateFooter();
});
```

The click event handler then calls the `remove` method in the `TasksStore` class to delete it in the object store:

```
Future remove(Task task) {
    var transaction = _db.transaction(TASKS_STORE, 'readwrite');
    transaction.objectStore(TASKS_STORE).delete(task.key);
    return transaction.completed
      .then((_) {
      task.key = null;
      tasks.remove(task);
      });
}
```

Clicking the checkbox to signal a task as complete invokes an update on the object store:

```
taskElement.query('.task-completed').onClick.listen((MouseEvent e)
{
    task.completed = !task.completed;
    task.updated = new DateTime.now();
    tasksStore.update(task);
});
```

The `update` method transforms the `Task` object to a map (which is needed to store it in IndexedDB) and calls the `put` method on the object store:

```
Future update(Task task) {
    var taskMap = task.toDb();
    var transaction = _db.transaction(TASKS_STORE, 'readwrite');
    transaction.objectStore(TASKS_STORE).put(taskMap, task.key);
    return transaction.completed;
}
```

Spiral s03

The new elements in this spiral are: a checkbox above the textbox to mark all the tasks as completed, the number of active (incomplete) tasks shown at the bottom, and a button to clear (remove) all the completed tasks (their number is indicated in the parentheses) are added. The active and completed tasks are returned by the getters in the `TasksStore` class, for instance:

```
List<Task> get activeTasks {
    var active = new List<Task>();
    for (var task in tasks) {
      if (!task.completed) {
        active.add(task);
      }
    }
    return active;
}
```

In `_initDb`, we create a new database by changing the name and creating a unique index on the title by calling `createIndex` on the object store:

```
store.createIndex(TITLE_INDEX, 'title', unique: true);
```

This speeds up the search on tasks' titles. The click handler for the **complete all tasks** button calls the following method:

```
Future completeTasks() {
    Future future;
    for (var task in tasks) {
      if (!task.completed) {
        task.completed = true;
        task.updated = new DateTime.now();
        future = update(task);
      }
    }
    return future;
}
```

In fact, this will only return the `Future` object of the last update. In this example, it will be the last one to get completed. However, it would be more correct to return a `Future` objects that completes when all the updates are complete. We'll make improvements in spirals s06 and s07.

All kinds of detailed screen updates are now assembled in `_updateDisplay()` in `view.dart`.

Spiral s04

Now, our `todo` application is getting more and more functional with nice links to all the active and completed task lists, the possibility of editing the task's title, and the persistence for the data in IndexedDB, as shown in the following screenshot:

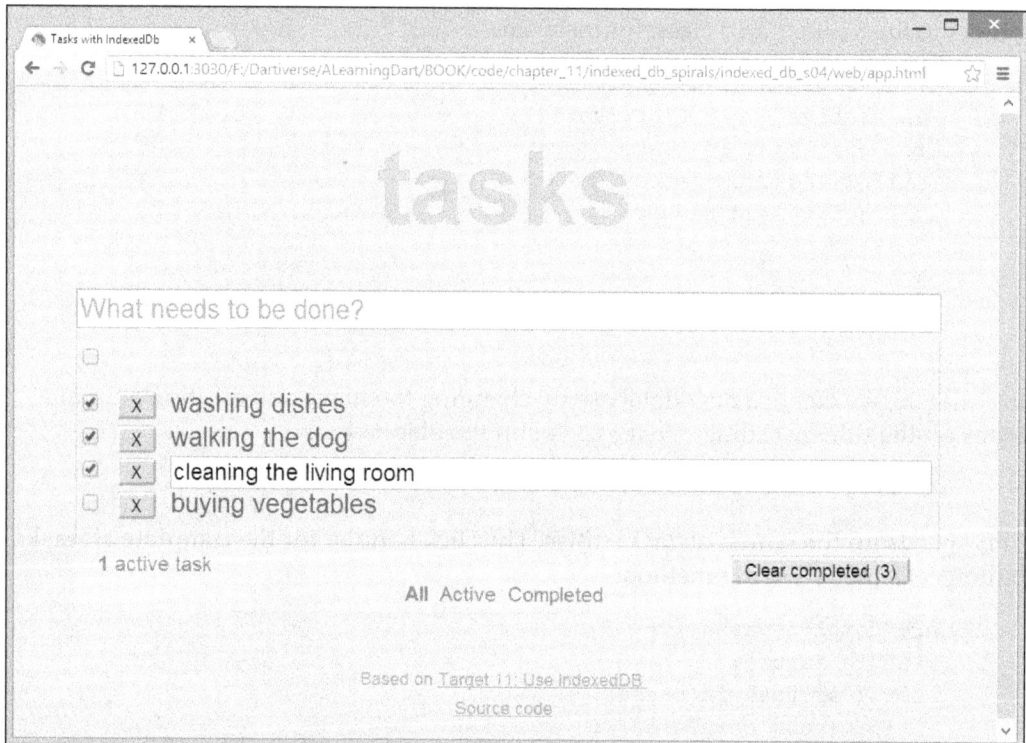

The screen of Spiral s04

The following code changes are worth discussing. In the previous spiral, a unique index on the title was created. However, no error message was shown when a duplicate task was entered; the double task was simply not added and the IndexedDB error was ignored. Now, we do better by using the `catchError` method in line (1) and changing the `Keypress` event handler of the input field to:

```
InputElement newTask = query('#new-task');
newTask.onKeyPress.listen((KeyboardEvent e) {
  if (e.keyCode == KeyCode.ENTER) {
    var title = newTask.value.trim();
    if (title != '') {
      _tasksStore.add(title)
        .then((task) {
```

```
            _addElement(task);
            newTask.value = '';
            _updateFilter();
         })
       .catchError((e) {  // IndexedDB error unique index      (1)
            newTask.value = '${title} : title not unique';
            newTask.select();
         });
     }
   }
});
```

The edit functionality is coded as follows, when the task title is double-clicked on in line (2) and a `editTitle` textbox, in line (3), is selected:

```
Element title = taskElement.query('.task-title');
InputElement editTitle = taskElement.query('.edit-title');
editTitle.hidden = true;
title.onDoubleClick.listen((MouseEvent e) {                     (2)
  title.hidden = true;
  editTitle.hidden = false;                                     (3)
  editTitle.select();
});
```

The `editTitle` variable also has an `onKeyPress` event handler that calls an update on the store and shows a nonunique error when this occurs.

The model now has a `find` method based on querying the index in line along with `get` in line (4):

```
Future<Task> find(String title) {
    var trans = _db.transaction(TASKS_STORE, 'readonly');
    var store = trans.objectStore(TASKS_STORE);
    var index = store.index(TITLE_INDEX);
    var future = index.get(title);                              (4)
    return future
      .then((taskMap) {
        var task = new Task.fromDbWoutKey(taskMap);
        return task;
      });
  }
```

This is used in the _showActive and _showCompleted methods of the view:

```
_showCompleted() {
  _setSelectedFilter(_completedElements);
  for (LIElement element in _taskElements.children) {
    Element titleLabel = element.query('.task-title');
    String title = titleLabel.text;
    _tasksStore.find(title)
      .then((task) {
        element.hidden = !task.completed;                    (5)
      })
      .catchError((e) {});
  }
}
```

In line (5), we see that the task in the list is hidden when it is not yet completed.

Spiral s05

In this spiral, the UI and functionality remain the same, but the model is reorganized. The model code, which contains the Task class and a Tasks collection class (with methods such as sort, contains, find, add, remove, and display0 in lib/model/model.dart), is cleanly decoupled from the data access code: the TasksDb and TasksStore classes in lib/model/idb.dart. This makes it easier to change or enhance the model code, or use another data source by switching to a different data access layer, which is what we do in **Spiral s05_1**.

Using Lawndart

IndexedDB doesn't (yet) work on all browsers. What if we don't know what browser our clients will use? Can we still provide universal offline key-value storage? The solution is Lawndart (https://github.com/sethladd/lawndart), a pub package that you can import in your app, which has been developed by Seth Ladd as a Dart reworking of Lawnchair. Lawndart presents an asynchronous, but consistent interface to local storage, IndexedDb, and Web SQL. Your app simply works with an instance of the Store class and the factory constructor will try IndexedDB, Web SQL, and then, finally, local storage. This is implemented in **Spiral s05_1**; the only change with **Spiral s05** is that IndexedDB (idb.dart) is replaced with Lawndart (lawndart.dart). For example, the load method is now written as:

```
Future load() async {
  await for (var taskJsonString in _store.all()) {
    var task = new Task();
```

```
            task.fromJsonString(taskJsonString);
            tasks.add(task);
        }
    }
}
```

Study `lawndart.dart` to see how the interface code changes.

A Dart web server

The Dart VM can also run as a server application on the command line or as a background job. While creating the application, choose the command-line application template. Most of Dart's server functionality lives in the `dart:io` library, which cannot be used in writing browser Dart apps; in the same way, `dart:html` cannot be used on the server. The `HttpServer` class is used to write Dart servers; a server listens on a particular host and port for incoming requests and provides event handlers (also called request handlers) that are triggered when a request with incoming data from a client is received. The latter is described by the `HttpRequest` class, which is an asynchronous API provided by the browser (formerly known as Ajax) and has properties, such as method, path, query parameters, and `InputStream` with the data. The server responds by writing to `OutputStream` of an `HttpResponse` object. The following is the code of the `webserver` project, where you can easily see all the parts interacting:

```
import 'dart:io';

main() {
  print('simple web server');
  HttpServer.bind('127.0.0.1', 8080).then((server) {
    print('server will start listening');
    server.listen((HttpRequest request) {
      print('server listened');
      request.response.write('Learn Dart by Projects, develop in
        Spirals!');
      request.response.close();
    });
  });
}
```

Firstly, start the server from the editor or on the command line with `dart webserver.dart`. Then, start a (any) browser with the `http://localhost:8080` URL to see the response text appear on the client; the print output will appear in the server console.

Using JSON web services

In this section, we code a web server that communicates with our clients and runs the `todo` app; the `todo` data is sent to and from the web server in the JSON string format. **Spiral s06** consists of a server and a client part. To run it, first start the server (`lib/server/server.dart`) in Dart Editor or from the console; it runs when you see in the `server.dart` tab in Dart Editor: **Listening for GET and POST on http://127.0.0.1:8080** (If it does not run, use run/manage launches). Then, start one or more clients (`web/app.html`) in Dartium. Locally, the client still saves the data in IndexedDB. Our screen has two new buttons:

- **To server**: The client converts the data into the JSON format and sends it to the server, where the data is stored in the main memory (post data to server)

- **From server**: Another client (on a different machine) can request the server data to update its local database (get data from the server)

This is how the `tasks` application at this stage looks like:

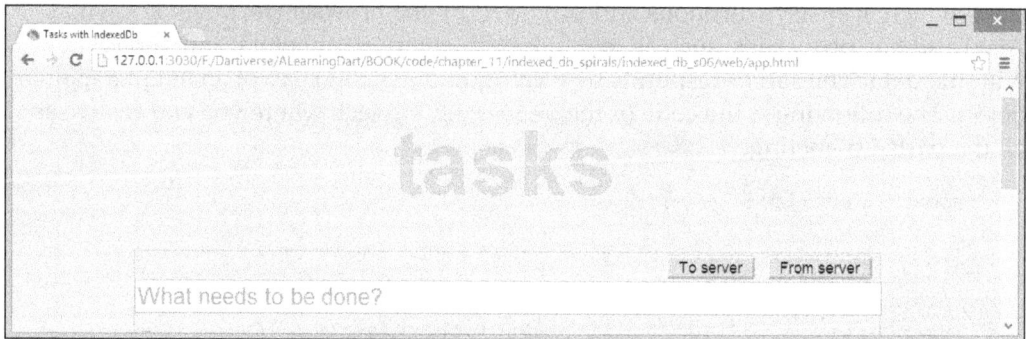

Server communication in Spiral s06

The following is the client code (from `lib/view/view.dart`) for **To server** (posting data):

```
ButtonElement toServer = querySelector('#to-server');
    toServer.onClick.listen((MouseEvent e) {
      var request = new HttpRequest();                          (1)
      request.onReadyStateChange.listen((_) {                   (2)
        if (request.readyState == HttpRequest.DONE &&
            request.status == 200) {
          // Data saved OK on server.
          serverResponse = 'Server: ' + request.responseText;
        } else if (request.readyState == HttpRequest.DONE &&
            request.status == 0) {
          // Status is 0...most likely the server isn't running.
```

```
            serverResponse = 'No server';
        }
    });

    var url = 'http://127.0.0.1:8080';
    request.open('POST', url);                                          (3)
    request.send(_tasksStore.tasks.toJsonString());                     (4)
  });
```

In line (1), a new client request is made. From line (3), we see that the method is POST. In line (4), the data from the tasks collection is sent to the server. Then, the client listens to a possible server response (status and responseText) in the onReadyStateChange event. HttpStatus 200 indicates that everything went fine. The code for fromServer (getting data) is shown as follows:

```
ButtonElement fromServer = querySelector('#from-server');
fromServer.onClick.listen((MouseEvent e) {
    HttpRequest.getString('http://127.0.0.1:8080')
      .then((result) {                                                  (5)
        String jsonString = result;
        serverResponse = 'Server: ' + result;
        print('JSON text from the server: ${jsonString}');
        if (jsonString != '') {
          List<Map> jsonList = JSON.decode(jsonString);      (6)
          print('JSON list from the server: ${jsonList}');
          _tasksStore.loadFromJson(jsonList)                 (7)
            .then((_) {
              var tasks = _tasksStore.tasks;
              _clearElements();
              loadElements(tasks);
            })
            .catchError((e) {
                          print('error in loading data into
                                 IndexedDB from JSON list');
          });
        }
    });
  });
});
```

We get the data in the JSON format from the server with the getString method. The response from the server containing the data is stored in result in line (5), decoded in List<Map> in line (6), and added to IndexedDB through the loadFromJson method (line (7)). Of course, the print statements are only needed as a way to log what takes place and what can be left out. We will improve this code in **Spiral s07**.

However, what happens on the server? The server is started through the
following code:

```dart
import 'dart:io';
import 'dart:convert';

const String HOST = "127.0.0.1"; // or: "localhost"
const int PORT = 8080;
List<Map> jsonList;

void main() {
  start();
}

start() {
  HttpServer.bind(HOST, PORT).then((server) {
    server.listen((HttpRequest request) {
      switch (request.method) {                               (1)
        case 'GET':
          handleGet(request);
          break;
        case 'POST':
          handlePost(request);
          break;
        case 'OPTIONS':
          handleOptions(request);
          break;
        default: defaultHandler(request);
      }
    },
    onError: print);                                          (2)
  })
    .catchError(print)
    .whenComplete(() => print('Listening for GET and POST on
      http://$HOST:$PORT'));
}
```

In line (1) in the listen handler, we match the method of the request. Notice in
line (2), the onError handler, which is, in fact, the second optional parameter of
the listen method (onError: print could also be written as onError: (e) =>
print(e) to see an error while trying to start the server on port 80. Then, you get
SocketException). Everything between lines (1) and (2) is the (anonymous)
onData handler of listen.

In the **To server** situation, `handlePost` is executed:

```
void handlePost(HttpRequest request) {
  print('${request.method}: ${request.uri.path}');
  request.listen((List<int> buffer) {                          (3)
    var jsonString = new String.fromCharCodes(buffer);
    jsonList = JSON.decode(jsonString);                        (4)
    print('JSON list in POST: ${jsonList}');                   (5)
  },
  onError: print);
}
```

Here, in the `listen` handler the client data is loaded in the buffer in line (3). It is then decoded to the `List<Map>` `jsonList` variable on the server storing the data in memory (line (4)). The server prints to its console in line (5):

POST: /

JSON list in POST: [{title: washing dishes, completed: true, updated: 2013-08-08 15:40:51.999}, {title: walking the dog, completed: true, updated: 2013-08-08 10:30:47.794}, {title: cleaning the kitchen, completed: false, updated: 2013-08-08 15:21:44.626}, {title: buying vegetables, completed: false, updated: 2013-08-08 10:32:20.707}]

In the **From server** situation, `handleGet` is executed:

```
void handleGet(HttpRequest request) {
  HttpResponse res = request.response;                         (6)
  print('${request.method}: ${request.uri.path}');
  addCorsHeaders(res);                                         (7)
  res.headers.contentType =
      new ContentType("application", "json", charset: 'utf-8');(8)
  if (jsonList != null) {
    String jsonString = JSON.encode(jsonList);                (9)
    print('JSON list in GET: ${jsonList}');
    res.write(jsonString);                                     (10)
  }
  res.close();                                                 (11)
}
```

Here, the response is prepared from line (6) onwards; line (8) sets the content type of the server response to the JSON text. In line (9), the `jsonList` server variable is encoded to a JSON string and written into the response stream in line (10), which is then closed in line (11). The server prints out the following:

```
GET: /
```

```
JSON list in GET: [{title: washing dishes, completed: true, updated:
2013-08-08 15:40:51.999}, {title: walking the dog, completed: true,
updated: 2013-08-08 10:30:47.794}, {title: cleaning the kitchen,
completed: false, updated: 2013-08-08 15:21:44.626}, {title: buying
vegetables, completed: false, updated: 2013-08-08 10:32:20.707}]
```

The client then prints out:

```
JSON list from the server: ... same list as above ...
```

In line (7), the `addCorsHeaders` method adds the following so-called **CORS (Cross Origin Resource Sharing)** headers to the response:

```
    void addCorsHeaders(HttpResponse response) {
      response.headers.add('Access-Control-Allow-Origin', '*, ');
      response.headers.add('Access-Control-Allow-Methods', 'POST,
        OPTIONS');
      response.headers.add('Access-Control-Allow-Headers', 'Origin, X-
        Requested-With, Content-Type, Accept');
    }
```

In order to prevent cross-site scripting attacks, browser vendors have added a **same origin policy** to their browsers. If your web page comes from a server at URL domain1, you can only send requests to the same domain1 (remember that a domain consists of a name and port, and not just name — `localhost:8080` and `localhost:8081` are two different domains). If the server sends CORS headers back in the response, the client can also send requests to other servers. In general, it is not safe to use CORS headers. However, for development purposes, it is useful to allow them so that you can run apps from Dart Editor that uses `3030` by default for its internal server.

Spiral s07

But wait! Something is not yet right; the data of a new client overwrites on the server the data from a previous client, so we have to implement some form of data integration:

- **To server** (POST) adds local tasks without conflicting titles to data on the server
- **From server** (GET) removes tasks with conflicting titles from local data and adds tasks without conflicting titles to local data

In handlePost on the server (bin/server.dart), we will now call _integrateData
FromClient(jsonList), which contains the algorithm for the merging of tasks:

```
_integrateDataFromClient(List<Map> jsonList) {
  var clientTasks = new Tasks.fromJson(jsonList);
  var serverTasks = tasks;
  var serverTaskList = serverTasks.toList();
  for (var serverTask in serverTaskList) {
    if (!clientTasks.contains(serverTask.title)) {
      serverTasks.remove(serverTask);
    }
  }
  for (var clientTask in clientTasks) {
    if (serverTasks.contains(clientTask.title)) {
      var serverTask = serverTasks.find(clientTask.title);
      if (serverTask.updated.millisecondsSinceEpoch <
          clientTask.updated.millisecondsSinceEpoch) {
        serverTask.completed = clientTask.completed;
        serverTask.updated = clientTask.updated;
      }
    } else {
      serverTasks.add(clientTask);
    }
  }
}
```

This means that the server now has to know about the model (class Task/Tasks)
to realize that we share the model between the client and server by making it into a
library (lib/shared_model.dart):

```
library shared_model;
import 'dart:convert';
part 'model/model.dart';
```

By importing this in server.dart and idb_client.dart as well:

```
import 'package:client_server/shared_model.dart';
```

First, start the server and then two or more clients, for example, the first in Dartium
and the second in Chrome or another browser (run as JavaScript) (see doc/use.txt).
Then, juggle a few tasks between them!

As an improvement to the `completeTasks` method in **Spiral s03**, we now have the `complete` method, which guarantees that it will wait until all the update tasks are finished by using `Future.wait` on a `futureList` list of all the following tasks:

```
Future complete() {
    var futureList = new List<Future>();
    for (var task in tasks) {
      if (!task.completed) {
        task.completed = true;
        task.updated = new DateTime.now();
        futureList.add(update(task));
      }
    }
    return Future.wait(futureList);
}
```

Summary

In this chapter, you got acquainted to using the `Future` objects in order to call methods asynchronously. We discussed the pros and cons of browser storage mechanisms and used the best mechanism (IndexedDB) extensively in a complete reworking of our `todo` app. We also looked at Lawndart for times when you want to program against a uniform local storage interface. Then, we started with Dart on the server: how to write a web server and how to communicate between clients and the server. With it, we rewrote our app into a real client-server app and stored data locally on the clients and in the memory on the server.

However, any system failure can have server memory loss as a result. Mostly, we want to have more persistent central data storage; this is the topic we will cover in the following chapter.

11
Data-Driven Web Applications with MySQL and MongoDB

Data is usually stored on a server in a database; in order to do this, our Dart app needs a middle layer called a **database driver**. We'll review which drivers are already available and then see how you can store and access your data on the server with MySQL and MongoDB. These are two of the most popular databases: MySQL is a typical relational database, and MongoDB is a NoSQL database (according to the following link, http://db-engines.com/en/ranking, MySQL is second in popularity after Oracle, and MongoDB occupies the sixth place). The following topics will be covered in this chapter:

- Database drivers for Dart
- Storing the todo data in MySQL
- Dartlero tasks — a many-to-many model in MySQL and JSON
- MongoDB — a NoSQL database
- Using the mongo_dart driver to store the todo data in MongoDB
- Running a Dart server on an App Engine Managed VM

Database drivers for Dart

The amazing Dart community has already provided a whole spectrum of drivers (here **P** means published in the pub repository, https://pub.dartlang.org/).

For the relational databases, we have:

- **MySQL**: An actively developed connector called `SQLJocky` (P) by James Ots (`https://github.com/jamesots/sqljocky`); we will use this driver in the next section

- **PostgreSQL**: A driver called `postgresql` (P) by Greg Lowe (`https://github.com/xxgreg/postgresql`)

- **SQLite**: A native extension library called `Dart-sqlite` by Sam McCall (`https://github.com/sam-mccall/dart-sqlite/`)

- **ODBC-driver**: A library called `dart-odbc` (P) by Juan Mellado; this allows connections to any database vendor (Oracle, MySQL, PostgreSQL, SQLServer, and so on) with legacy ODBC drivers (`http://code.google.com/p/dart-odbc/`)

For the NoSQL databases, the choice is even greater:

- **MongoDB**: This is a driver called `mongo_dart` (P) by Vadim Tsushko, Ted Sander, and Paul Evans (`https://github.com/vadimtsushko/mongo_dart`); we'll use it in this chapter. Another client by Vadim Tsushko is an object document mapper tool called `Objectory` (`https://github.com/vadimtsushko/objectory`), which can be used on the client as well as the server.

- **CouchDB**: This is a driver called `couchclient` (P) by Henri Chen from Rikulo (`http://rikulo.org`). Another driver called `wilt` (P) is created by S. Hamblett (`https://github.com/shamblett/wilt`).

- **Redis**: This is a driver called `redis-dart` by Adam Singer (`https://github.com/financeCoding/redis-dart`). Another Redis client called `DartRedisClient` (P) is created by Dartist (`https://github.com/dartist/redis_client`).

- **Riak**: This is a driver called `riak-dart` (P) by Istvan Soos and Ian Jones (`https://code.google.com/p/riak-dart/`).

- **RethinkDB**: This is a driver called `rethinkdb` (P) by Dave Bettin (`https://github.com/dbettin/rethinkdb`).

- **HashMap**: This is a driver called `dart-dirty` (P) by Chris Strom (`https://github.com/eee-c/dart-dirty`), a dirt simple NoSQL DB that is a persistent, server-side HashMap.

There also exists an **Object Relational Mapper (ORM)** framework:

- **Dorm**: This framework is created by Frank Pepermans (`https://github.com/frankpepermans/dorm`). It provides an ORM mapping on the client. The goal is to hook it up with existing server-side ORM solutions (Hibernate, Entity Framework, and so on).

Storing todo data in MySQL

Building further on **Spiral s07** from the previous chapter, we will now add the functionality to store our data on the server in a MySQL database. The project is named `todo_mysql` and the code can be obtained from `https://github.com/dzenanr/todo_mysql`.

It contains three subprojects: one for the client, which is the same as the client portion of `client_server_db_s07` in the `indexed_db_spirals` project from *Chapter 10*, *Local Data and Client-Server Communication*; and two server projects with MySQL. The server projects are equivalent in functionality: `todo_server_mysql` uses MySQL directly and `todo_server_dartling_mysql` is built with a task model in dartling to show how the database is updated by reacting to the changes in the model. Both the server projects need to talk to MySQL, so they have the `sqljocky: any` dependency in their `pubspec.yaml` to import the MySQL driver. However, of course, we also need the database software, so we have to download and install the MySQL Community Server installer from `http://dev.mysql.com/downloads/mysql/`. This is straightforward; in case you need any help with the installation, visit `http://dev.mysql.com/doc/refman/5.7/en/installing.html`.

Be sure to start the MySQL server process (`mysqld`) before going further. Then, start the MySQL Workbench tool (contained in the download) and create a new database (also called a **model** or a **schema**) with the name `todo`. We need only one table, `task`, which you can easily drag and drop using this tool; you can also run the Dart script from `test/mysql_test.dart` to create and populate the table with some initial data.

You can now run the app as follows. Run the server first:

```
todo_server_mysql/bin/server.dart
```

Alternatively, you can run the following in the **Dart Editor**:

```
todo_server_dartling_mysql/bin/server.dart
```

When you run, the output you see in the `server.dart` tab in **Dart Editor** is as follows: **Listening for GET and POST on http://127.0.0.1:8080**.

If it does not run, use the run/manage launches (put a path to the project folder; for example, `d:\todo_mysql\todo_server_mysql` in the working directory field in the run/manage launches in order to have access to the `connection.options` file). Run the first client in Dartium (`todo_client_idb/web/app.html`) and the second client as JavaScript (`todo_client_idb/web/app.html`) in Chrome.

Use the client app in Dartium to add, update, or remove a task. The screen hasn't changed since the screenshot shown in **Spiral s04** and the server communication in **Spiral s06** (*Chapter 10, Local Data and Client-Server Communication*). Send it by pushing the **To Server** button where it is stored in the database; check this by viewing the task table data in MySQL Workbench. The second client can then retrieve this data using the **From Server** button. Experiment with the data by adding other clients; remember, that all the clients also store the data locally in `IndexedDB`.

How do we go about storing our data in MySQL? We'll first examine the `todo_server_mysql` project. The code that interacts with `sqljocky` sits in `lib/model/mysql.dart` and contains the `TodoDb` and `TaskTable` classes. The model, together with the data access layer, is contained in `library todo_server_mysql`, which is imported in `bin/server.dart`.

The code starts executing with the `main()` function in `server.dart`: a `todoDb` object is made on which (asynchronously) the open method is called, a connection is made with MySQL and the task data is loaded in `taskTable`, and finally the webserver is started:

```
void main() {
  var todoDb = new TodoDb();
  todoDb.open().then((_) {
    taskTable = todoDb.taskTable;
    start();    // start webserver
  });
}
```

In order to connect to a MySQL server and database, we need a minimal set of configuration settings that our app needs to read: a username, password, database, hostname, and a port number. These are stored as the `key=value` pairs in the `connection.options` file:

```
# connection.options defines how to connect to a MySQL db
user=root
password=xyz # fill in your own password
port=3306
db=todo
host=localhost
```

In a production environment, `host` would be the name of the MySQL server as shown here:

```
host = ndb_mgmd.mysql.com
```

The `connection.options` file sits right beneath the `project` directory. In order to have access to it from our app, or any file, with a `main` method that you run, we need to create the run/manage launches from the **Dart Editor** menu and put a path to the project folder (`todo_mysql`) in the working directory field. The quickest way to do this is to run it first; it will fail because it doesn't find the file, but then you have a readymade **Manage Launch** window to insert the right path.

To read the contents of such a file in Dart, create an object of the `OptionsFile` class, passing it the filename (see line (1) in the upcoming code). This class comes from the `options_file` package by James Ots available from pub; in order to use it, we must include the following line of code in our library file:

```
import 'package:options_file/options_file.dart';
```

Line (3) and onward, the `getString` or `getInt` method is used, which, given the key name, provides the value. Here is how it is done in the `TodoDb` class from `lib/model/mysql.dart`:

```
class TodoDb {
  TaskTable _taskTable;
  TaskTable get taskTable => _taskTable;

  Future open() {
    var pool = getPool(new OptionsFile('connection.options')); (1)
    _taskTable = new TaskTable(pool);
    return _taskTable.load();
  }

  ConnectionPool getPool(OptionsFile options) {                  (2)
    String user = options.getString('user');                     (3)
    String password = options.getString('password');
    int port = options.getInt('port', 3306);
    String db = options.getString('db');
    String host = options.getString('host', 'localhost');
    return new ConnectionPool(                                    (4)
      host: host, port: port, user: user, password: password,
        db: db);
  }
}
```

With these values, the `getPool` method (starting in line (2)) builds a `ConnectionPool` object in line (4), which knows everything needed to connect to the MySQL database. It is returned from this method and assigned to the `pool` variable in line (1). In the next line, a `TaskTable` object is constructed on which the `load` method is called. When the server starts, it loads data from MySQL to the model in the main memory. When the model changes, the database is updated. Our code continues executing in the `TaskTable` class:

```
class TaskTable {
  final ConnectionPool _pool;
  Tasks _tasks;

  TaskTable(this._pool) {
    _tasks = new Tasks.withTable(this);
  }

  Tasks get tasks => _tasks;
  bool get isEmpty => tasks.length == 0;

  Future load() {                                       (1)
    Completer completer = new Completer();              (2)
    _pool.query(                                        (3)
      'select t.title, t.completed, t.updated '
      'from task t '
    ).then((rows) {                                     (4)
      var taskMap;
      rows.stream.listen((row) {                        (5)
        taskMap = {
          'title'    : '${row[0]}',                     (6)
          'completed': '${row[1]}',
          'updated'  : '${row[2]}'
        };
        var task = new Task.fromDb(taskMap);            (7)
        tasks.load(task);
      },
        onError: (e) => print('data loading error: $e'),  (8)
        onDone: () {
          completer.complete();                         (9)
          print('all tasks loaded');
        }
      );
    });
    return completer.future;                            (10)
  }
```

The `load` method in line (1) executes asynchronously, so it returns a `Future` object (so do all the methods accessing the database). However, we also see, in line (1), the use of an intermediate instance of the `Completer` class from the `dart:async` library. When the asynchronous code becomes more complex, the use of a `Completer` method helps write more maintainable and readable code. Using the `Completer` method, you can explicitly indicate when the `Future` value will be available by calling the `complete` method as in line (9) in the `onDone` handler (a `Completer` object is also useful in converting synchronous code into asynchronous while using asynchronous API's). This signals the `Future` object that the asynchronous operation has been completed. At the end of the `load` method, the `Future` object value is returned, in line (10), as `completer.future`. The code of the `load` method can seem daunting at first sight; let's analyze it step by step with the help of the many built-in functions in the editor (another visual theme from **Tools | Preferences** can also be useful). MySQL is a relational database, so at some point, our code will have to construct the SQL statements to be sent to the database for execution. In line (3), the `query` method (defined in `sqljocky`) is called on the `pool` object with a SQL string as the parameter. The following is the signature taken from the pop-up window when the cursor hovers over query:

```
Future<Results> query(String sql)
```

As we expected, query returns a `Future` object; so, a `then` clause has to follow in line (4). The following is the signature:

```
Future then( onValue(Results) -> dynamic, { onError(Object) ->
    dynamic})
```

From this, we see that it has an `onValue` handler to process the results and an optional `onError` handler. In our code, we have an anonymous `onValue` handler that runs all the way down to stop just before line (10):

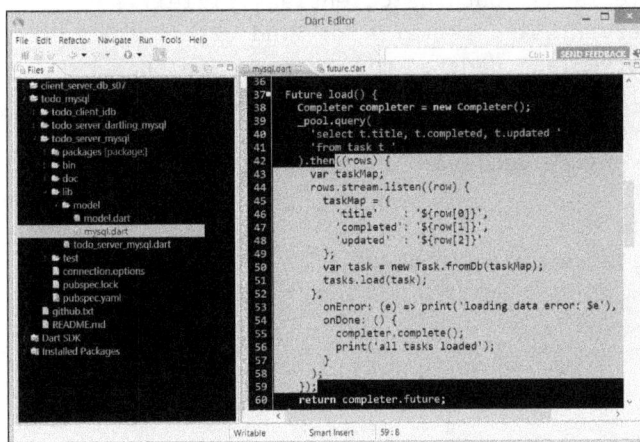

The onValue handler in the load method

The retrieved rows come in like a stream; the `stream` getter has a `listen` method to subscribe to this stream with the signature:

```
StreamSubscription<Row> listen( onData(Row) -> void, {
   onError(dynamic) ->  void, onDone() -> void, bool  cancelOnError}
   )
```

It has an `onData` handler that is called for every row that comes in, and the optional `onError` and `onDone` handlers. The `onData` handler is again an anonymous method and it stretches from line (4) just up to line (8). Here, the data is extracted using a `row[i]` indexing operator. With string interpolation, we construct a literal map, `taskMap`, from which a `Task` object is made and added to the tasks collection; so, all the task data is in the server memory. Then, we see `onError`, which prints possible errors, and `onDone`, which signals the completion of the `async` operation in line (9). The value of the `Future` object is returned in line (10).

The `_integrateDataFromClient` method in `bin/server.dart` updates the data in the server memory and the database (we'll see this shortly):

```
_integrateDataFromClient(List<Map> jsonList) {
  var clientTasks = new Tasks.fromJson(jsonList);
  var serverTasks = taskTable.tasks;
  var serverTaskList = serverTasks.toList();
  for (var serverTask in serverTaskList) {
    if (!clientTasks.contains(serverTask.title)) {
      serverTasks.remove(serverTask);                              (1)
    }
  }

  for (var clientTask in clientTasks) {
    if (serverTasks.contains(clientTask.title)) {
      var serverTask = serverTasks.find(clientTask.title);
      if (serverTask.updated.millisecondsSinceEpoch <
          clientTask.updated.millisecondsSinceEpoch) {
        serverTask.completed = clientTask.completed;
        serverTask.updated = clientTask.updated;
      }
    } else {
      serverTasks.add(clientTask);                                 (2)
    }
  }
}
```

The `remove` and `add` methods in lines (1) and (2) are found in `model.dart` (use **Open Declaration** from the context menu). In turn, they call the `delete` and `insert` methods from `mysql.dart`. The `update` method gets called in the completed and updated setters in `model.dart`. Let's look a bit deeper at these methods, for example, the `insert` method:

```
Future<Task> insert(Task task) {
    var completer = new Completer();
    var taskMap = task.toDb();
    _pool.prepare(                                                (1)
      'insert into task (title, completed, updated) values (?, ?,
        ?)'
    ).then((query) {
      print("prepared query insert into task");
      var params = new List();                                    (2)
       params.add(taskMap['title']);
       params.add(taskMap['completed']);
       params.add(taskMap['updated']);
       return query.execute(params);                              (3)
    }).then((_) {
      print("executed query insert into task");
      completer.complete();                                       (4)
    }).catchError(print);                                         (5)
    return completer.future;
}
```

Here, we see that the SQL of the query is first prepared in line (1) (a sort of a parse step in the database), which returns a `Future` object. In the returned result, the task data is inserted in the `?` placeholders using a list that contains the parameter values. This list is constructed in line (2) and the subsequent lines. Then, the `execute` method is called on the query in line (3), returning a `Future` object again. The `async` operation is marked as completed in line (4). Note, the error handling in line (5); always include it while dealing with the database access. Now, you'll be able to understand the `update` and `delete` methods by yourself, as shown in the following code:

```
Future<Task> update(Task task) {
    var completer = new Completer();
    var taskMap = task.toDb();
    _pool.prepare(
      'update task set completed = ?, updated = ? where title = ?'
        ).then((query) {
      print("prepared query update task");
      var params = new List();
      params.add(taskMap['completed']);
```

```
      params.add(taskMap['updated']);
      params.add(taskMap['title']);
      return query.execute(params);
  }).then((_) {
    print("executed query update task");
    completer.complete();
  }).catchError(print);
  return completer.future;
}


Future<Task> delete(Task task) {
  var completer = new Completer();
  var taskMap = task.toDb();
  _pool.prepare(
    'delete from task where title = ?'
  ).then((query) {
    print("prepared query delete from task");
            var params = new List();
      params.add(taskMap['title']);
    return query.execute(params);
  }).then((_) {
    print("executed query delete from task");
    completer.complete();
  }).catchError(print);
  return completer.future;
}
```

You have now seen a complete data access layer to a relational database in action!

The second `todo_server_dartling_mysql` project builds upon the `dartling_todo_mvc_spirals` project in *Chapter 9, Modeling More Complex Applications with dartling*. The dartling was used to model tasks and generate a code basis; so the `lib/gen` code is the same. The data access code lives in `lib/persistence/mysql.dart`. With dartling, a model is not dependent on MySQL—the model does not call insert, update, and delete methods (with the SQL code). The `TodoDb` class, in its constructor, starts listening to the actions of the dartling model:

```
domain.startActionReaction(this);
```

In the `react` method, the `TodoDb` class reacts to actions in the dartling model:

```
react(ActionApi action) {
  if (action is AddAction) {
    taskTable.insert(action.entity);
  } else if (action is RemoveAction) {
```

```
        taskTable.delete(action.entity);
    } else if (action is SetAttributeAction) {
        taskTable.update(action.entity);
    }
  }
```

In this way, one may use more than one database with dartling without updating the model code. The _integrateDataFromClient method in bin\server.dart now works with the model's actions (such as AddAction and RemoveAction):

```
_integrateDataFromClient(List<Map> jsonList) {
  var clientTasks = new Tasks.fromJson(db.tasks.concept,
jsonList);
  var serverTaskList = db.tasks.toList();
  for (var serverTask in serverTaskList) {
    var clientTask =
        clientTasks.singleWhereAttributeId('title',
          serverTask.title);
    if (clientTask == null) {
      new RemoveAction(db.session, db.tasks, serverTask).doit();
    }
  }
  for (var clientTask in clientTasks) {
    var serverTask =
        db.tasks.singleWhereAttributeId('title',
          clientTask.title);
    if (serverTask != null) {
      if (serverTask.updated.millisecondsSinceEpoch <
          clientTask.updated.millisecondsSinceEpoch) {
        new SetAttributeAction(
          db.session, serverTask, 'completed',
            clientTask.completed).doit();
      }
    } else {
      new AddAction(db.session, db.tasks, clientTask).doit();
    }
  }
}
```

To experiment with this version, first run the bin/server.dart server and then one or more clients from todo_client_idb.

Dartlero tasks – a many-to-many model in MySQL

A one table project is quite unrealistic; let's now revisit the `dartlero_project_tasks` application in *Chapter 8, Developing Business Applications with Polymer Web Components*. This has a many-to-many relationship between the `project` and `employee` concepts, `task` being the intermediate concept; data is stored only in the browser's local storage. In the `dartlero_tasks` project (code can be cloned from `https://github.com/dzenanr/dartlero_tasks`), we have the same model built on Dartlero, but the data can be stored on the server either in the JSON format or in a MySQL database. The startup script for both the options is `bin/dartlero_tasks.dart`. The model and the data access layer are defined in `library dartlero_tasks lib/model/darlero_tasks.dart`.

The JSON storage

If you want to use the JSON file storage, you have to create a command-line launch for the `bin/dartlero_tasks.dart` script. In the run/manage launches of Dart Editor, enter two script arguments (`--dir` and `path`), for example:

- `--dir C:/Users/"username"/git/dartlero/dartlero_tasks/json_data` (on Windows)
- `--dir /home/username/git/dartlero/dartlero_tasks/json_data` (on Linux)

By running the `main` function in the `bin/dartlero_tasks.dart` file, a model with two entry points will be initialized and saved in the given directory. For each entry concept, a file with the concept name and the `.json` extension will be created. The next time the program is run, data from the two files will be loaded. View the data in the JSON documents with a text editor, or use a JSON pretty printer. Let's dig into the code and examine `bin/dartlero_tasks.dart`:

```
import 'package:dartlero_tasks/dartlero_tasks.dart';          (1)

void main(List<String> arguments) {
  var model = TasksModel.one();

  try {
    if (args.length == 2 && (args[0] == '--dir')) {
      model.persistence = 'json';
      model.jsonDirPath = args[1];
      if (!model.loadFromJson()) {                            (4)
        model.init();
```

```
        model.saveToJson();
      }
      model.display();
    }
  } else if (args.length == 1 && (args[0] == '--mysql')) {
        // code for MySQL storage
    } else {
      print('No arguments: consult README');
    }
  } catch (e) {
    print('consult README: $e');
  }
}
```

Line (1) imports the model. The `loadFromJson` method from `lib/model/model.dart` reads in the JSON files with:

```
File employeesFile = getFile(employeesFilePath);
// ... code left out
String employeesFileText = readTextFromFile(employeesFile);
```

The `getFile` and `readTextFromFile` variables are defined in `lib/model/file_persistence.dart`. This file contains all the methods from the project that directly use `dart:io`:

```
part of dartlero_tasks;

Directory getDir(String path) {
  var dir = new Directory(path);
  if (dir.existsSync()) {
    print('directory ${path} exists already');
  } else {
    dir.createSync();
    print('directory created: ${path}');
  }
  return dir;
}

File getFile(String path) {
  File file = new File(path);
  if (file.existsSync()) {
    print('file ${path} exists already');
  } else {
    file.createSync();
```

```
      print('file created: ${path}');
    }
    return file;
  }

  addTextToFile(File file, String text) {
    IOSink writeSink = file.openWrite();
    writeSink.write(text);
    writeSink.close();
  }

  String readTextFromFile(File file) {
    return file.readAsStringSync();
  }
```

The methods in dart:io work asynchronously by default; for example, the create, exists, open, read, and write methods return a Future object. These should be used in the real production apps. To simplify the code in our case, we used their synchronous counterparts, createSync and existsSync, for the directory, reading the entire content of the file as a string with readAsStringSync. Writing the files is done when the model saves itself with the saveToJson method in model.dart. This calls addTextToFile; here, we see that openWrite is called on the file object returning an object of the IOSink class, a helper class that is used to write to a file. It contains a buffer, which must be closed explicitly when the writing is completed. Take some time to explore the API for dart:io at http://api.dartlang.org/docs/releases/latest/dart_io.html, especially the file methods and properties.

MySQL storage

For using the MySQL storage, use the --mysql script argument in **Run | Manage Launches** of Dart Editor. There is no need to create a new database (the default database test will be used), but do not forget to start the MySQL server. Before running a Dart file with main, put a path to the dartlero_tasks project folder in the working directory field in **Run | Manage Launches** to have access to the connection.options file.

Run example/mysql/example.dart to drop and create all the tables; the following output appears (every script produces some output to monitor its execution):

```
opening connection
connection open
running example
dropping tables
```

```
dropped tables

creating tables

executing queries

created tables

prepared query 1

executed query 1

prepared query 2

executed query 2

prepared query 3

executed query 3

querying

got results

bye
```

In the following screenshot, you will see the `project` table contents in SQL Workbench after execution:

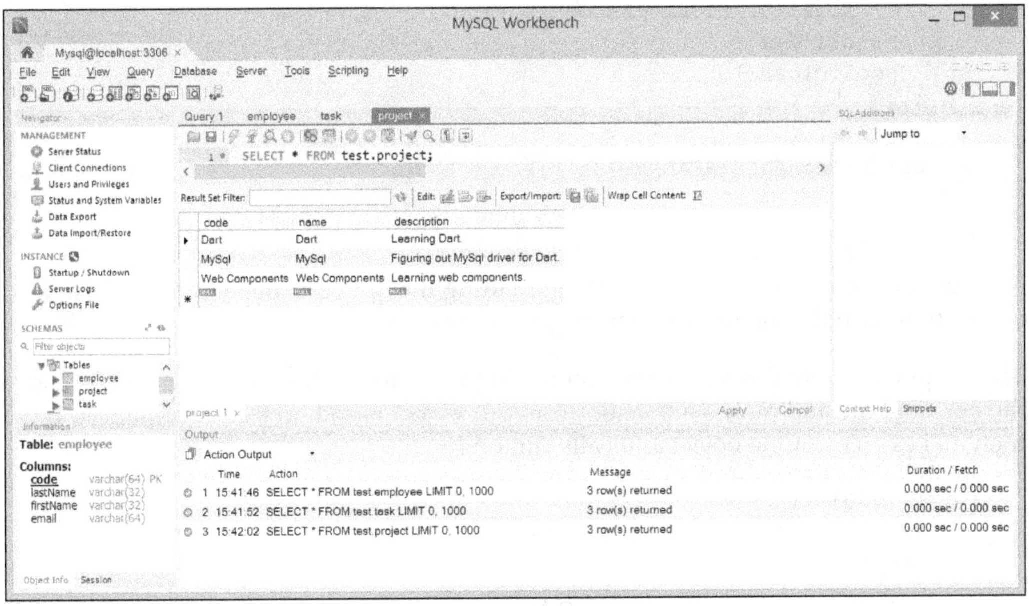

Data in the project table

The following is the `main` method:

```
void main() {
  try {
    OptionsFile options = new OptionsFile('connection.options');
    String user = options.getString('user');
    String password = options.getString('password');
    int port = options.getInt('port', 3306);
    String db = options.getString('db');
    String host = options.getString('host', 'localhost');
    // create a connection
    print('opening connection');
    var pool = new ConnectionPool(host: host, port: port, user:
      user, password: password, db: db);
    print('connection open');
    // create an example class
    var example = new Example(pool);
    // run the example
    print('running example');
    example.run().then((_) {
      // finally, close the connection
      print('bye');
      pool.close();
    });
  } catch(e) {
    print('consult README: $e');
  }
}
```

Note the `try`/`catch` exception handling; reading the `options` file and opening a connection with the database can both generate an exception.

The script itself contains some new interesting ways to work with `sqljocky`. It reads the `options` file and makes a `ConnectionPool` object based on this information. It then makes an example object and calls run on it:

```
Future run() {
  var completer = new Completer();
  dropTables()
    .then((_) => createTables())
    .then((_) => addData())
    .then((_) => readData())
    .then((_) => completer.complete())
    .catchError( (e) => print(e) );
  return completer.future;
}
```

This is a good example of how methods that return a `Future` object can be chained in a succession of the `then` calls. This produces elegant and readable code. The `dropTables` method uses a `TableDropper` object to drop a list of tables:

```
Future dropTables() {
    print("dropping tables");
    var dropper = new TableDropper(pool, ['task', 'employee',
      'project']);
    return dropper.dropTables();
}
```

`Future createTables` uses a `QueryRunner` object. Its `executeQueries` method can execute a list of SQL statements:

```
Future createTables() {
    print("creating tables");
    var querier = new QueryRunner(pool,
        [
          'create table employee (code varchar(64) not null, '
          'lastName varchar(32) not null, '
          'firstName varchar(32) not null, '
          'email varchar(64) not null, '
          'primary key (code))',

          'create table project (code varchar(64) not null, '
          'name varchar(64) not null, '
          'description varchar(256), '
          'primary key (code))',

          'create table task (code varchar(128) not null, '
          'projectCode varchar(64), '
          'employeeCode varchar(64), '
          'description varchar(256), '
          'primary key (code), '
          'foreign key (projectCode) references project (code), '
          'foreign key (employeeCode) references employee (code))'
        ]);
    print("executing queries");
    return querier.executeQueries();
}
```

Future addData shows how a prepared SQL statement with parameters (as before, each ? is a parameter that needs a value) can be given a list of Lists, where each inner list contains all the parameter values for one statement. The executeMulti method on the query executes the statements in succession:

```
Future addData() {
    var completer = new Completer();
    pool.prepare(
        "insert into employee (code, lastName, firstName, email)
          values (?, ?, ?, ?)"
        ).then((query) {
      print("prepared query 1");
      var parameters = [
          ["dzenanr@gmail.com", "Ridjanovic", "Dzenan",
            "dzenanr@gmail.com"],
          ["timur.ridjanovic@gmail.com", "Ridjanovic", "Timur",
            "timur.ridjanovic@gmail.com"],
          ["ma.seyer@gmail.com", "Seyer", "Marc-Antoine",
            "ma.seyer@gmail.com"]
        ];
      return query.executeMulti(parameters);
    }).then((results) {
      print("executed query 1");
    // code left out
```

The other scripts in the example/mysql folder use the same techniques to populate each table separately.

The project also contains test scripts exercising Dart unittest; for example, test/mysql/employee_test.dart for employee data. The following is the main method's code:

```
main() {
  try {
    var pool = getPool(new OptionsFile('connection.options'));
    dropTables(pool)
      .then((_) => createTable(pool))
      .then((_) => initData(pool))
      .then((_) => testProjects(pool));
  } catch(e) {
    print('consult README: $e');
  }
}
```

The testing output is shown as follows:

```
PASS: Testing employees Select all employees
PASS: Testing employees Select Ridjanovic employees
PASS: Testing employees Select all employees, then select Ridjanovic
employees


All 3 tests passed.
unittest-suite-success
selected all employees
count: 1 - code: dzenanr@gmail.com, last name: Ridjanovic, first
name: Dzenan, email: dzenanra@gmil.com
 // other data.
```

The following is the code of the `testing` method:

```
testEmployees(ConnectionPool pool) {
    group("Testing employees", () {
    test("Select all employees", () {
      var count = 0
      pool.query(
          'select e.code, e.lastName, e.firstName, e.email '
          'from employee e '
      ).then((rows) {
        print("selected all employees");
        rows.stream.listen((row) {
            count++;
          print(
              'count: $count - '
            'code: ${row[0]}, '
            'last name: ${row[1]}, '
            'first name: ${row[2]}, '
            'email: ${row[3]}'
          );
        }).onDone(() => expect(count, equals(3)));
      });
    });

    test("Select Ridjanovic employees", () {
      pool.query(
          'select e.code, e.lastName, e.firstName, e.email '
          'from employee e '
          'where e.lastName = "Ridjanovic" '
```

```
    ).then((rows) {
      print("selected Ridjanovic employees");
      rows.stream.listen((row) {
          expect(row[1], equals('Ridjanovic'));
        print(
            'code: ${row[0]}, '
            'last name: ${row[1]}, '
            'first name: ${row[2]}, '
            'email: ${row[3]}'
        );
      });
    });
});


test("Select all employees, then select Ridjanovic employees",
() {
  var futures = new List<Future>();                        (1)
  var completer = new Completer();
  futures.add(completer.future);                           (2)
    var count = 0;
  pool.query(
      'select e.code, e.lastName, e.firstName, e.email '
      'from employee e '
  ).then((rows) {
    print("selected all employees");
    rows.stream.listen((row) {
     count++;
      print(
          count: $count - '
        'code: ${row[0]}, '
        'last name: ${row[1]}, '
        'first name: ${row[2]}, '
        'email: ${row[3]}'
      );
       }).onDone(() {
          expect(count, equals(3));
          completer.complete();
      });
  });

  Future.wait(futures).then((futures) {                    (3)
    pool.query(
        'select e.code, e.lastName, e.firstName, e.email '
        'from employee e '
```

```
                  'where e.lastName = "Ridjanovic" '
            ).then((rows) {
              print("selected Ridjanovic employees");
              rows.stream.listen((row) {
                  expect(row[1], equals('Ridjanovic'));
                print(
                    'code: ${row[0]}, '
                    'last name: ${row[1]}, '
                    'first name: ${row[2]}, '
                    'email: ${row[3]}'
                );
              });
            });
          });
        });
      });
    }
```

In the ("Select all employees, then select Ridjanovic employees") test, we see how we can wait for the execution of the code until all the Future objects contained in a list are terminated. In line (1), List<Future> is defined and, in line (2), a Future object is added to the list. In line (3), the wait static method is called on Future object: it waits until all the methods in its List argument (here, only one) have returned their Future value. Run test/mysql/project_test.dart to test the projects table:

dropping tables

creating project table

initializing project data

prepared query insert into project

executed query insert into project

unittest-suite-wait-for-done

PASS: Select all projects

All 1 tests passed.

unittest-suite-success

selected all projects

count: 1 - code: Dart, name: Dart, description: Learning Dart.

count: 2 - code: MySql, name: MySql, description: Figuring out MySql driver for Dart.

count: 3 - code: Web Components, name: Web Components, description: Learning web components.

MongoDB – a NoSQL database

Many NoSQL databases exist in the market today, but MongoDB, by the company with the same name (http://www.mongodb.org/), is the most popular among them. An important distinction between relational and NoSQL databases is that NoSQL databases are **schema-less**; this means you don't have to define the tables before inserting data. This in itself, of course, adds a lot to the flexibility and agility while using these databases; for example, adding a new field no longer means that you have to alter the table and run the SQL update commands. As there are no SQL queries to be used here, all the data retrieval happens via standard **CRUD** calls (create, read, update, and delete). In MongoDB, this is known as insert, find, update, and remove. MongoDB presents itself as an open source, distributed, document-oriented database—each data record is actually a document. A table is called a **collection** in MongoDB. Documents are stored in a JSON-like format called **Binary JSON (BSON)**. BSON documents are objects that contain an ordered list of saved elements; each element comprises of a field name and a value, which is of a specific type. BSON is designed to be more efficient than JSON, both in storage space and reading speed, adding to the performance MongoDB is known for. In a MongoDB database, you can query data not only through keys and secondary keys, but also with ranges and regular expressions; indexes can be applied to pretty much everything, such as 2D and 3D spatial data; there's absolutely no limitation.

To guarantee high availability, a master-slave replication (also called **replica-sets**) is built. For big data applications, support to spread data across multiple servers (also called **auto-sharding**) is a key feature, making MongoDB a very scalable solution. Install the latest production release for your system from http://www.mongodb.org/downloads.

This is easy; for details, refer to http://docs.mongodb.org/manual/installation/. A number of binaries are installed in the bin map; among them are mongod, which is the server (or daemon) process, and mongo, which is a command-line client. The http://docs.mongodb.org/manual/tutorial/getting-started/ link is a good tutorial to get started. Start the mongod server process (for example, from c:\mongodb\bin on Windows) before you go further. If all is well, you should see an output, similar to the following, on the console:

```
Fri Aug 23 10:57:19.256 [initandlisten] MongoDB starting : pid=1568
port=27017 db

path=\data\db\ 64-bit host=predator

Fri Aug 23 10:57:19.258 [initandlisten] db version v2.4.5
```

To close the MongoDB server safely, issue *Ctrl + C* in the console. Before using a Dart driver, let's get acquainted a bit with the Mongo shell, which works with JavaScript and communicates directly with MongoDB. Open a console window and start the `mongo` command. The following output appears, telling us that we are using the default database test and showing us a prompt:

```
MongoDB shell version: 2.4.5
connecting to: test
>
```

Suppose we want to save stock data; for example, GOOG (the symbol), Google Inc. (the company's name), and its current rating of 13. We will call our database invest. Switch to that database with `use invest`, which returns `switched to db invest`. At this point, the database doesn't really exist, as it doesn't contain any data. In MongoDB, data is stored in collections, allowing you to separate documents if required. Let's create a document and store it as a new collection named `stocks`:

```
db.stocks.save({symbol:"GOOG",name:"Google Inc.",rating:13});
```

Save some other data as follows:

Symbol	Company	Current rating
MSFT	Microsoft Technologies	7
KOG	Kodiak Oil & Gas Corp	11
AAPL	Apple Inc	11
CSCO	Cisco Systems	12

Our collection now contains five documents. Retrieve them with `db.stocks.find()`:

```
{"_id" : ObjectId("521df951abd1215f4673c8ed"), "symbol" : "GOOG",
  "name" : "Google Inc.", "rating" : 13 }
{ "_id" : ObjectId("521df997abd1215f4673c8ee"), "symbol" : "MSFT",
  "name" : "Microsoft Technologies", "rating" : 7 }
{ "_id" : ObjectId("521df9caabd1215f4673c8ef"), "symbol" : "KOG",
  "name" : "Kodiak Oil & Gas Corp", "rating" : 10 }
// 2 other documents left out
```

The `_id` attribute is a unique identifier generated by MongoDB and it will be different in your result. Documents can be way more complex than these, storing various datatypes including strings, integers, floats, dates, arrays, and other objects. Suppose we only want to see the stocks with a rating greater than 11; the query gives us GOOG and CSCO:

```
db.stocks.find({rating:{$gt:11}});
```

For example, sorting on the symbol is also easy:

```
db.stocks.find().sort({symbol: 0});
```

Add `.count()` at the end of any find command that will give the number of documents found. If Microsoft's new CEO comes along and the company's rating rises to `12`, how do we change it in our database via the shell? First, we must get a variable reference to the document we want to change:

```
var ms= db.stocks.findOne({symbol: "MSFT"});
```

Then, we make the change as we would in the code:

```
ms.rating = 12;
```

Then, we save the change with:

```
db.stocks.save(ms);
```

Verify with `find()` that the change is stored. You can create an index in the symbol field with:

```
db.stocks.ensureIndex({symbol: 1});
```

To create a backup, issue the `mongodump` command. To explore the shell and its commands further, visit the MongoDB website. The following screenshot illustrates the Mongo shell displaying the stocks collection:

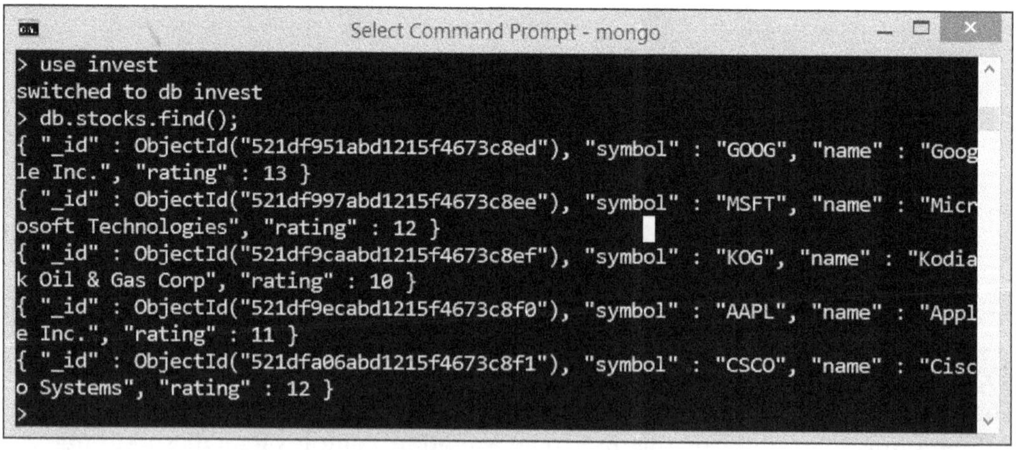

The Mongo shell showing the stocks collection

Using the mongo_dart driver to store the todo data in MongoDB

MongoDB drivers exist for a whole range of programming languages, including Dart. We will use `mongo_dart` in our app, which is a server-side driver implemented purely in Dart. Simply add `mongo_dart: any` to your app's `pubspec.yaml` and issue pub install. In the code, write:

```
import 'package:mongo_dart/mongo_dart.dart';
```

The `todo_mongodb` version is a version of `todo_server_dartling_mysql`, but we will now use MongoDB as a persistent data source (clone the project from `https://github.com/dzenanr/todo_mongodb`). It contains a `todo_client_idb` client app identical to the one in the previous section, which stores data in `IndexedDB`. The `todo_server_dartling_mongodb` server part can be started by running `bin/server.dart`. You should see the following output in the editor or the console:

Server at http://127.0.0.1:8080;

If you see the following exception, it means that the `mongod` server has not yet been started:

SocketException: Connection failed (OS Error: No connection could be made because the target machine actively refused it., errno = 10061), address = 127.0.0.1, port = 27017.

Run a Dartium client (`todo_client_idb/web/app.html`) from the editor and a JavaScript client in Chrome or any other browser. Fill in some tasks if you see nothing to do and click on the **To Server** button. The `mongod` console outputs that it has created a data file with index, and that it has inserted a number of rows:

Fri Aug 23 11:19:55.839 [FileAllocator] allocating new datafile \data\db\todo.1,

filling with zeroes...

Fri Aug 23 11:19:55.842 [conn1] build index todo.tasks { _id: 1 }

Fri Aug 23 11:19:55.844 [conn1] build index done. scanned 0 total records. 0.002

 secs

Fri Aug 23 11:19:55.846 [conn1] insert todo.tasks ninserted:1 keyUpdates:0 locks(

micros) w:412870 412ms

Fri Aug 23 11:19:56.466 [FileAllocator] done allocating datafile \data\db\todo.1,

 size: 128MB, took 0.625 secs

Synchronize the other clients by clicking on their **From Server** button. To verify that the data is actually in MongoDB, open a Mongo shell by typing `mongo` in a console and issuing the commands to retrieve the documents from the `tasks` collection in the `todo` database:

```
> use todo
```

The output will be as follows:

```
switched to db todo
```

The command to retrieve the documents is as follows:

```
> db.tasks.find()
```

The output will be as follows:

```
{ "_id" : ObjectId("5217293b479e4132cdecef0e"), "title" :
"administration", "comp

leted" : false, "updated" : ISODate("2013-08-16T09:14:50.569Z") }
```

Running `test/mongodb_test.dart` is an alternative to create and populate the `todo` database with a tasks collection. From the structure of our app, we can deduce that the data access code resides in `lib/persistence/mongodb.dart`, which contains the `TodoDb` and `TaskCollection` classes. Let's now see how our Dart code reaches out to MongoDB. In the `main` method of the server script (`bin\server.dart`), we see:

```
    void main() {
      db = new TodoDb();                              (1)
      db.open().then((_) {                            (2)
        start();
      });
    }
```

Line `(1)` calls the constructor from `TodoDb` and, in line `(2)`, the database is opened. The following is the code from the `TodoDb` class:

```
    class TodoDb implements ActionReactionApi {
      static const String DEFAULT_URI = 'mongodb://127.0.0.1/';
      static const String DB_NAME = 'todo';

      TodoModels domain;
      DomainSession session;
      MvcEntries model;
```

```
  Tasks tasks;

  Db db;

  TaskCollection taskCollection;

  TodoDb() {                                                    (3)
    var repo = new TodoRepo();
    domain = repo.getDomainModels('Todo');
    domain.startActionReaction(this);
    session = domain.newSession();
    model = domain.getModelEntries('Mvc');
    tasks = model.tasks;
  }

  Future open() {
    Completer completer = new Completer();
    db = new Db('${DEFAULT_URI}${DB_NAME}');                    (4)
    db.open().then((_) {                                        (5)
      taskCollection = new TaskCollection(this);               (6)
      taskCollection.load().then((_) {                          (7)
        completer.complete();
      });
    }).catchError(print);
    return completer.future;
  }

  close() {
    db.close();
  }

  react(ActionApi action) {
    if (action is AddAction) {
      taskCollection.insert((action as AddAction).entity);
    } else if (action is RemoveAction) {
      taskCollection.delete((action as RemoveAction).entity);
    } else if (action is SetAttributeAction) {
      taskCollection.update((action as
  SetAttributeAction).entity);
    }
  }
}
```

The constructor starting in line (3) does everything necessary to start up the dartling model. The `open` method creates a new MongoDB database in line (4) (with the substituted value):

```
db = new Db('mongodb://127.0.0.1/todo );
```

The `Db` class comes from `mongo_dart`; it has an `open` method called in line (5). From the `then` keyword, we see that it returns a `Future` object as expected. As dictated by dartling, any change in the app's data calls react to update the model and the database, as `TodoDb` listens to the actions in the model through the line:

```
domain.startActionReaction(this));
```

When an action happens, all the listeners are informed about the action in the `react` method for listeners. The `TaskCollection` class, whose object is constructed in line (6), is the closest we will get to MongoDB in this project, again, using `Future` objects throughout. The code is as follows:

```
class TaskCollection {
  static const String COLLECTION_NAME = 'tasks';
  TodoDb todo;
  DbCollection dbTasks;

  TaskCollection(this.todo) {
    dbTasks = todo.db.collection(COLLECTION_NAME);            (8)
  }

  Future load() {                                             (9)
    Completer completer = new Completer();
    dbTasks.find().toList().then((taskList) {
      taskList.forEach((taskMap) {
        var task = new Task.fromDb(todo.tasks.concept, taskMap);
        todo.tasks.add(task);
      });
      completer.complete();
    }).catchError(print);
    return completer.future;
  }

  Future<Task> insert(Task task) {
    var completer = new Completer();
    var taskMap = task.toDb();
    dbTasks.insert(taskMap).then((_) {
      print('inserted task: ${task.title}');
      completer.complete();
```

```
  }).catchError(print);
  return completer.future;
}


Future<Task> delete(Task task) {
  var completer = new Completer();
  var taskMap = task.toDb();
  dbTasks.remove(taskMap).then((_) {
    print('removed task: ${task.title}');
    completer.complete();
  }).catchError(print);
  return completer.future;
}


Future<Task> update(Task task) {
  var completer = new Completer();
  var taskMap = task.toDb();
  dbTasks.update({"title": taskMap['title']}, taskMap).then((_){
    print('updated task: ${task.title}');
    completer.complete();
  }).catchError(print);
  return completer.future;
  }
}
```

It contains a DbCollection object (also defined in mongo_dart) called dbTasks, which mirrors the tasks collection in the database through the assignment in line (8) of the constructor. In line (9), its load method (called in the previous code snippet in line (7)) calls find() on dbTasks. When the results return, a new Task object is made for each document, found, and added to the tasks collection. The insert, delete, and update methods, respectively, call insert, remove, and update on the DbCollection object dbTasks. Notice the exceptional handling clause that will signal any error:

```
.catchError(print);
```

When a server starts, all the data from a database are loaded into the model in the main memory. When the model changes, these changes are propagated immediately to the database through actions/reactions. In this approach, a database system is used only minimally — all the searches for the data are done in the main memory without using the slower database system. With dartling, a model is not dependent on MongoDB — the model does not call the `insert`, `update`, and `remove` methods. The use of (only a few methods of) the `mongo_dart` driver shields us from using and knowing the slightly more elaborate MongoDB commands in our Dart code. The complete API reference of the driver can be found at `http://vadimtsushko. github.io/mongo_dart/mongo_dart/Db.html`.

Again, we clearly see the advantages of using a modeling framework and a well-structured library; our data access code in `lib/persistence` was all we needed to adapt while changing from the MySQL version to the MongoDB version!

Running a Dart server on an App Engine Managed VM

Dart applications can be hosted on the Google Cloud Platform — they run in a custom runtime on **App Engine Managed VM**. In contrast to the secure, **sandboxed environments** in which Python, Java, Go, and PHP are run, Dart runs in a VM-based hosting environment, which is more flexible, providing more CPU and memory options.

In the previous chapters, we learned how to write HTTP clients and servers in Dart, which is exactly what we need for a Dart app running in a managed VM.

This environment uses the *Docker* cloud service to distribute applications. Docker is a tool, written in the Go programming language, to package an application and its dependencies in a virtual container that can run on any Linux server. Docker can be used with various infrastructure tools besides Google Cloud Platform, a few being Amazon Web Services, Chef, Jelastic, Jenkins, Microsoft Azure, OpenStack Nova, OpenSVC, Puppet, and Salt. If you do not develop on Linux, you will need a VM running Linux; `boot2docker` is a pre-packaged Linux VM image for *VirtualBox*.

Go through the following steps to deploy Dart on App Engine:

1. To install and configure Docker and related tools, visit `http://docs. docker.com/installation/windows/`.

2. To install and set up a Google Cloud SDK project, visit `https://www. dartlang.org/server/google-cloud-platform/app-engine/setup.html`.

Use the following steps to create your Dart project:

1. You need a dependency on the `appengine` package, so add this to your `pubspec.yaml` file.

2. You need an `app.yaml` file with the following as minimal content:
    ```
    version: app_name
    runtime: custom
    vm: true
    api_version: 1
    ```

3. Your server code must reside in a `bin\server.dart` file and contain the following start up code:
    ```
    import 'dart:io';
    import 'package:appengine/appengine.dart';              (1)
    main() {
      runAppEngine((HttpRequest request) {                  (2)
        request.response.write(My first Dart App Engine App!')
                        .close();
      });
    }
    ```

    In line `(1)`, the `appengine` package is imported. This includes the top-level `runAppEngine()` method, which starts Dart's runtime and connects it to App Engine. This takes an HTTP request handler as callback, which creates the response for the browser.

4. To start the app using App Engine, run on a command line:
    ```
    gcloud preview app run app.yaml
    ```

5. Navigate to `http://localhost:8080` using your browser to see the result and start developing and testing it locally.

6. When you are satisfied, you can deploy your app to App Engine using the following command:
    ```
    gcloud preview app deploy app.yaml
    ```

    After deployment is completed your app can be reached on the **World Wide Web (WWW)** via `http://app_name.appspot.com/`.

Before embarking on your own project, study and experiment with a worked out example of a client-server app available at `https://www.dartlang.org/server/google-cloud-platform/app-engine/client-server/`. Other examples can be found at `https://github.com/dart-lang/appengine_samples`.

> You can find the latest news on Dart in App Engine on `https://www.dartlang.org/server/google-cloud-platform/app-engine/`.
>
> For more information on App Engine, consult at `https://cloud.google.com/appengine/docs/managed-vms/`.

Summary

This chapter gave you the tools necessary to write the client-server Dart applications that store their data in the server databases. You learned how to work with command-line arguments by using the `Options` class, and how to work with files, storing data in the JSON format. We stored our data in a typical relational database (MySQL), using the `sqljocky` driver for Dart. Then, we gave you an introduction to the document database system MongoDB, and showed you how to use it from a Dart app with the `mongo_dart` connector.

This brings us to the end of our Dart journey in this book. We hope you've enjoyed it as much as we enjoyed developing the code and writing the text for it. You now have the tools to develop all sorts of apps using Dart. Join the Dart community and start using your coding talents! Perhaps, we'll meet again in the Dartiverse.

Index

A

abstract classes **61, 62**
abstract methods **61, 62**
App Engine Managed VM
  about 346
  Dart server, running 346-348
  reference link 348
asynchronous calls 292-295
asynchronous programming
  reference link 85
  with async 84, 85
  with await 84, 85
attributes
  about 99
  modifying, of elements 120-124
  reference link 124
auto-sharding 338

B

Binary JSON (BSON) 338
Bitbucket
  URL 94
browser storage
  options 292
built-in types
  about 27-29
  conversions 29
  dates 33
  lists 34, 35
  maps 36, 37
  methods 27-29
  operators 29-31
  String methods 31, 32
  times 33

C

callbacks 293
CamelCase notation
  URL 20
canvas
  about 137
  ball, moving 142-144
  bouncing ball, creating 145
  circle, drawing 137-141
  code, reorganizing 144, 145
  colored circles, displaying 141, 142
  colored rectangles, displaying 141, 142
  game, developing 149
  master version, creating 150, 151
  racket, displaying 146, 147
  racket, moving with keys 147, 148
  racket, moving with mouse 148
  rectangle, drawing 137-141
  reference link 137, 142
  replay option, adding 150
  title, adding 150
cascade operator 55
categories and links application 114-117
category links project
  local storage, adding 231-233
  Polymer.dart, using 224-230
classes
  about 54
  abstract classes 61, 62
  abstract methods 61, 62
  collections 66
  constructors 57
  generics 66
  inheritance 60
  interface 63

[PACKT] open source *
PUBLISHING   community experience distilled

Thank you for buying
Learning Dart
Second Edition

About Packt Publishing

Packt, pronounced 'packed', published its first book, *Mastering phpMyAdmin for Effective MySQL Management*, in April 2004, and subsequently continued to specialize in publishing highly focused books on specific technologies and solutions.

Our books and publications share the experiences of your fellow IT professionals in adapting and customizing today's systems, applications, and frameworks. Our solution-based books give you the knowledge and power to customize the software and technologies you're using to get the job done. Packt books are more specific and less general than the IT books you have seen in the past. Our unique business model allows us to bring you more focused information, giving you more of what you need to know, and less of what you don't.

Packt is a modern yet unique publishing company that focuses on producing quality, cutting-edge books for communities of developers, administrators, and newbies alike. For more information, please visit our website at www.packtpub.com.

About Packt Open Source

In 2010, Packt launched two new brands, Packt Open Source and Packt Enterprise, in order to continue its focus on specialization. This book is part of the Packt Open Source brand, home to books published on software built around open source licenses, and offering information to anybody from advanced developers to budding web designers. The Open Source brand also runs Packt's Open Source Royalty Scheme, by which Packt gives a royalty to each open source project about whose software a book is sold.

Writing for Packt

We welcome all inquiries from people who are interested in authoring. Book proposals should be sent to author@packtpub.com. If your book idea is still at an early stage and you would like to discuss it first before writing a formal book proposal, then please contact us; one of our commissioning editors will get in touch with you.

We're not just looking for published authors; if you have strong technical skills but no writing experience, our experienced editors can help you develop a writing career, or simply get some additional reward for your expertise.

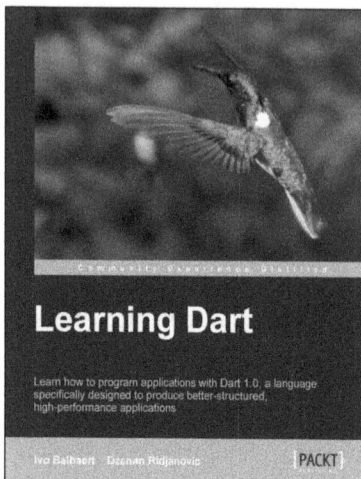

Learning Dart

ISBN: 978-1-84969-742-2   Paperback: 388 pages

Learn how to program applications with Dart 1.0, a language specifically designed to produce better-structured, high-performance applications

1. Develop apps for the Web using Dart and HTML5.

2. Build powerful HTML5 forms, validate and store data in local storage, and use web components to build your own user interface.

3. Make games by drawing and integrate audio and video in the browser.

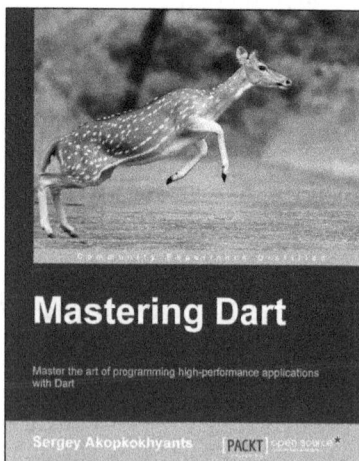

Mastering Dart

ISBN: 978-1-78398-956-0   Paperback: 346 pages

Master the art of programming high-performance applications with Dart

1. Improve the performance of your Dart code and build sophisticated applications.

2. Enhance your web projects by adding advanced HTML 5 features.

3. Full of solutions to real-world problems, with clear explanations for complicated concepts of Dart.

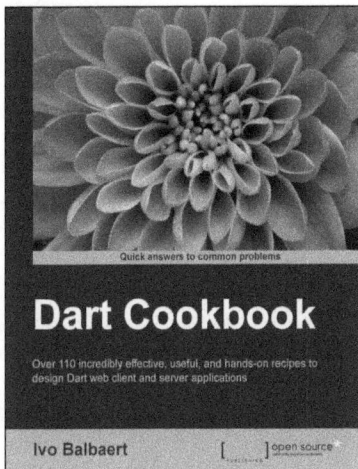

Dart Cookbook

ISBN: 978-1-78398-962-1   Paperback: 346 pages

Over 110 incredibly effective, useful, and
hands-on recipes to design Dart web client
and server applications

1. Develop stunning apps for the modern web
   using Dart.

2. Learn how to store your app's data in common
   SQL and NoSQL databases with Dart.

3. Create state-of-the-art web apps with Polymer
   and Angular.

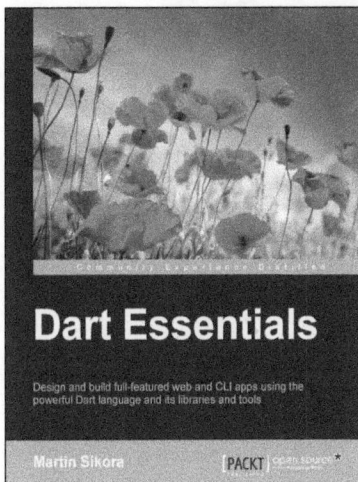

Dart Cookbook

Over 110 incredibly effective, useful, and hands-on recipes to
design Dart web client and server applications

Ivo Balbaert

Dart Essentials

ISBN: 978-1-78398-960-7   Paperback: 232 pages

Design and build full-featured web and CLI apps
using the powerful Dart language and its libraries
and tools

1. Build sophisticated, powerful apps using
   Dart 1.9; learn about the newest libraries and
   asynchronous APIs.

2. Write encapsulated components and apps
   with Web Components, polymer.dart,
   and AngularDart.

3. Explore Standalone Dart VM with CLI apps,
   unit testing, and server-side scripting and
   discover Dart's full potential with C/C++
   native extensions.

Dart Essentials

Design and build full-featured web and CLI apps using the
powerful Dart language and its libraries and tools

Martin Sikora

Please check **www.PacktPub.com** for information on our titles

www.ingramcontent.com/pod-product-compliance
Lightning Source LLC
Chambersburg PA
CBHW080711220326
41598CB00033B/5375